THE COLLECTED POEMS

BOOKS BY

REYNOLDS PRICE

LETTER TO A MAN IN THE FIRE 1999

LEARNING A TRADE 1998

ROXANNA SLADE 1998

THE COLLECTED POEMS 1997

THREE GOSPELS 1996

THE PROMISE OF REST 1995

A WHOLE NEW LIFE 1994

THE COLLECTED STORIES 1993

FULL MOON 1993

BLUE CALHOUN 1992

THE FORESEEABLE FUTURE 1991

NEW MUSIC 1990

THE USE OF FIRE 1990

THE TONGUES OF ANGELS 1990

CLEAR PICTURES 1989

GOOD HEARTS 1988

A COMMON ROOM 1987

THE LAWS OF ICE 1986

KATE VAIDEN 1986

PRIVATE CONTENTMENT 1984

MUSTIAN 1983

VITAL PROVISIONS 1982

THE SOURCE OF LIGHT 1981

A PALPABLE GOD 1978

EARLY DARK 1977

THE SURFACE OF EARTH 1975

THINGS THEMSELVES 1972

PERMANENT ERRORS 1970

LOVE AND WORK 1968

A GENEROUS MAN 1966

THE NAMES AND FACES OF HEROES 1963

A LONG AND HAPPY LIFE 1962

REYNOLDS PRICE

THE COLLECTED POEMS

SCRIBNER POETRY

SCRIBNER POETRY
SCRIBNER
1230 Avenue of the Americas
New York, NY 10020

First Scribner Poetry edition 1999

Set in Adobe Electra

Manufactured in the United States of America

1 3 5 7 9 10 8 6 4 2

The Library of Congress has cataloged the Scribner edition as follows:
Price, Reynolds, 1933.
[Poems. Selections]
The collected poems / Reynolds Price.
Includes index.
p. cm.
I. Title.
PS3566.R54A6 1997
811'.54—dc21 96-53117
CIP

ISBN 0-684-83203-8
ISBN 0-684-86002-3 *(Pbk.)*

CONTENTS

Preface *xv*

I. VITAL PROVISIONS
(1982)

ANGEL 2

ONE

THE DREAM OF A HOUSE 5
THE DREAM OF LEE 8
THE DREAM OF FOOD 12
SEAFARER 14
QUESTIONS FOR A STUDENT 17
THE ALCHEMIST 18
AT THE GULF 19
LEAVING THE ISLAND 22
ANNIVERSARY 23
ATTIS 24
BETHLEHEM — CAVE OF THE NATIVITY 26
JERUSALEM — CALVARY 27
PURE BOYS AND GIRLS 28
NIGHT SPEECH 29
TEN YEARS, FOUR DAYS 30
RESCUE 31

TWO : NINE MYSTERIES

ANNUNCIATION 39
REPARATION 41
CHRIST CHILD'S SONG AT THE END OF THE NIGHT 43
DEAD GIRL 44
NAKED BOY 46
SLEEPING WIFE 51
RESURRECTION 53

INSTRUCTION 55
ASCENSION 58

THREE

PICTURES OF THE DEAD 63
1. ROBERT FROST, 1951 63
2. W. H. AUDEN, 1957 64
3. ROBERT LOWELL, 1968 65
ARCHAIC TORSO OF APOLLO 66
FOUND, FOR MY BROTHER 67
TO MY NIECE—OUR PHOTOGRAPH IN A HAMMOCK 68
I SAY OF ANY MAN 70
AURORA 71
A RAINBOW AND A DAY-OLD CALF 72
MAN AND FAUN 73
TOWN CREEK 75
DIVINE PROPOSITIONS 76
YOUR ELEMENT 77
BLACK WATER 78
MEMORANDA 79
TOWARD JUNCTION 79
MEMORANDUM 1 80
MEMORANDUM 2 81
MEMORANDUM 3 82
MEMORANDUM 4 83
MEMORANDUM 5 84
THE FIELD 85
CUMAEAN SONG 86
FOR LEONTYNE PRICE AFTER *Ariadne* 88
THE ANNUAL HERON 89

II. THE LAWS OF ICE
(1986)

PRAISE 98

ONE

AMBROSIA 101
WHAT IS GODLY 103

GOOD PLACES 104
1. WARM SPRINGS 104
2. RINCÓN 1 105
3. RINCÓN 2 106
4. CHEROKEE 108
5. LIGHTHOUSE, MOSQUITO INLET 109
6. HAWK HILL 110
BEFORE THE FLOOD 111
1. HER CHOICE 111
2. HIS DISCOVERY 112
DROWNED 113
JONATHAN'S LAMENT FOR DAVID 114
DAVID'S LAMENT FOR SAUL AND JONATHAN 116
PORTA NIGRA 117
LAST CONVERSATION 118
REMEMBERING GOLDEN BELLS 120
DEAD MAN, DYING GIRL 121
SLEEPER IN THE VALLEY 122
A HEAVEN FOR ELIZABETH RODWELL, MY MOTHER 123
EPITAPHS FROM THE GREEK ANTHOLOGY 128
THE LAWS OF ICE 129

TWO : DAYS AND NIGHTS

PREFACE 133
1. SALAMANDER 134
2. FLOOD 135
3. COOL 136
4. HMMMM 137
5. LUNA 138
6. LETTER MAN 139
7. RELIC 140
8. PRAISE ON YOUR BIRTHDAY 141
9. HECATOMB 142
10. WARNED 143
11. A POLAR SIMPLE 144
12. RIDDLE 145
13. THE AIM 146
14. SAME ROAD 147
15. LATE 148
16. EELS 149

17. FOR VIVIEN LEIGH 150
18. SECRET 152
19. FOR LEONTYNE PRICE 153
20. CAUGHT 154
21. CAW 155
22. TRANSATLANTIC 156
23. A LIFE IN DREAMS 157
24. REST 158
25. FOR JAMES DEAN 159
26. THE CLAIM 160
27. TV 162
28. NEIGHBORS 163
29. PEARS 164
30. VISION 165
31. THE DREAM OF REFUSAL 166
32. OCTOBER SUN 168
33. MOTHER 169
34. TURN 170
35. LATE VISIT 171

THREE

LINES OF LIFE 175
THREE SECRETS 176
1. JOSEPH 176
2. MARY 179
3. JESUS 180
ROAD 183
THREE VISITS 184
1. DIONYSOS 184
2. APHRODITE 187
3. HERMES PSYCHOPOMPOS 190
YOUR BLOOD 193
HELIX 194
I AM TRANSMUTING 195
A TOMB FOR WILL PRICE 196
MIDNIGHT 199
HOUSE SNAKE 200
WATCHMAN. TOWER. MIDNIGHT. 212

III. THE USE OF FIRE
(1990)

ONE

UNBEATEN PLAY 217
SOCRATES AND ALCIBIADES 221
THREE DEAD VOICES 222
1. DIRECTOR 222
2. PHOTOGRAPHER 223
3. TEACHER 224
HALF OF LIFE 226
THE EEL 227
1. 25 JULY 1984 227
2. 26 JULY 1984 229
3. 26–30 JULY 1984 230
SIX CONSOLATIONS 231
1. AUGUST 1939 231
2. JULY 1946 232
3. JULY 1956 233
4. SEPTEMBER 1961 234
5. OCTOBER 1976 235
6. NOVEMBER 1989 236
INITIATION 237
MORTAL SEVEN 238
1. PRIDE AND SLOTH: 1985 238
2. ENVY AND COVETOUSNESS: 1952 239
3. ANGER: 1985 240
4. LUST AND GREED: 1962 241
WINTER 242
TWO SONGS FOR JAMES TAYLOR 243
1. HYMN 243
2. DAWN (JOHN 21) 244
DREAM ELEPHANTS 246
NOON REST, BEST DAY 249

TWO : DAYS AND NIGHTS 2

PREFACE 253
1. PRAISE 254
2. AGAIN 255

3. REX 256
4. THE DREAM OF SALT 257
5. NOCTURNE FOR A WEDDING 258
6. THE DREAM OF FALLING 259
7. BEN LONG'S DRAWING OF ME 260
8. 31 DECEMBER 1985 261
9. THICKET 262
10. SAMUEL BARBER 263
11. STEPHEN SPENDER 264
12. VALENTINE. HERON. 265
13. NEAR A MILESTONE 266
14. PAID 267
15. GOOD FRIDAY 268
16. EASTER SUNDAY 1986 269
17. BACK 270
18. AT SEA 271
19. SKY, DARK 272
20. TWO CAVES, A HOUSE, A GARDEN, A TOMB 273
    1. NAZARETH, MARY'S HOUSE 273
    2. BETHLEHEM, BIRTHPLACE 274
    3. CAPERNAUM, PETER'S HOUSE 275
    4. GETHSEMANE, GARDEN 276
    5. JERUSALEM, JESUS' SEPULCHER 277
    6. MOUNT OF OLIVES, ROCK OF THE ASCENSION 278
21. A HERON, A DEER—A SINGLE DAY 279
22. FIRST GREEN 280
23. 15 MARCH 1987 281
24. 16 MARCH 1987 282
25. SPRING TAKES THE HOMEPLACE 283
26. THE RESIDENT HERON 285
27. LIGHTS OUT 286
28. THE RACK 287
29. JIM, WITH AIDS 288
30. TOM, DYING OF AIDS 289
31. FISHERS 290
32. YOM KIPPUR 1983–1988 292
33. JIM DEAD OF AIDS AN HOUR AGO 293
34. TWO 294
35. EASTER SUNDAY 1989 295
36. TOM DEAD 297
37. DOWN AND BACK 298

38. THANKS 299
39. SCANNED 300
40. THE NET 301
41. *New Music* IN CLEVELAND 302
42. J.H. 303
43. MOB QUAD, OCTOBER 1955 304
44. AT HEAVEN'S GATE, MAY 1956 305
45. BOAR'S HILL, SPRING 1958 306
46. A HERON, A DEER—AGAIN 308
47. SPIRIT FLESH, 1960 309
48. ANTIPODES, 1969 AND ON 310
49. FREE FUEL, BYRD STREET, 1948 311
50. FIRST LOVE, HAYES BARTON, 1948 312
51. ELEGY, BYRD STREET 313
52. 1 JANUARY 1990 314
53. SAFEKEEPING, 1963 AND ON 315
54. GIANT 316
55. MAYA 318
56. 13 FEBRUARY 1984–1990 319

THREE

JUNCTURE 323
YOUR EYES 327
LOST HOMES 328
1. AN IRON BED IN GRANVILLE COUNTY.
A GIRL AGED TWELVE. 328
2. A SINGLE BED. A BACK STREET IN VENICE.
TWO YOUNG MEN. 334
3. A CLEARED RING IN THE BLUE RIDGE MOUNTAINS.
A BOY AGED TWELVE, NOW A MIDDLE-AGED MAN. 336
SIX MEMORANDA 340
1. IMPRECATION 340
2. BED 341
3. YOUR LIES 342
4. YOUR DEBT 343
5. MONDAY, JUNE THE SIXTH 344
6. FAREWELL WITH PHOTOGRAPHS 345
WINTER 2 346
LAST VISIT 347
AN AFTERLIFE, 1953–1988 348

IV. THE UNACCOUNTABLE WORTH OF THE WORLD
(1997)

ONE

AN ACTUAL TEMPLE 359
NEW ROOM 362
THE DREAM OF THE COURT 364
FIRST CHRISTMAS 366
LEGS 367
THE DREAM OF ME WALKING 369
MID TERM 370
ALL WILL BE WHOLE 372
ENTRY 373
TO MUSIC 375

TWO : DAYS AND NIGHTS 3

PREFACE 379
1. FOR K.W. ON HER BIRTHDAY 380
2. F.H. AGAIN 381
3. DURHAM, 4 JUNE 1984 - FORT WORTH, 4 JUNE 1993 382
4. HOME FROM THE CLIBURN PIANO COMPETITION 383
5. TWENTY-ONE YEARS 384
6. RECUMBENT, SLEEPING 385
7. INDOORS 386
8. LUCK 387
9. A CHIPMUNK GONE AT CHRISTMAS 388
10. LION DREAM 389
11. FOR HUBERT DILWORTH DEAD IN HIS SLEEP 390
12. BACK AT MERTON COLLEGE 391
13. AFTER THE ANNUAL MRI SCAN, CLEAR 392
14. LIGHTNING BROWN DISCOVERS HE SHARES A BIRTHDAY WITH EMILY DICKINSON 393
15. AFTER AN AIDS BENEFIT 394
16. NEAR THE DEATH OF THE SUN 395
17. ON THE ROAD NORTH 396
18. THE DYING BELT, DOUGLAS PASCHALL GONE 397
19. ANNIVERSARY, 9 JANUARY 1995 398
20. BESIEGED BUT STRONGER 399

21. MERE FACT 400
22. THE WHEELED EROS 401
23. TWO FRIENDS, PARTING 402
24. BACK, D.V. 403
25. SAFE HOME 404
26. ON THE ROAD 405
27. STEPHEN SPENDER DEAD 406
28. NAPALM 407
29. WITH A.T.M., BALTIMORE 408
30. WITH T.M., BALTIMORE 409
31. TENTH MRI 410
32. IN THE FALL 411
33. NEAR THANKSGIVING 412
34. TOWARD AN ENDING 413
35. THE DREAD 414
36. BIRTHDAY PARTY 415
37. FORTY-EIGHTH BIRTHDAY 416
38. THE DAY ITSELF 417
39. TURTLE DANCE, SAN JUAN PUEBLO 418
40. A LONG STORM PASSING 419
41. SNOW 420
42. A CLASSICAL FRIEND 421
43. THE ISSUE 422
44. A VISIT THAT FEELS LIKE THE LAST 423
45. GONE 424
46. SCATTERING LIGHTNING IN THE SLAVE CEMETERY 425
47. EROS TYRANNOS 426
48. AN UNEXPECTED PARENT 427
49. SCOURED 428
50. A READING 429
51. BRIEF VISIT 430
52. SMALL ASTONISHMENTS 431
53. ECLIPSE 432
54. WANT 433
55. STUCK IN GEAR 434
56. QUIET EVENING 435
57. WHO? 436
58. MAY DAY 437
59. AT FEARRINGTON 438
60. LEFT 439
61. THE SWAP 440

62. WESTWARD 441
63. FROM HERE 442
64. NOB HILL 443

THREE

THE DANCING AT CANA 447
THIS FIELD 449
ANOTHER MEAL 450
THE LIST 451
FROM SO FAR 452
A HAVEN 453
THE DREAM OF MOTHER AND MY CANE 455
THE BUDDHA IN GLORY 456
SCORED BY LIGHT 457
THE PROSPECT 460
THE CLOSING, THE ECSTASY 462

Acknowledgments 465
Index of Titles 467

PREFACE

I WAS TWELVE years old when I began to encounter poems more demanding than the jingles of childhood or the nonsense lyrics of popular songs. Those first serious poems were introduced to me and my colleagues in a seventh-grade public-school classroom by Jane Alston, our teacher. She was an imposingly tall, middle-aged and never-married woman of dauntless gravity and rare but keen delight; and she was generous with praise when surprised by a sign of thoughtful imagination from her students. A superb sergeant for our maneuvers through arithmetic, reading, geography and natural science, she possessed as well a simple method which I've never met with elsewhere for building poetry into young human bones.

From a slender volume called *Best Loved Poems*, she'd read us a favorite of her own—brief lyrics from poets of genius like Wordsworth, Keats and Tennyson and from lesser but often rousing lights like Elizabeth Barrett Browning, Longfellow, Whittier, Eugene Field and John McCrae. Then she'd write the day's poem on the blackboard for us to copy into our notebooks (the copying became, simultaneously, an exercise in the now lost art of legible penmanship). Every few days Miss Alston would lead the class in reading, aloud in unison, all the poems we'd copied. Occasionally she'd have us copy the words of a well-known song, and we'd add a cappella musical renditions to our repertoire—the song that's haunted me longest is the Scottish "Annie Laurie" (a majority of my classmates had Scottish roots, as I do). The vigor and swing of those performances suggested that far more members of the class than I had discovered a welcome new form of play. And given our widespread enthusiasm and the porous eagerness of young minds, we likewise found that in a matter of only a few such performances, all the poems were locked into place in our heads.

In my case, most of them wait there still; and on numerous occasions of boredom, fear or foundering spirits, I've brought them forward for silent assistance. Mostly when I call them to mind, I feel again the rise of my boyhood zeal, a pleasure which can suddenly flow from the presence of that benign conjunction of word, image and rhythm which poetry offers more liberally than other forms even in lines of a minor distinction like those I first learned in 1945 (from John McCrae's "In Flanders Fields")—

Take up our quarrel with the foe;
To you from failing hands we throw
The torch; be yours to hold it high.
If ye break faith with us who die
We shall not sleep, though poppies grow
In Flanders fields.

Some three years after that introduction, I made my first independent contact with a poet who—though she'd been dead for sixty-two years—would lure me to study all the available work of a particular lifetime. That contact was made not only in independence but in solitude and apparent coincidence. It was in 1948; my family had recently moved from a town with no bookstore to Raleigh, and the capital city boasted two stores which offered a secular stock. Though they maintained a pitifully small range of new titles, each offered a shelf of inexpensive Modern Library editions.

Early on I'd acquired two schoolboy favorites, *The Prophecies of Nostradamus* and W. H. Hudson's *Green Mansions*; but one gray Saturday afternoon when I was fifteen, I chanced on *The Selected Poems of Emily Dickinson.* I doubt I'd heard Dickinson's name till then; and I was unaware that her nearly two thousand poems had still not appeared in a chronologically arranged and textually faithful edition. But on that lucky afternoon, as the small selected volume fell open, I read to myself

Success is counted sweetest
By those who ne'er succeed.
To comprehend a nectar
Requires sorest need.

Not one of all the purple Host
Who took the Flag today
Can tell the definition
So clear of Victory

As he defeated – dying –
On whose forbidden ear
The distant strains of triumph
*Burst agonized and clear!**

The fact that I was only beginning to emerge from a gloomy stretch of early adolescence—one that had left me feeling powerless and defeated among my

*Here, and in a second Dickinson poem below, I quote the text established later by Thomas H. Johnson. I no longer have my copy of the old Modern Library edition; but my recollection is that the Johnson text—prepared directly from the manuscripts—differs from the Modern Library only in matters of punctuation, capitalization and in a single verb. In "Success" the verb in the final line was "Break."

contemporaries—meant that I was ideally braced by temperament, recent experience and a still uncrowded sensibility for such a rich discovery. With a sharp clarity, I recall the inexplicable elation of that moment as one of the two or three high points in a lifetime's reading.

I bought the book, read Conrad Aiken's preface that night and gradually consumed the remainder of the poems over coming weeks. The childhood rhymes and radio songs and the memorized poems from Jane Alston's class had entered my mind as all but inhuman objects. They'd felt more like tangible specimens for my growing boy's museum—with Indian arrowheads, stamps and old coins—than like durable forms of help from another member of my species. Dickinson's poems were the first that struck me as not only important and memorable in their own mysterious right (and without the prior endorsement of my teachers); they were also my introduction to the idea that a particular solitary human being might actually make such practical and lasting objects—someone who, in Dickinson's one surely attested photograph, looked much like any number of my distant cousins or teachers.

Again I committed many of the poems to memory; I consulted other editions; I read biographies of Dickinson, wrote a poem of my own about her, made her the subject of my junior-year term paper for the American literature class taught by a fervent apostle of poetry named Phyllis Peacock; and I delivered a lengthy presentation to my classmates on the phenomenon of Dickinson's lone brave existence and the wealth she made of it. Never quite saying so to a group of contemporaries who were visibly ready to lunge into laughter at any whiff of pretense, I managed to get away with implying for myself a degree of privileged kinship with this woman and the body of her work. Even in the presence of Dickinson's most opaque riddles, after all, I'd mostly sensed that I penetrated her veiled sanctuaries through a near-blood bonding. (Interestingly, in the upper South of those years, none of my classmates seemed to find anything strange in Dickinson's withdrawal from society—few extended families then lacked their own eccentric but tolerable aunt or cousin, usually a widow, spinster or bachelor.)

Privately I'd also begun—as eros swamped me in its first riptides—to guess what depths of transport and darkness lurked at the edge of even the most sequestered human mind, one that demanded such a broad range of response from itself. What acts, mental or physical, could have lain for instance behind Dickinson's consumingly erotic

Wild Nights – Wild Nights –
Were I with thee
Wild Nights should be
Our luxury!

Futile – the Winds –
To a Heart in port –
Done with the Compass –
Done with the Chart!

Rowing in Eden –
Ah, the Sea!
Might I but moor – Tonight –
In Thee!

Led on in the hunt for comparably successful shocks, by the time I entered the final year of high school, my battery of favorites had expanded to include a few prose works—*Madame Bovary*, *Anna Karenina*, the early stories of Hemingway and his *A Farewell to Arms*—but for a good while, nothing equaled for me the poems and plays of a still-writing contemporary, T. S. Eliot. That attraction developed even as one of my senior teachers guided me in another direction by showing me her autographed copy of the poems of A. E. Housman, whom she'd met in the thirties on a trip to Cambridge. In part, my curiosity about Eliot was kindled by the unprecedented public attention paid to him in the wake of his Nobel Prize (1948) and the immediately subsequent success of his play *The Cocktail Party*. No other poet writing in English since the dazzling youth of Lord Byron can have had such fame and attention as Eliot received in the late 1940s and 50s. Another part of my own early fascination lay, as it did for legions of older readers, in Eliot's notorious obscurity—poetry as puzzle can be as riveting a game for a bookish child as it was then for thousands of scholars.

But I also know that the seeds of a lasting debt were sown in my first baffled readings of "Sweeney Among the Nightingales" and "The Waste Land." Those seeds lay in a boy's dim perception of the unfeigned and luminous awe which poured—in verse of such bare strength—into Eliot's middle and late work from his passionate but long-chilled hunger for transcendence. From my first encounter with the work, it struck an unlikely harmony to already-old longings in me; and from that time on, the mind and the piercing voice of Eliot's eerie unaccompanied quest were my close companions. Few months have passed in ensuing years in which I have not read one or more of the *Four Quartets* or heard them in Eliot's fierce, though desiccated, voice on his recordings.

Toward the end of my freshman year at Duke University, I encountered yet a third poet who'd soon blank most others in my study and pleasure. In an introductory course of Major British Authors, I first read quantities of the work of John Milton. A few years earlier I'd heard the sonnet on his blindness over the radio, but I knew little else about him. So launching at the age of nineteen into the swirl and swagger of his "On the Morning of Christ's Nativity" (written to celebrate his twenty-first birthday) and, above all, his grieving "Lycidas" had the overwhelming and hallucinatory effect of a month spent prowling the floor of the sea—somehow safe but rapt in the effort to absorb and retain every sight and sound for the later hours when I'd surface and could sort my findings.

In my sophomore year I enrolled for a semester's work in Milton with Florence Brinkley, a respected scholar of seventeenth-century English poetry and another Southern spinster who combined the iron strength of her devotion to poetry with a quizzical social mildness that reminded me of so many of my earlier teachers and made her both an intimate guide and a chaste but oddly radiant priestess. My engagement with Milton's early poems continued—and a sense of kinship, however distant, with Milton's awareness, from his early school days, of high vocation as a poet and teacher—but months of gradual immersion in *Paradise Lost* were like an obsessive love affair or a low-grade fever that refused to remit in its heightening of my senses: above all the mind's love of thought and its relish for language deployed with the strut and potency of grand architecture yet the translucent line of the simplest ballad.

Toward the end of that term, Miss Brinkley urged me to read a book called *Poetry as a Means of Grace* by C. G. Osgood. Conceived in 1940 as lectures to young Princeton theologians, Osgood's still keenly provocative chapters propose that, in a hectic and book-filled world, a thoughtful person might well choose a single inexhaustible poet and fix upon that poet's work as a lifelong spring of refreshment in the driest times. From his own obviously immense knowledge, he suggests four candidates—Dante, Spenser, Milton and Samuel Johnson—and proceeds to define the offerings of each. Of Milton he concludes,

> . . . *I know him as an older friend and brother from whose presence I never depart without a sense of expansion, and enlargement, of clarification of mind and accession of power, together with an exaltation of spirit.*

Still short of twenty, I harbored suspicions about the source of grace that were fairly unshakable, but Osgood's old-style avuncular tone deepened and clarified my attraction to Milton. Neither Osgood nor Miss Brinkley were the first sane persons I'd known who freely confessed that poetry—even the poetry of others—was worth a whole life; but there beside the lifework of Milton, they made their point convincingly and permanently.

The giant battery of Milton's skills, his fevered steady drive to know and consume and present all life, from ant to seraph, in its native splendor fired my own diffuse will to write; and the polyphonic richness of his language, with its ready access to the eloquence of plain speech, rang familiarly in the ears of one raised, as I'd been, in a society all but drunk on its craving for a spoken and written language equal to the coiling emotional and moral needs of a life as complicated as that of my own kin and friends in the upper South, less than a century after a devastating war we'd conceived for an evil purpose. Milton's voice, after all, rose from the same Anglo-Celtic-Norman springs that had shaped—with beneficent African additions—the tongue and tone of my home place. The demands and rewards of that voice continued to hold me through a further Milton course at Duke with the doughty Allan Gilbert, through a senior thesis on Milton's entry into public life, then a graduate thesis at Oxford on his dramaturgy (with the formidable Helen Gardner, a guide whose unpredictable compound of gentleness and rigor most usefully echoed Milton's vehement amiability).

By the end of three years in the now-lost England of the 1950s—an England much like Milton's own—my early allegiance to poetry had been hammered into what would amount to a sleepless, if sometimes distant, companionship. And for all my growing interest in the writing of prose fiction, I'd begun to suspect that I was also fitted with a hunger for the small and large satisfactions that appeared to be offered only—in the English language at least—by the audible human voice as it creates or reproduces in verse one of an infinite variety of thoughts while that thought forms itself into words and is simultaneously formed by those words, by that rhythm and all the other possibilities of verbal music: rhyme, assonance, dissonance, modest plainchant and incantatory ecstasy.

Full attention to the hunger would wait through more than an otherwise busy decade. Meanwhile, none of those concerns interfered with my having a normal young life of laughing friendship with my friends, my first reciprocated loves, domestic duties and the eventual and ominous necessity to choose a profession and earn both my own keep and a share of my mother's (my father had died when I was a junior at Duke). Meanwhile, I was generally lucky in having friends my own age who were struck with similar compulsions. Our long talks prompted me further; and soon like many of them, I'd begun to eke out attempts at poems of my own. A sizable handful of those efforts survive. They cast me, more than a little melodramatically, as the loneliest soul on the planet yet one prepared to gamble on the power of language to bridge most gulfs if the words are got right.

Of those brief poems, none is right enough to offer here, even as juvenilia. The earliest included are "The Sleeper in the Valley" after Rimbaud and "I Say of Any Man" after Hölderlin. Small as those two versions are, they were not completed until 1961 after more years of formal and informal study—I was then twenty-eight. And perhaps, since they came shortly after the completion of my first book, a novel, the long span of focus on prose narrative had silently demonstrated how much of my life was likely to prove of no use to my fiction.

It would be misleading not to acknowledge that such a late beginning came after the gradual encouragement of a few exemplary practitioners. Among them, in my early adult years, Robert Frost was frequently available in public readings and for one memorable small seminar in Chapel Hill. W. H. Auden was among my teachers in graduate school, at a time when I was immersed in continued study of Milton. Shy, though hilarious and profoundly instructive, Auden sought out those of us with an interest in the writing of poetry and—with no insistence whatever—became at once an enduring example. Stephen Spender published my first fiction in *Encounter*, a journal which he was then coediting, and for the remainder of his long life was the source of unabashed advice, keen-eyed warning and generous friendship. His own seven decades of work have proved an invaluable guide to the outer reaches of a poetry of unrelenting self-inspection.

The other poems collected here have gathered in the nearly four succeeding decades—sometimes in rapid clusters, sometimes sparsely and with lengthy pauses. Through most of the 1960s and early seventies, my energies continued to concentrate on the writing of more novels, stories, plays and essays. Yet my reading and teaching kept the prospect of poetry clear before me, however distant (I'd begun to teach the thoughtful reading of prose and verse at Duke University in 1958); and a new poem sometimes made its way through the prevailing prose—generally a short poem that meant to preserve some small incident which seemed in imminent danger of vanishing if not reproduced quickly in the most precise sentences available.

It was only in the late 1970s, however, that I found myself more and more subject to the arrival of poems and to the eventual awareness that many of my experiences had begun to present themselves in the shapes and tones of verse. I suspect that the gradual ambush of middle age had much to do with the development. A certain kind of person, made keenly aware of growing age and mortality, is likely to find himself in search of a means to fix those maybe significant memories that become increasingly fugitive or less inclined to merge into the longer colonnades of prose fiction and memoir.

Then in the mid-1980s, when I stalled in the straits of an illness that refused to admit more expansive work, I turned frequently toward the drafting of short poems. Most of them were composed for a notebook or journal, called *Days and Nights*, which I'd begun to keep only a few months earlier. Though work in that notebook has continued till now, I've by no means written for it daily. Still its steady presence on my desk has allowed me to secure, in stripped-down but occasionally fuller poems, a few striking aspects of random experience which might otherwise have faded from my memory.

Those poems outside the journal differ markedly in their occasions, and their procedures have varied considerably through a working span of thirty-five years. The first three-quarters of this collection comprise the contents of three earlier volumes—*Vital Provisions, The Laws of Ice* and *The Use of Fire*. Anyone familiar with those collections will note that there are no omissions here. However tempted I am to reprint only those poems that attain their full ambition, it has finally seemed preferable to persist in laying out the broad spread, not a tidied or camouflaged garden. The few original poems that occur in my volumes of fiction were written, or adapted, for the needs of a particular character and situation and are not included here; several poems published in journals but not previously collected are again excluded as unsatisfactory.

There is also, in previously published work, only the barest minimum of correction (the temptation to realign a few early heavily stressed passages into what now seems a more natural metrical order has been resisted; punctuation and spelling have not been homogenized; and at the risk of repetition, I've retained in my notes to the first two parts of *Days and Nights* a few matters that are dealt with more amply here). An obligation in being a writer of any sort, as of being human, is the owning up to the final outcome of one's range and choices. I've long felt that, once a poem has made its initial appearance in a book, it has ceased to be the author's creature to change at will. However small its audience, the poem has entered public life and almost surely cannot be profitably changed by its author, a person who has gone on to become someone else. Modern poetry is rife with examples of poets who have deformed good early work through later revision—Whitman, Yeats, Ransom and Auden are prime examples and have served as warnings against the occasional itch to smooth an earlier roughness or a hapless vulnerability. So I have not only resisted substantial change, I have left in place the initially unconscious repetitions of word and image that become in time one more form of confession.

I have likewise retained, and augmented, a scattered body of poems which are American versions of poems by writers in other languages. Since some of those poems have occurred in languages that I barely know, if at all, I discovered many of them in translation and have resorted freely to literal-sense versions made for me by knowledgeable friends and scholars. In every case, my versions and variations were made from poems that—so far as I comprehended them—were relevant to live concerns of my own. That the versions are often so free as to constitute scarcely recognizable variations is no less a gesture of homage to their originals.

The most literal transcriptions in the volume are grounded in another source—the intimate yet alien nightly dream. All but one of the poems entitled "The Dream of [So and So]"—or, in one case, "Lion Dream"—reproduces as faithfully as possible a dream I experienced, one that seemed of more weight and interest than the average run of my nocturnal narrative sessions and that I transcribed no more than a few days later. ("The Dream of Me Walking" reproduces a frequently reported dream of my friends.)

The final quarter of the volume, entitled *The Unaccountable Worth of the World,* consists of new and previously uncollected poems, including a third substantial group from the ongoing *Days and Nights*. Though the new poems sketch a few comic gestures, the fact that many concern themselves with the deaths of friends is not so much a function of a darkening turn of mind as it is the natural result of my age. I was born in 1933; my contemporaries have begun to fail and die with some frequency; and the AIDS disaster of recent years has, with monstrous cruelty, taken younger friends. A number of new poems expose the same elations and quandaries of desire and need as my earliest poems of isolated boyhood. That longing, however, has now lost much of its power to humiliate, coming as it does as a welcome sign of life.

From the start—perhaps in an unconscious effort to establish independence from the pentameter of Milton and so much other early reading—many of the poems are linked by a family resemblance in their tendency to volunteer in the oldest of English-language rhythms, the relentlessly powered four-stress line of *Beowulf* and other Anglo-Saxon survivals: a line in which the number of syllables is relatively immaterial and may be widely varied. Though my own poems have mostly come without the heavy Saxon regularity and alliteration, my version of the Old English poem "Seafarer" attempts to recall that propulsion and those hammering echoes at their ancient height. Earlier and elsewhere, Samuel Taylor Coleridge found the same line productive of a natural but heightened diction. In 1815 in the preface to his poem "Christabel," Coleridge defended his revival of an apparently irregular meter with the claim that "this occasional variation in number of syllables is not introduced wantonly, or for the mere ends of convenience, but in correspondence with some transition in the nature of the imagery or passion."

I've mentioned that a few of my early poems attempt to insist that the reader employ a high degree of accentual emphasis. Elsewhere, my less insistent versions of the four-stress rhythm rely on a choice of systolic variations in speed; and close attention is given to line endings and enjambments in the hope of avoiding an unduly po-faced plainness. A number of poems have arrived with other rates of stress and regularity, and a few have come with no predictable meter. But the four-stress rhythm—since it is seldom prone to the prolixity that threatens longer lines and since it allows for unanticipated moments of emphasis on a varying ground of syllables—has felt closely allied to the wary economy and dignity of those kinds of speech that, in my lifetime, have been most concerned for lucid and memorable communication with sundry but alert listeners.

Subject as the four-stress line is to shortening or lengthening, that intense and often eloquent native speech frequently offers, in its robust candor, to make a last step into narrative verse. More than many of my American colleagues, I've distrusted the lyric poem which is not braced on an armature of tellable story (the stride of narrative being a born dispeller of the clandestine and hermetic). My continuous effort has been to assist that last step onward from speech into comprehensible and useful story; and I've tried to remember that even narrative verse must work to be as well written as good prose, as detaining as good talk and no more subject to private quirk than any other would-be communicative act.

Finally, I note that my allegiance to poetry and my hope to write it were formed in a physical, human and artistic world very different from today's. While I continue to read some contemporary poets with enjoyment, the work that caught my attention early, and goes on holding it, was and is the work of Dickinson, Eliot, Frost, Housman, Milton, Herbert, Donne, Wordsworth, Keats, Hopkins, Yeats, Rilke, Rimbaud, Auden and Robert Lowell (I name them in the order of encountering their poems). In its concerns and results, my work is patently different from any of theirs; but their examples of self-reliance, sleepless curiosity about the world and its creatures, and an insistent concern to be heard and remembered have remained strong standards for me.

Though my young interest in poetry coincided with the late phases of the arch high-modernists, my own poems are often skeptical of the modernist demand that *Make it new* be the banner aim of poetry. It has often seemed to me that a more productive aim might be *Show it old and vital;* and a few poems here have the express aim to echo, while revising, older but still rewarding voices. If occasional other poems and lines have the air of a former time and idiom—if they take a wider view than is presently common of the desirable range, altitude and depth of poetic subjects and of the instruments by which those subjects may be observed—then that air is not necessarily the result of conscious archaism, verbal exhaustion or rampant nostalgia but of the deep-cut impressions of youth, of youth's most durable alliances, and of the actual timbre of a voice formed in an earlier school of what is believed to be reliable and perennial language.

R.P.

I

VITAL PROVISIONS

(1982)

ANGEL

Every angel from its height
Sheds a pure though blinding light,
Intermittent noon and night.
Yet—or therefore—it deserves
Thanks, attentions, steady loves:
Every angel on its height
Burns itself, itself its light.
Burn, clear angel—I observe,
Thank, attend, attempt to serve.

ONE

THE DREAM OF A HOUSE

There seems no question the house is mine.
I'm told it first at the start of the tour—
"This is yours, understand. Meant for you.
Permanent." I nod gratitude,
Containing the flower of joy in my mouth—
I knew it would come if I waited, in time.
It's now all round me—and I catalog blessings
Tangible as babies: the floors wide teak
Boards perfectly joined, the walls dove plaster.
At either end a single picture,
Neither a copy—Piero's *Nativity*
With angel glee-club, Vermeer's pregnant girl
In blue with her letter. Ranks of books
On the sides—old Miltons, Tolstoys, *Wuthering*
Heights, Ackermann's *Oxford*. A holograph
Copy of Keats's "To Autumn." All roles
Of Flagstad, Leontyne Price in order
On tape, with photographs. Marian Anderson
At Lincoln Memorial, Easter 1939.
A sense of much more, patiently humming.
My guide gives me that long moment,
Then says "You've got your life to learn
This. I'll show you the rest."

I follow and the rest is normal house.
Necessary living quarters—clean,
With a ship's scraped-bone economy. Bedroom
Cool as a cave, green bath,
Steel kitchen. We end in a long
Bright hall, quarry-tiled—
Long window at the far end
On thick woods in sunlight.
The guide gives a wave of consignment—
"Yours"—though he still hasn't smiled.
I ask the only question I know—
"Alone?" He waits, puzzled maybe

(For the first time I study him—a lean man,
Ten years my junior, neat tan clothes:
A uniform?). So I say again
"Alone?—will I be here alone?"
Then he smiles with a breadth that justifies his wait.
"Not from here on," he says. "That's ended too."
But he doesn't move to guide me farther.
I stand, thinking someone will burst in on us
Like a blond from a cake; and I reel through
Twenty-six years of candidates,
Backsliders till now. Silence stretches
Till he points to a closed door three steps
Beyond us.

I cannot go. After so much time—
Begging and vigils. He takes my elbow
And pulls me with him to an ordinary door,
Black iron knob. I only stand.
He opens for me—an ordinary hall
Closet: shelf lined with new hats,
Coats racked in corners. In the midst
Of tweeds and seersuckers, a man is
Nailed to a T-shaped rig—
Full-grown, his face eyelevel with mine,
Eyes clamped. He has borne on a body
No stronger than mine every
Offense a sane man would dread—
Flailed, pierced, gouged, crushed—
But he has the still bearable sweet
Salt smell of blood from my own finger,
Not yet brown, though his long
Hair is stiff with clots, flesh blue.

The guide has never released my arm.
Now he takes it to the face. I don't resist.
The right eyelid is cool and moist.
I draw back slowly and turn to the guide.

Smile more dazzling than the day outside,
He says "Yours. Always."

*

I nod my thanks, accept the key.
From my lips, enormous, a blossom spreads
At last—white, smell strong as
New iron chain: gorgeous,
Lasting, fills the house.

THE DREAM OF LEE

I'm driving from Durham, North Carolina
To Lexington, Virginia to get General Lee.
He'll be spending two days at Duke University,
Meeting with students and giving one formal
Evening lecture. Time is the present—
Dull end of the seventies, unaccustomed
Relative peace in a world where
Danger is individual again:
Mad or malevolent single bodies
Of human beings no stronger than we,
Hurtling in dark (or broad daylight)
Through the final membrane that has kept us ourselves—
But nothing seems strange in the General's lasting
Well over a century past Appomattox.
The strangeness inheres in the land I speed through—
Hills hid in pines big as old redwoods,
No soul in sight for the whole four hours:
Vacuum containing just me and this quiet,
Though round every bend I expect some
Glittering messenger to hail me with urgent
News of grace, extinction or company.
None volunteers, today anyhow;
And at three o'clock I pull up behind
The President's House at Washington College,
And the General emerges from a stable to greet me.
Meet would describe the moment more nearly—
He is dressed in a deep-blue suit,
Wide lapels, gold chain cross the vest;
And he offers his hand and says "Mr. Price"
With a still grave beauty as rare as the land
I've approached him through and as fevered with promise
Or threat to help. But he says no more
Then. He motions toward the house
And I follow him there. He seats me
In a rocker on the wide porch, facing
The chapel where his white tomb will be.

He says a good deal in the next
Quarter-hour, inside in the hall
(I've angled to see through the open door)—
It takes him that long to extricate himself
From the famously hypochondriac Mrs. Lee,
Who seems in her wheelchair the statue
Of Obstinate Triumph I'd rather expected
Him to be. From her I can hear
Only "Robert, Robert." From him only "Mary,
I'm pledged to return." When he comes out finally
With his small black country-doctor's satchel,
He's shed one or two of the skins of calm
And shows round his eyes those crevices helplessly
Opened on *appall*, the toothless mouth
Of utter loss, abandonment
That make Michael Miley's last photographs
Of him such satisfactory likenesses of Lear.
But he smiles slightly and says "Lead on."

I lead him back down through the same
Dazed country—vacancy parting
Silent as water to accept our journey,
Shutting silent behind us. But he never mentions
The emptiness; and I only speak
When spoken to, which—after an hour
Of decorous grooming, more small
Talk than I'd guessed him good for—
Is a level question poured straight
At my profile in the tone of courteous command:
"We know my story. I would like to know yours."
I don't imagine he means a curriculum
Of places, dates; but no story
Comes—none that seems mine.
So I drive us, not speaking, to the Carolina
Line when he faces me again. I try
Not to look, pretend the wide
Vacant road requires my total
Attention (he knows it doesn't).
He says "I would be grateful to hear."
Still not facing him, I say "Tell
Me" and smile at the road. I mean

My story and I think he's
Answered when he gives a slow rub,
With his palm in the air, over half the visible
Arc of our view and says "Something
Very much like this here."
I know he means the view, the element
That's borne our journey till now—patient
Broadbacked unworked beast—
And dodging his eyes, I know he's right
Though I don't think "Why?" or ask
Him to paraphrase his gesture or the land.
I say "Yes sir" and the one
Other thing he asks awhile later is
The size of my family. I say "It's here
On the seat beside you. I bivouac light,
Vanish at will." I rub my chest
And smile again. He says "Mrs. Lee's
Life stopped years ago," but by then
We're there.
                    The next two days
I stand as his aide through duties he's agreed to—
Several history classes with excellent
Questions on the details of campaigns,
Struggles with Jeff Davis, agonies
Of choice. He wears his perfect blue
Suit and answers perfectly, perfectly
Consistently—seamless as a river rock,
As shut to entrance; yet tall in impotence
As old Chief Joseph or a captive pope.
We fall back on pleasantry in what few minutes
He has between stints; he eats alone
In a hotel coffee-shop.
                                He's ready
At the curb when I call to take him
To his formal lecture; and as I approach
Down the evening street, it seems the strangest
Thing of all that no single
Passer on a crowded pavement gives any
Sign of seeing, much less
Recognizing a face as beautiful
As any human feasible vision

Of any god in charge of Fate
And Mercy—serene now, omniscient,
The flare of wildness quenched or banked.

I introduce him to the crowded hall
And, reaching my conclusion, know I've forgot
To ask him his subject; so I end by telling
The audience I'm sure it awaits
The lecture as eagerly as I.
When oceanic welcome subsides,
The General rises, steps to the lectern,
Slowly unties a black leather case,
Then looks back to me and says "I regret
Not telling you. I hope my changed
Plan will cause you no pain." I smile.
He doesn't. He faces his crowd and says
"I shall read from my poems tonight."
Slightly chilled, I think "*The Poems of Lee*—
Is there any such book?" Before I decide,
The great voice starts—"First a poem I composed
Two days ago for my friend Mr. Price."
He waits, puts a fist to his lips and coughs,
Then reads a poem one line long—
"*A country emptied by the fear of war.*"
I turn translucent with discovery,
Story told; then transparent as a glass
Anatomical man, a lesson for children—
All organs (less genitals) blasted
By white magnesium glare as every
Eye in the hall scans me, smiles.

THE DREAM OF FOOD

The room is dark and is all your body.
In the single buttress of late light strained
Through the porous roof, I see you are all—
You constitute space, the walls of space,
Air (I breathe clean safety)—yet
You're plainly yourself, recumbent below me:
Irregular glory of bone and rind,
Bronze island of hair.
                                        I wait in the door—
Not quite afraid, hoarding a dim
Astonishment, unsure of having
Or wanting permission.
                                        You stir your left
Arm, the entrance wall; it oars me
In. Fluid, I lie on the floor—your
Breast (you're larger than I by maybe
Half and warmer by maybe a full
Degree, this side fever).
I pause incredulous, crouched on the tide
Of respiration; then accept your will
And stretch my legs down yours. My thighs
Discover a yielding terrain in your fork—
Mounds, channels. I calmly know you
Are utterly strange—not father, mother,
Girl or boy, though your skin is the standard
Pliant leather I recall as human.
I doubt my purpose but lighten my weight
For your next requirement. You cup the crown
Of my head and press. It descends in an arc,
Hours or days; is stopped on the field
Between your sternum and the dark past your
Belly. Total night.
                                My mouth
Rests precisely in a bowl of flesh off-center
In your side. My dry lips scout—perfect
Rim, scar-slick; scooped

Sides, in the pit a complicated
Knot. I test it with my teeth—apparently
Flesh, apparently plaited in three
Equal strands round a denser
Core.
        It silently feeds me.
My tongue is bathed in more than spit.
I draw back. Your hand presses
Firmly again. I submit and am given
A thread of what I decide is nourishment—
Thinner than milk and mildly bitter
With occasional grains I grind to paste.
In maybe a year I rise enough to thank you.
You press then with mammoth urgency, saying
"Never leave."
                        I don't but endlessly
Consume your gift, growing at a glacial
Rate of my own and seeing each dawn
That the nearest wall is all your eyes,
All lashed like horsetails and flicking in random
Harmonies I scan for news
Of a world beyond us, if any
Survive.

SEAFARER

I can make one true song about myself—
Sing voyages, how I worked through Hell,
Tunneled my grief in bowels of ships
(Deep waves sucking) or above
When I drew dark watch at prow:
We sheering loud cliffs, feet locked in frost,
Heart scalded in grief, hunger ravening
Sea-wild soul.
 No man who draws land-luck can guess
How, crazed, I plowed desperate winter
Through rimey sea on exile road.
Stripped of kin, swathed in ice,
I'd strain to hear past crashing wave
And sometime catch swan call for solace,
Gannet, curlew for company,
Gull's caw for drink.
Storm pounded stone, cold tern answered,
Tattered horn-beaked eagle screamed,
But no kind kin warmed harassed heart.
So he who tastes in guarded towns
Glee of wine, homebound pride,
Who never treks bitter trails—
How can he guess how hard I rode
When forced to take sea's long path
Through night, north snow, all shore ice-barred
In stinging hail, coldest seed?
 Yet now my heart drums out thought
To taste again steep salt waves.
Famished heart yearns to fare
Forward toward homes of strangers,
Stranger lands—though can there be
Man so grand (free with gifts,
Flushed with youth, brave in deed,
Loved by his lord) that will not
Always dread his sail toward
What God dooms? For him can be

No thought of harp, winning of rings,
Joy in woman, joy in world—
Only waves. He who's sailed
Will long to sail.
   Trees burst with bloom, towns with beauty,
Fields freshen, life hastens—
All things drive eager soul
To wander, him who dreams of flood.
So cuckoo moans, summer's scout;
Sings harsh sorrow into hearts.
Men lapped in ease never know
What wretches know on exile road.
Still my mind roams past my heart.
My dreaming now on ocean flood
Roams wide—whale haunts,
Earth's skin—comes back
Unfed. Lone flier cries,
Whets heart for whale's way,
Ocean's breast, because God's joys
Weigh more with me than this dead loan
Of life on land.
   I here deny earth's riches last.
One thief of three will seize all men—
Plague, old age, hate—and only praise
From them who stay is fame past death,
Fame won in deeds from foes on earth,
Fiend in dark: fame among hosts of God,
Bright angels.
   Days are done now, all earth's glories.
Kings are gone now, Caesar's gone—
Great gold-givers cloaked in splendor,
Fallen, gone: old joys gone.
Weaklings last and swarm the world,
Win it with sweat. Pride is shamed.
Lords of life age and parch
Like other men in middle earth—
Ambush of age, face pales,
Hair grizzles, dim eyes watch
Sons of princes rendered to dark:
Flesh numb to sweets, hands still, mind still.
And though a brother long to sow

His brother's grave with gold—death-hoard
Guarded by him while he drew breath—
To go with him and his sinful soul
For help against God's awfulness,
He cannot now.
   Great is the Judge's awfulness—
World turns from it though he founded firm
Earth's skin and sky. Fool is he
Who does not dread his Lord.
Death will teach him.

after the Anglo-Saxon

QUESTIONS FOR A STUDENT

Nine months after I published a novel called
Love and Work, you woke me at 1 a.m. by phone
From Charlottesville; and we talked twenty minutes—
You talked; I held in groggy misery,
Unable to ask why, for this first favor,
You couldn't keep human time or what you wanted.
(I'd heard two years before when you were my student
That you'd been the youngest recipient
Of electroshock in Tarheel manic-depressive
Annals—a spunky file that holds its own—
But all I noticed as you talked a straight path
Through my thorny genre-course in the novel
Was the nails on your stub fingers,
Wolfed to the quick). And all I remember your saying
That night is "Do you really mean
What you say in the book?" I said I did—
True enough for the hour, I must have thought,
Though in my stupor I failed to ask
What you thought I said or why that mattered.

Three days later in afternoon light, you phoned
Your estranged wife; begged her to come back and—
When she refused for the umpteenth time—blew your brains out
With her on the line, a pause in your plea.

Even I don't assume the burden of that;
But ten years on, from a deep of my own
(Maybe no match for your Mindanao
But an honorable trench that sinks as I move),
May I ask these questions, awake at least?
Did I say Death and Silence?
If so was I wrong? If—as older books than mine
Predict—your agony lasts, can it help any way
If I offer here (late to be sure but in a safer genre)
This peace to your ruins, your bloody nails?

THE ALCHEMIST

Laughing, the chemist set the hot alembic
Where it could cool, fuming at his grin.
Now he knew what—simply—he would need
To force the thing he coveted to come:

Mind as girdling as the zodiac,
Free and sovereign but fiercely ruled,
Glomerate with power, a private sea;
Eons for seething down this crystal crib

—In which the monster of his yearning lay
(Got now, blind, by him on this blind night),
Prima Materia: rose past him to God

While, babbling like a drunk, he lay among
His magic-set, his priceless brittle gear,
And craved the crumb of gold he'd just now had.

after Rilke

AT THE GULF

The night I arrived you fed me grandly
At the new French restaurant—a hippie chef
Four thousand miles from Avignon (home),
The image of Courbet and as good at his work:
Champignons à la grecque, veal *cordon bleu.*
Then led me through alleys empty at ten—
Steaming palms, bananas, reek of shrimp—
To a pier from which you said we'd swim
Tomorrow (I'd flown since dawn to be here).
A strip of boardwalk ten yards long,
Not even a jetty, land itself roofed
In lazy confidence, well-placed apparently—
Six feet beneath us the hot brown Gulf
(The day had hit ninety, was only now dying)
Hunched impotent at pilings, force discharged
On reefs I'd seen from the plane, bone
Shield, gorget five miles out:
Making us the gorge.

Alone, grogged, we bulged round dinner
And—however dark and dead, too early to sleep—
Looked down dumb at the grateful sea,
Tamed shallow flank of the Mother, decrepit,
Whispering denials of her history.
Yet when I spoke first (to speak at all,
More than airport chatter, tabletalk),
I said "Not tomorrow. Forgot my armor."
You laughed—"It's safe, roped for swimmers"—
Then pointed outward. I strained to see,
Seine safety from night. None. Night.
The sounds—our breaths, water's helpless thanks
That we stood here for stroking. I said "Rope or nets?"
—"One rope."
                    I laughed. "And a sign saying
SHARKS KEEP OUT?"
                    You nodded.

"They can read. They know. Old enough to know."
—"Know what?"
"What's meat, what's bone." You faced me.
—"Which am I?"
Your turn to work; you smiled—
I was darker than you, you faced the light—
"Can't read," you said. "Not old enough."

—"You or I?" I thought but didn't ask.
We looked down again as though water were legible,
Engaged in clear signals, high-noon and help.
There was light—amber, the one you faced,
Bare bulb high on a shed behind me—
Invading the water till a thin layer phosphored,
Membrane the depth of muscles at work,
Achieving nothing, massage for plankton.

So you said "Ready?" to the water not me.
It had stroked me to a calm so anesthetic
That I never thought "For what?" but had stepped
To say "Yes"—to movement, reunion,
Repair, forgiveness, sleep—when you said
"No" and pointed with your turned face,
Dark, down. Below, a shape
Parallel to us in the burning water,
Slow and writhing without clear bounds,
Black, refusing light and name,
Condensation of crowded night.
Or—I knew at your left, one hand away—
A messenger sent with my answer to your "Ready?",
Coming since dawn (dawn of what?),
Arriving now. Five feet long, clearer
Since it rode higher toward us, undulant,
Still refusing, anonymous, black.
"What is it?" I said, also to the water,
And hoped "A saving dolphin in the wiggle-dance
Of bees" (saving who from what?).

When you knew, you turned again, bore the light,
Smiled—"One too young to read."
"You're sure?"

I needed phylum, species, order.
—"A nurse shark prowling, a hungry baby."
It sounded—gone, message offloaded,
Return begun—and was instantly followed
By a second, leaner, priest to the oracle,
Interpreter, scourer.

He also writhed. Redundant—I'd learned,
Knew, looked up to ask "Do we swim?"
—"In the morning, after breakfast." You smiled.
—"Then there's time," I said to the water. "Grow."
You laughed. Our growing baby sank, offended.
You watched its mute plunge. Had you watched me,
Strained to see me (I was half to the light
For that one purpose, that you take the joke),
I was smiling in response, exhaustion, relief.

Idiot relief. For when we turned
(You took the first step, the lead toward home),
We turned again apart. Not at once—
One room, one struggle to join, stay joined,
But separate sleep where (drowned, in no light)
Smiles are less defense than a child's left hand,
Where we are no longer feeders but food
(Your cries woke me twice, your seizing hand),
Where meat and bone are nightly assaulted,
Rent past healing, abandoned diminished
In morning light.

LEAVING THE ISLAND

Even the coral reeks of us.
Alleys furred with rot burn our light.

We have done that kindness to several places—
Some of them common beds stripped quickly
Of visible spoor (invisibly salved, precious
With joy), actual cells cast off our juncture,
Fossil markers (to what? for whom?):
One block of a street, a shack on stilts,
An airport lobby where we passed like strangers,
A post-office table across which we spoke
(Spontaneous, hopeless) perfect words of total pardon—
Grand in memory as any in Genesis, *Cymbeline*.

The places are speechless with gratitude,
Heard by me.

ANNIVERSARY

Three years ago this week,
    You found an egg
Beside a hot crossroad,
    Pierced, drained but spared;
Intact—and no known hen
    For four, five miles.
How? Who? and Why? I took it
    As you gave it—
Silent gift—and propped it
    In a window.
Those years pass. Its eyeless
    Muddy gaze
Survives and says this much—
    "Function can change,
Form persevere,
    Fragile wholes
Be ruined yet outlast lives."

ATTIS

Borne over high seas in swift ship
To Phrygia, Attis urgent on hungry feet
Fled to black-shagged home of Goddess,
Rabid with need, mind choked on need.
There with flint unloaded his sex;
Then borne on lightness of her new freed body—
Fresh blood blotching earth, feet—
Seized light tambor (your tambor,
Cybele, Your mystery, Mother), struck it, rung it
In tense hand of snow, howled tight-throated
Song to sisters. "Up. Go. Scale
Crags of Cybele, clamber beside me—
Queen's prize herds hunting exile home,
Flock at my heels who've taken my lead
Through boiling surf on cruel sands,
Gouged Venus from thighs in excess loathing:
Feed Queen's heart with laughter of flight!
Now. To Cybele's piney home
Where cymbals crash, hard tambors answer,
Phrygian flutist blows curved calamus,
Maenads in ivy fling hot in ring,
Keen as they brandish sacred signs,
Where tramps of the Queen crowd to dance.
With me, beside me—run to join!"
When Attis—forged woman—summoned sisters,
Quivering tongues hissed Yes from dance,
Pocked cymbals crashed, tambors rang glad.
Ida's green sides bore clutching climb
After Attis—quickest, gasping, lost—
Still leader howling through thickening pines,
Unplowed heifer scared, lurching in harness.

There—spent—they dropped at Cybele's door,
Slept hungry blinding sleep that smoothed
Clenched minds, locked limbs.
But—dawn: gold Sun, His scalding eye

Struck air, packed ground, ferocious sea,
And Attis' sleep. Calmed, sealed eyes
Slit, Attis saw act and losses, saw
Puckering scars, raced in mind
To empty shores, wailed lost home.
"Home that made me, bore me, that I fled,
Hateful slave, to roam waste Ida—snow-choked,
Ice-ribbed caves of beasts, my own mind beast.
How?—where?—to reclaim you?
For this instant soul is sane, let eyes
See you once. Not again?—home,
Goods, parents, friends, market, ring,
Wrestling pit? Agony. Groan grinds groan.
What have I not been, what form not filled?—
I woman, cocked boy, boy-child, baby,
Crown of the track, oiled glory of the pit,
Warm doorsills ganged with friendly feet,
Garlands round me to deck my house
At dawn when I stood from my own wide bed:
Now priestess to gods, slavegirl to Cybele, maenad,
Scrap of myself, gored man, dry girl,
Chained—no hope—to green frigid Ida
With deer grove-haunting, rooting boar,
Each thin breath poisoned by memory."

Noise of her pink lips—news to gods.
Cybele, bending to lion at Her left, terror of herds,
Said "Now. Go. Hunt Attis
Toward Me. Drive him through woods till, mad, he heels;
Goes down appalled, lashed by your tail
To My ring where pines stagger at your voice."
Wild, She unharnessed yoke, lion crouched,
Roused rage, charged woods toward Attis, tender
By marble sea—slave, girlslave all his life.

Strong Goddess, Goddess Cybele, Goddess Lady of Dindymus—
Spare my house, Queen, from total fury.
Hunt others. Seize others. Others appall.

after Catullus

BETHLEHEM—CAVE OF THE NATIVITY

The air of this cave
Is actual substance,
Nearly transparent but grained
Like an oak wall or
Braided like water in a weir
Though still.

The blade of rust
That scores your tongue
Is atoms of iron—
Girl's blood on that rock
Where she spread,
Subliming at a constant rate
Two thousand years
Though tossed by flame
Of adoring lamps.

Taste slowly,
Drink.

JERUSALEM—CALVARY

Beyond this aromatic Greek monk
With the roll of toilet paper by his foot
(You must pay him to stand here)—
An altar on legs, beneath it a disc,
In the disc a hole.
                                        If you've paid enough
(He names no sum), he'll say as you crouch
"Reach in. Golgotha.
Hole for cross."
                                   Beware.
Eight empty inches, then live rock—
Cooling mouth, still raw
At the lip. One whole arm inserted
Would reach dead center.

PURE BOYS AND GIRLS

Pure boys and girls,
Diana's wards,
We praise her thus—
  Best seed of Jove,
Latona's child,
Cradled by her
Near Delian grove
(So You be Queen of Mountains,
Woods, Deep Glades,
Queen of Rivers crashing in their course),
Mothers in birth-groan
Call you Queen of Light,
Others Dark Lady,
Moon of Stolen Gleam.
Goddess, by months
You measure out our year,
Filling the honest farmer's house with store.
Holy—whatever name
You please to wear—
Save as you once saved
Romulus' big brood.

after Catullus

NIGHT SPEECH

In ten years of this
The most you've said
Is the odd "I'm glad"
To my declarations.
The rest is silence and
Its works—
Your silence, open as
Our window toward the sea
And above it your whole
Face charged
Again with my
Visitation: raft
Combusting in the night,
Moored to me.

TEN YEARS, FOUR DAYS

1. Petroleum dark.
   I pierce maybe you.
   Cries maybe your voice.

2. Greek cross—
   Equal arms, legs,
   Dense crown at the joint—
   Your thatch, my thorn.

3. You
   Through glaze
   Of maybe transport.
   Repeatable saint,
   Fugitive text.

4. Grinder.
   Who will eat this bread?

RESCUE

Something I never told you—I watched, hardly blinking,
Each moment of the morning you were nearly drowned
Or taken by moray, shark, barracuda
As you tested yourself in the half-mile channel
Between our room and Advent Island.

You know this much—that you walked down that morning
(A Monday in March) after breakfast on the beach,
Calm as a sleeper, to the hot smooth sea;
Fell forward on the water and dug your way
With no visible effort to a coral bone
Two hundred yards long: scene of nocturnal
Drinking parties and home to a huddle
Of scrub evergreens raided at Christmas
By natives of the larger bone, where we stayed.
You swam twenty minutes—past the odd flotilla
Of junk boats, sleek yachts—then walked up
Out of the sea as rested as a child at dawn,
Your back straight and steady, or like one of a number
Of maritime gods with grace to bestow
If they turn and look. You stood a few seconds,
Made two deep bows which were either obeisance
To what I could not see or simple stretches;
Then ran up the white beach, rounded the far end,
And vanished in cedars.
                                        I said to myself
Something very much like "The perfect soul"—
You, I meant, and *perfect* for me;
A statement untouched by the five years since—
Then turned to my reading, an hour of watching
Imagined souls secrete real lives
On my hands: peaceful joy.
                                        When I looked again
You were vanished still, no sight of you
On land or water. I think I felt
A quick chill in the morning,

Viscid bubble blown by a corpse.
I say *I think* when what I recall
Is I stood to wash and was clean again
Of the traces of you and well into dressing
When a workman knocked and entered to fix
The glass-door lock (we'd been open to passers).
I finished; he tinkered in admirable silence
Till he said—over some twenty feet between us—
"That child's a goner less he's stronger than he looks"
And aimed at the Gulf a finger cold
As the first hump of fear I'd ignored
Awhile back.
                    I braced and came forward. You were midway
Between the island and me, stroking
Slowly. I could not see your face but you seemed
Safe enough. I asked the man "Why?"

He was back at his work and did not look again—
"Tide's turned against him and that's a shark channel."

In a minute's wait I confirmed the tide.
You were steadily draining-off to my left,
Nothing between you and Mexico but
Three hundred miles of thick green Gulf;
The sharks were a guess, though a native's guess
(Roughly half the American shark-attacks
Of the twentieth century occurred hereabouts).
I said "Who could help him?"
                                        He said "God Above
Or the U.S. Coast Guard if they're not at lunch"
And left, door fixed.
                          The options were plain—
One, walk eight feet and phone the Coast Guard;
Ask them to rescue a single swimmer
In the tidal rush (it was sliding now
Toward some wide mouth in its hidden floor)
And risk your refusal, embarrassment.
Or *Two,* stand still.
                          You were not advising—
No sign of distress, no pause or look,
Just a constant slap at the gorgeous face

Consuming you. Two safe yachts passed
In practical reach; you asked them nothing.

So for once myself I stood and offered
Nothing, having offered my life the night
Before and for some years past.
                                        You held
Your own through the next few minutes.
I could gauge you against the one visible buoy,
Knobbed with the standard pelican dozing
Near the spot you'd seized in the silent flux—
Expensive, I knew.
                            I held mine.
By then I was on our midget porch—
A squad of poolside lunchers behind;
Palms to left, coral boulders to right
(To form which, billions of sentient lives
Had volunteered bodies less fragile than yours).
You were only a hundred yards away.
Did you see me at all? I waved one time—
A modified Indian-greeting, palm-out,
Inviting an answer.
                            Nothing, I thought.
Did I miss some plea? I waited two minutes,
Monstrous gap.
                        Then you vanished;
Were swept down left past the pelican,
Still afloat but not stroking, arms abandoned.
The next pier hid you.
                                I must have prayed.
But what I remember is combing my hair
And walking at a sane brisk clip out the door
Into sun—past the pool and a girl mock-drowning
A boy who'd seemed all week her brother;
Then into the street past the First Shell Shop
And its grimy display of the Giant Clam,
Threat to Pearl Divers; then on to the pier
Behind which you'd vanished two minutes before.
I thought you were dead. I was calm with the thought.
It filled my skull like a plug of gelid fat,
Room for nothing else.

At the pier there was
One boat, a forty-foot ancient—*Proud Mari*—
And on it a middle-aged woman in a 1940s
Tank suit, coiling rope. I stopped.
She looked and awarded my wait a grin
Bleak as her timbers. Helpless, I smiled—
The hulk had blanked my view of the water—
And gathered to ask if she'd seen a swimmer
In trouble just now.
You rose at the far side—
Her port rail, soaked: your hands, head, face.
You didn't see me. You said to the woman
"Can I land here please? I'm a little bushed."
You were ivory, translucent in the final seconds
Of total exhaustion.
She said "Help yourself"
And went on coiling.
You managed to haul
Your legs aboard (there were still two, intact).
They bore you the moments you shuddered in glare,
Lovely as anything borne by the earth
That noon—any noon—and *seen*
By me in lucid perfection of love
That moment, though I'd watched you drown.
Then you strode
Forward, frail as a calf on your pins,
And were over the near side and six feet away
Before you saw me, your disyllabic "Hi"
Preserved in its brightness and plunging distance.
You might well have asked "What are you here for?"—
I needed proof you were really alive—
But you said "Lunch time"
And I said "True."
It was true; we ate it by the pool—shrimp
Salad and a butterscotch pie so rich
I expected a carbohydrate fit any instant.
It never struck and when (over coffee)
You lightly sketched your recent dilemma,
I concealed my witness, listened rapt,
And expressed post-facto restrained delight
At your narrow luck.

My full delight
Poured freely after dark when, stronger, you rose
On cool sheets above me and rode through
Twelve long minutes of danger toward another
Wordless rescue, borne by me
(The next word was *Thanks*, conceded by both).

I was also asking pardon in every cell,
And I felt you give it from an endless horde.
But I never spoke my offer again—
Simply my life—and never confessed
That paralyzed witness of your capture by the sea,
Its release or abandonment of what it had left you.

What had it left you? Tell me
That please. What have we left you?

Telling you now, I find what's left
In my own swept head—my silent knowledge
As you vanished in cedars years ago:
I required your life.
The offer stands.

TWO

NINE MYSTERIES

(Four Joyful, Four Sorrowful, One Glorious)

The Angel Gabriel was sent from God to a city in Galilee named Nazareth to a virgin promised to a man named Joseph of the house of David. The virgin's name was Mary. Coming in on her he said "Rejoice, beloved! The Lord is with you."
LUKE 1:26–28

ANNUNCIATION

The angel tries to imagine *need.*
Till now he has not stood near a girl—
Odd generals, magistrates, prophets in skins—
And since his mission is to cry "Beloved!"
And warn of the coming down on her
Of absolute need, he pauses to study
Her opaque hands—both open toward him—
And strains to know what need could draw
The Heart of Light to settle on this
Dun child, clay-brown, when curved space
Burns with willing vessels compounded of air.
He feels he is failing; is balked by skin,
Hair, eyes dense as coal.
"Beloved" clogs his throat. He blinks.
Nothing needs this. He has misunderstood.

The girl though has passed through shock to honor
And begins to smile. She plans to speak.
Her dry lips part. "*Me.*" She nods.

The low room fills that instant with dark
Which is also wind—a room not two
Of her short steps wide, plugged with dark
(Outside it is three, March afternoon).
In the cube, black as a cold star's core,
One small point shines—her lean face
Licked by a joy no seraph has shown,
An ardor of need held back for this
And bound to kill.
But slowly she dims,
The room recovers, she opens a fist.

*

The angel can speak. “Rejoice, beloved!”

The girl laughs one high note, polite—
Cold news—then kneels by her cot to thank him.

Now the birth of Jesus Messiah was like this. When his mother Mary was promised to Joseph before they came together she was found big-bellied by the Holy Spirit.

Now Joseph her husband being good and not wanting to disgrace her decided secretly to dismiss her.

But while he considered these things—look—an angel of the Lord appeared to him in a dream saying "Joseph son of David, don't fear to accept Mary your wife since the thing fathered in her is from the Holy Spirit." MATTHEW 1:18–20

REPARATION

I'm not especially known for dreams—
There is one though that has had some fame
In which the angel visits me, sleeping,
And says I'm to marry the girl anyhow;
That her story is true.
The dream was true—
I had it, I mean: angel-visit and explanation,
That I choose to believe as far as it went.
What is not so famous (entirely secret
Till now in fact) is a second dream
That, the more I think, I think came first.

We were in a room—her mother's house—
In natural light, some distance apart.
Her mother had left us a moment before,
And we were alone for the first time really—
(I'd watched her alone at the well, in her garden;
But always till now in open space,
No walls round us).
Our arms were down
But our eyes met closely. I knew two things—
That her body, small for her age though sturdy,
Was an adequate hive for making the boy
I'd failed to make on my late dry wife;
That I'd fail again. I wondered *why?*
There was ample evidence my body worked—
Ducked and nodded at appropriate sights—
But no cause dawned: just desolate news
That nothing would come of this, not from me.

I didn't move. I said "Is it true?"
She said a plain "No" and made one move—
One step that consumed the space between us,
One hand to raise my cold right wrist
And spread my palm, one finger pressed
In the palm, then gone.
                                        Alone in the room
I watched what I had—the hand, broad hand
That had howled, blank *howled*, for a thing to hold.

I was given two things. The spot she'd touched
Blistered and burst; a brown stem rose
And ramified slowly in tiers of thorns—
Desert shrub. Then beneath the shrub
A child condensed, size of the second
Joint of my thumb, with a manchild's organs—
Perfect, the size of three barley grains:
The thing I'd get. So I shut my hand
Upon it gently and have lived with that.

The more I've thought, the more that seems
My only dream—untold till now,
As I said; now told. My hand has adequately
Held it till now.
                                Look here. Still mine.

She bore her firstborn son and wrapped him and laid him in a manger since there was no room for them in the inn. LUKE 2:7

CHRIST CHILD'S SONG AT THE END OF THE NIGHT

I have, to be sure, enjoyed the event
And am conscious of various efforts involved—
Trips by ass, foot, camel,
Wing—to welcome what must necessarily
Seem a bafflement (a normal
Boy, ten fingers and toes, brown eyes
And hair) at the narrow end
Of angel prophecies, celestial consorts,
Stellar anomalies, perturbations.

None seemed perturbed. All grinned and bowed;
All left some token of satisfaction—
Free-will offerings in lieu of tickets
To the single display that will not recur.

Now in late quiet, my parents
Asleep, I'm free to think the last
Free thought I'll be allowed. Let it stand,
Grateful chord to the evening's music—
Grateful, short, unavoidably true—

Though handsomely asked, every other one here
Could have stayed at home—Joseph, my mother,
Could still be single in Nazareth: barren.
Shepherds and magi consented with near-
Unseemly ease. Angels themselves were
Free to choose—note the famous
Dissenter, hid there by the door.
I am the one in the reach
Of time who is given no choice,
The chosen child.

They came to the house of the synagogue leader. Jesus saw a commotion, people weeping and wailing hard. Entering he said to them "Why make a commotion and weep? The child is not dead but sleeps."

They mocked him.

But expelling them all he took the child's father, mother and those with him and went in where the child was. Grasping the child's hand he said to her "Talitha koum" which is translated "Little girl, I tell you rise."

At once the little girl stood and walked round—she was twelve years old—and at once they were astonished with great wildness. MARK 5:38–42

DEAD GIRL

I have died and am glad.
My body is twelve years old on my bed.
I can see it there and the room around it,
The hall outside, all the people I knew.
I am smaller than I thought—they are pressing me down
Like a bale with their eyes; and my father has brought in
Two old men with flutes, four expensive wailers
Who must be boys but look like dolls.
I am shrinking from that (I mainly loved music)
Or was shrinking when I died. I remember clearly.
My father kept asking if I was in pain;
And I nodded Yes, though I'd gone past pain.
Pain had passed on some good while before
When it dawned on me *No one will touch me.*
Once I died they would wash me and bind me tight.
Then no one would ever touch me again—
I would be unclean; men would walk
Whole miles not to touch my tomb (our family
Has a tomb: I will be on a slab in the dark tomorrow).
I was thinking that and may have been smiling,
So calm anyhow that the way I knew
I had finally died was having the bracelet
Cool on my wrist. I was standing outdoors
In light houseclothes and had on my arm
The big dark bracelet that had been Grandmother's
And would come to me on my wedding day—
Worked with monsters' heads and fiery leaves.
I was thoroughly glad and rubbed at the bronze

And smelled my finger and walked on forward
Past the well I would never drink water from again
Toward the edge of a lake.
                                        There is no one but me.
The dead world is empty and was made for me.
I will never be fed, talked to or touched.
I am glad, as I said, and have left them my body.
It is what they have waited twelve years to get.
I sit on the wet rocks and watch them have it
With their eyes—bats feeding—
Till almost dark. I am cool and calm.
I have seen a single star and thanked it.
They will wail all night.
                                        But the dead need rest.
When night is thoroughly down, I am tired.
I find a beached dry boat and enter.
I lie on a rag sail and press
My bracelet in on a chest where no
Heart beats, cold against me
(I have still not warmed it; I never will).
Then I shut my eyes and shut out all—
Stars, lake, that room, my twelve-year-old
Body bled by grief of men
Who needed me; will now never touch me.
I make one strong thrust out with my mind
And float on a rest I smile to meet—
Black water beneath me that bears my weight,
Alone in my wedding-ware for good.

This sleep will last till the end of things.

They got their hands on Jesus and seized him.

But one of the bystanders drawing a sword struck the high priest's slave and cut off his ear.

Speaking out Jesus said to them "Did you come out with swords and sticks as if against a rebel to arrest me? Daily I was with you in the Temple teaching and you didn't seize me. But the scriptures must be done."

Deserting him they all ran.

One young man followed him dressed in a linen shirt over his naked body. They seized him but leaving the shirt behind he fled naked.

Then they took Jesus off to the high priest and all the chief priests, elders and scholars gathered. MARK 14:46–53

NAKED BOY

He got to our house at ten that morning,
Alone, not hungry—first time
I'd seen him completely alone. The mob
That had trailed him all week—all year—
Was simply gone. He'd hid from them somehow
And turned up here—himself, no disguise:
Not even the famous adhesive woman
In sight or John. My mother and Rhoda
Had left a little before since shops
Would mostly close at noon, so I
Met him in the porch and said she was gone.
He nodded—"I came to help you."
I couldn't think how but my pleasure
Must have looked like bewilderment. He said
"The hen house." I remembered telling him
That Mother had asked me to build a coop,
That I'd gathered boards and would get to it soon.
But I hadn't meant this day—Passover
Ban began at noon, no work after noon.
I said "We'd never get it finished by noon."
He said "We'll finish." I'd have seized adders
For him, so I just led him out
To the yard; and with hens limping round us,
He carefully showed me how to start;
Then sat on a ledge to watch me at it,
Coming over occasionally to do something right.

*

I worked in a steady fever of joy,
Assuming and fearing he'd leave any minute
Or the friends would find him. He never
Went farther than three steps from me, and nobody
Came but Mother and Rhoda just before
Noon with all they'd bought
For the long weekend. He only told Mother
"I'm here to help him. We'll work till it's done."
She thanked him but said we should come in
At noon. He just said "We'll finish,"
And we worked right through the volley of horns
From Temple Hill announcing ban.
By the time we had got the job on its feet,
It was three o'clock; and nothing was left
But the hard part—the door, fitting
The door. He took over then and started
On that; but to keep me busy, he said
"Please tell me all your life."
I laughed but he said "No, please" so I did.
He listened as if my thin news
Was one last missing rail
For some bigger hut he had
In mind, though all I could tell was the trifling
Schedule of fifteen years in my father's
House, my father's death three months
Before.
          I'd got to that end when the twelve
Friends shuffled up by twos and threes
From whatever day they'd had without him.
I understood then that they'd known
Where he was and had kept their distance, which proved
More than ever he'd chosen the time
With me. They lay round the yard while
He hung the door, and Mother came out
And whispered to me to go to my uncle's
Downhill for seder—he'd asked to eat
Here with his friends, and her hands were full.
I said out loud "I'll stay close
And help." He heard me, faced me,

Shook his head once No. Then he set down
The knife he was trimming the door with,
Turned (no look back) and climbed
Eight steps to our high room,
Friends behind him.
                                        So I stayed
To finish the door he'd abandoned,
Put one scared hen in to give her
A lead, then ignored Rhoda's call
To wash for my uncle's and decided to walk
Out past Hinom to a cut in rock
Where I lie when I'm low and complain to bushes,
The odd lost goat or lunatic.
                                                    But the streets
Were solid with gentiles, soldiers and a few
Northern hicks who were in town
For more than lamb with herbs; and after
A few yards of bucking crowds—relays
Of hands plucking at me in dark till they came
To seem the promise I needed:
That the secret heart of town was tender,
Had reached for me and would fold me in
If I nodded or smiled—I bared my
Excellent teeth to the dry air
And grinned through a slow wide wheel
Round Zion.
                              No taker. I was all
One piece, back at Mother's—safe,
Entirely me. Caged, prowling in my bones,
And as likely to sleep as a tom in a ring
Of staring dogs.
                                But I climbed to my own
Room and, stripped on my mat, gave myself
To myself—not quite a cold supper, a meal
Nonetheless: short, soporific.

Mother touched me later—I'd dressed before sleep
In a clean nightshirt—and said, all dark,
"Quick. To the garden. Lead him here
Fast." She left as quickly.
                                                I lay still,

Understanding clearly—*Butchery, or the dream*
Of butchery, begins. I did not plan to move.
I planned to sleep and did; then dreamed
That my father had not died but, cured, sat
With Mother as I came down at dawn for food
And said "I have waited all night for you."

So I woke, sick with shame, and ran in my shirt
Through ways only slightly less packed than before—
Past three distinct voices requesting me—down and cross
Kidron, uphill to the garden.
They already had
Him (no sign of the others except for
Redhead, back on the rim of torchlight,
Explaining). A Temple guard held Jesus
By the elbows. I doubt he saw me, but he looked
My way very steadily.
So I went on toward him
And nobody stopped me. His gaze never broke—
No recognition, no warning—but when
I was three steps short of his face,
He said "Would the hens go into the house?"
I said "Yes." Then he said he was sorry.
I understood he didn't mean the hens;
But before I could ask "For what?" or forgive him,
The guard grabbed my shoulder with far more strength
Than he held Jesus with.
I stood a long moment,
Wrenched back hard. He held onto Jesus
But struggled with me enough to tear my shirt.
Then Jesus said "*Leave.*" I tore clean free,
Stood another instant naked. The guard
Called for help, but by then I was dark.

It had been a repeated dread of course—
Stripped in the streets, no cover near—
But nobody bothered following; and I ran
Through deeper black toward the edge of houses,
Then walked to my moaning place in the rock
And managed sleep—dreamless, cold.

*

When I woke, brown day was seeping up.
I stood, brushed grit from my side
And face and walked to my mother—bare
As she'd borne me, through streets as bare. I didn't
Think of him till, in sight of our gate,
A voice in a window—the one wake soul—
Said "You. Now. Please."
                                        I looked
And my mind stalled; but I never stalled,
Though a hand reached toward me—cupped and clean.
I strode in my cold skin the last steps home,
My dazzling hide.

Now when Pilate was sitting on the judgment bench his wife sent to him saying "Do nothing to that good man for I suffered much today in a dream because of him." MATTHEW 27:19

SLEEPING WIFE

We'd heard weird news all winter,
Filtered south—dead walking, wounds
Sealing—but I'd seen him just once
The previous morning as we crossed the Court
Of the Gentiles, bound for our Residence flat.
He lectured a modest huddle of rural
Pickers and scratchers (none visibly
Cured) and stood, arms up,
Spoon-thumbs, back to me—which helps
Explain his showing in the dream: younger,
Leaner, some distance from a man.

It was already light. My husband had
Left. I dozed, postponing the annual
Lamb-slaughter pending at our window.
He stood
In the door—black hair to his shoulders,
Stray wires on his chin: calm as wax.
I knew it was him when I called his name—
He'd made no noise, never did; the cries
Were mine. How I put that name to that
Face is still odd. Once named he could
Move. I was trusting he'd grin; but
The face rushed on, iron arrow. At
The bed he drew off the sheet, bowed my
Legs, bent, entered. Understand—no
Man's slim thrust, a child's clawing:
Dry fingers, arms, head,
Chest, hips, legs, feet.
I mentioned cries—*screams* (no help
Heard or came)—but I never objected;
And in maybe five minutes he'd packed me
Entirely with his crawl, fork to crown,
And rested at the absolute walls of my skin

So I only sucked spoonsful of air,
Bird-sips. I'd never breathe
Deep till I bore him somehow.

I woke, sent word (not detailing the dream);
And failed as has been fairly customary.
Our only child strangled inside me
Fourteen years ago—male, I was told.

Mary the Magdalene turned and saw Jesus standing, not that she knew it was Jesus.

Jesus said to her "Woman, why cry? Whom do you want?"

She thinking it was the gardener said to him "Sir, if you carried him off tell me where you put him and I'll take him."

Jesus said to her "Mary."

Turning she said to him in Hebrew "Rabboni" which means Teacher.

Jesus said to her "Don't touch me for I haven't yet gone up to the Father. But go to my brothers and tell them 'I'm going up to my Father and your Father, my God and your God.' " JOHN 20:14–17

RESURRECTION

She's come a last time before day to touch him.
Last and first. Till now she has not—
Though till him what she'd known
Was ways to touch, valuable ways
That got her her life: small life
Promising to end, early rest.
Friday they'd only had time to loop him
In myrrh and aloes with linen strips
When Sabbath stopped them.
She's filled thirty hours
With hope of this, a private end—
Five minutes alone at the instant of day
To find his face and feet, wash them.
Then the gang of others, parceling him
(She'd hid all Saturday to plan in secret,
To come here unfollowed in Sunday dark).
She even knows her way round guards,
Her way to move rock—her old way, her—
And have her chance and be gone by light
To whatever house will feed her now.

No guard, no rock. Her fast hands
Scratch at the small thick dark. No body
On the ledge—blank yards of linen, stiff
With blood.
Late, she thinks. She says "*Again.*"
All her life she has missed her needs
By moments. Simple needs.

She shudders as demons
Pluck at her face—blind cocks, horn beaks
That will gouge till they find old holes
In. They touch her at least, know her slick skin.
She half-grins in welcome, slumps on the ledge.
Hot padding. She gnaws it.
What she does not know—
Outside it is day. In the garden he hunts
Her, her first. He is stunned—
Calf, wet colt, boy dredged from sleep.
Each step toward her, he burns with fresh blood
Rushing his legs. He feels he has won
All he swore to win, can face her now.

When she steps from the grave, sees him, knows,
He will not let her touch him.

Throwing the coins down in the Temple Judas left and going off hanged himself. MATTHEW 27:5

INSTRUCTION

I'm given the time it takes to tell you
Precisely this. Ask no questions.
There was one sighting which
Has not been reported by loyalists.
Peter, John, Mary, James
Have milked tears enough with their
Reunions to farm a fair-sized
Salt-lick in Sodom. I don't grudge them
That. The one not reported however
Was to me.
I'd got out of town by Friday
Dawn to miss the dustup I launched
In the garden. The cash was slung in my left
Groin, nudging other privates,
For the seven-mile walk to Emmaus—
The inn. We'd never worked that.
I could sleep the hours it would take to kosher
Him white as veal, the loyalists to note they'd
Failed him equally and scuttle home—
Dried boats, nets, wives,
Mothers-in-law. Then I'd head back
To town for the sinecure they'd thrown in
To sweeten the cash—bookkeeper
At the licensed Temple lamb-and-dove
Purveyance: no one cracked a smile.
I'd start Monday morning, under light
Guard till Friday (they had a week's
Worth of anxiety for me; I'd
Known the eleven through a year on the road
And knew I was safe—they'd growl but
On fast feet: Parthian growls).
I slept
Two days, waking only to think I'd
Never slept better and gnaw
A flat cake I'd hooked on the way

And ask if the rest—alluvial mud—
Wasn't better reward than cash or job
Or memory of Peter's white face
In fireshine, slick with fright:
Blown hog's bladder burst
By boys (the answer was Yes and I'd sleep
Again).
Sunday evening I was sated but
Hungry. I skimmed my eyes with cool
Dry fingers, rehung the privates
And went down to eat in the common room—
Loud clutch of Passover pilgrims
Bound north, no face I knew.
I'd finished when another three entered
And sat—Klopas, his squat wife, a trim
Tan stranger. The Klopases had bankrolled
Us, steady but stingy, through Galilee.
My legs jerked to leave, then locked me
In. I was legal; I'd make my first
Stand here. But they talked to the stranger
And never looked up. I licked at
My bowl and filled my space—paid-up patron.
The window over them faced due-
West, so I fixed on that and bathed
In sunset.
The girl brought their food.
They groveled to bless it. The stranger stood,
Neat as a sprout sucked up in a morning.
It was him, no question—crammed-
Down, a little ashy at the gills but
Pleasant and coming toward me.
I tried again to rise in the days
It took him to reach my bench;
Legs refused.
His hands were ruined—
Brown holes, barely dry—
But otherwise fit. I begged not to touch
Them, though I didn't speak.
He kept silent too,
Kept hands at his thighs.
No pause or stare, the smile

Never quit. He bent
To my hair and pressed it once, quite lengthily,
With a mouth that seemed his usual mouth—
No stars or rays, no sizzling brand—
Then walked the breadth of the floor and out.
I had not had to touch him—
Not direct, not skin.
I waited for roars, leaps, laughs
From the room. Klopas and his wife were chewing
In tears, drowned in the gift.
No one else had looked.
I sat till the next gnat
Sapped my heel, then stood as I was—
Freed to stand into honor like rain—
And went through the same door,
Same empty yard.
                                        Halfway back
To town in dark dry as meal, I
Groped out a tree that promised to hold.
Honor had lasted a full three miles.
I lasted a full two minutes
By the neck, longer than planned—my well-oiled belt
(The privates were insufficient ballast).
Nobody claimed body or ballast;
We two were the bachelors.
                                                            You may now ask questions.

Saying these things—with them looking—Jesus was lifted up and a cloud took him from their eyes. ACTS 1:9

ASCENSION

I expected one question the moment I was back—
Where did you go? Nobody asked it.
In thirty-nine days of astounding them
At our various haunts from Jerusalem
To the Sea and demonstrating my obvious
Self—tangible as a good plow
And roughly as worn—I heard only
One thing in several forms:
Who are you? I continued to show them
The answer was plain—*I'm what I've been*
From the start. Feel me. Some were readier
Than others to accept—Magdalene, Thomas:
She grabbing, he gouging.
Some came forward scared as boys
That have turned up a snake in a gully,
Sleep or dead—Andrew, young Mark.
Some never came at all—my brother James,
Which was no great surprise; Levi and John.
I kept on thinking John was the hold-out—
Beloved John—that when he got his
Nerve up, felt me once more,
Proved to us both I was *me* but *leaving*,
Then I could leave.
                                        I'd prepared my speech.
John would step up and kiss my left
Cheek-bone (thereby canceling
Judas' last greeting, damp still
And cool though spring days blew past it,
Helpless to warm); then would step
Back and nod acceptance of change—
You, departing. Then I would say
In the thirty-nine hours when death
Begins, you do not sleep. You rest
And recall every living person
You loved and expected. *The rest comes in this*—

You no longer expect *them: no more*
Than horses eating in ditches expect
Other horses. You think "That was it.
Thirty years to learn that." Then you
Wake and are happy. I even tracked
Him down on a fishing trip; but he kept
Safe distance between us, two steps.
And I knew I shouldn't force him.
So the fortieth
Day I resigned myself to a longer
Wait. We were back in Jerusalem—over in
The celebrated terrible garden, just olive
Blooms now. Ten of the pupils were
Sitting with me, discussing escape—
I was hunted of course and was well-
Disguised as a touring Greek.
John was in town, tending my mother
Who was ailing slightly or so
We'd heard: I still hadn't seen her,
Avoiding evidence of my worst
Harm.
But here they came. Peter
Saw them first, at the foot of the hill,
And whispered to me. There was time
To leave. I'd have been overhill
In Bethany by the time they
Arrived if I'd left then, but
I held my ground—for John not
Her.
It should have been for her.
I sat in dread, hard as I'd known
Here the night they seized me, and let
Her come.
She was ruined as the town itself
Would be—sewn with salt, barren
By me: barely fifty, stunned
As eighty. Or so it looked at nearing
Range; but she walked on her own and hurried
A little the last few yards,
Stopping an instant three steps
From me; then coming the whole way,

Kissing my left cheek, taking my
Right hand and touching her finger
To the rosy scar. Then she laid the whole
Palm over her mouth, returned it
To me and said "*Promise me*
It is possible to bear."
                                        I thought she meant
Me, for her to bear the rest
Of me. I doubted I could promise that
Honestly.
                    But she said "*Leaving.*"
I could promise that, having undergone
Considerable pain to leave and return—
And answer this question, finally asked.
I could answer it. I laughed and nodded—
She could halfway smile—and found I was free
To leave, and left.

THREE

PICTURES OF THE DEAD

1. ROBERT FROST, 1951

Begin then, Sisters of the sacred well—
"Most beautiful line the world affords,
And it can be *learned*," you say and repeat
It three slow times in your world-
Famed curmudgeon growl.
                                        I'm
Eighteen, silent in a team of Chapel
Hill Ph.D.'s all
Pumping for inside dope on Ezra
Pound. You're seventy-seven, refusing,
Substituting Milton and making us
Take it—for the hour at least, all
You'll give.
                  On the spot, I
Take it for no better reason than
Your frightening face, beat of your elephant
Hide on pine, unanswerable voice.
I was right. Still am, still
Learning the line.

2. W. H. AUDEN, 1957

We're dining alone at The Bear in Woodstock.
You've drunk your regulation two gins-and-
French, then insisted on buying the wine—
Lafite. I remember no other word you
Said nor what we ate in the packed
Small room (I'm to pay for the food);
Only that after in late spring
Evening, you seem to see nothing
As I drive us through Blenheim Park: still
Earth's clear apex for me.
                                        Back at my
Rooms in mean brick Headington—
A few yards down from mean
Tolkien, secreting his dream—I produce
A friend's gift from a Christmas
Nervous collapse in Madeira: hand-
Lettered 1930 Madeira,
Year of your *Poems.* You seem not
To notice; say only as you taste
"It's turned to gin." You sit in my chair,
I at your knees on the leatherette
Hassock. We drink all the gin.
I remember we laughed but again
No word of all we said; only that
At one unheralded moment, mid-sentence,
You lean with the grace of an oak umbrella-
Rack, kiss me twice rapid-fire
On the dry right cheek.
They remain—and my thanks.

3. ROBERT LOWELL, 1968

The night you died in a New York cab,
Here in my bed (oblivious) I dreamt
We were on my terrace again—you,
Jack Knowles, Charlie Smith and
I.
  We eat my leftover
Curry and rice, lie back to laugh
In April sun under baby leaves
While you read us Auden's "On the Circuit"—
I shift so frequently, so fast,
I cannot now say where I was
The evening before last,
Unless some singular event
Should intervene to save the place,
A truly asinine remark,
A soul-bewitching face.
The place (recent scene of a love
Entertaining as the Dresden fire-storm)
Is saved again by your broad mug—
Half-Homeric, half-mad,
Burnt over by intermittent winds
That will get you yet. Still the dream is
Happy and oddly actual, mere
Memory.
            I wake refreshed,
Do a good morning's work,
Drive in for mail, then on to the shop
To buy your new *Selected Poems.*
As I pay, the clerk says "Too
Young to die"—the news on you.
Home I tell the maid my dream
And how you died while it came.
She says "That was nothing but his
Spirit as it left, passing through places
It had been happy in."
                                You were
Welcome both times.

ARCHAIC TORSO OF APOLLO

Look. You'll never conceive his head.
Eyes blank as apples ripen to this day
Under Greek junk, were crushed to lime for mortar.
But here the body burns, amends for blindness.
Legs, arms, thrust down—torches for his dark.

So he blinds you. So his smile survives
In wings of muscle lifting from his sex.
Permit his shining. Otherwise he'll hulk,
Another mineral bore cooling his heels.

Wait. If not he'll never break his chains
And stalk—now!—one step crams the room with light.
A star swells madly, famished for what fuel?
You. His chest, legs, haunches, sex—now eyes.
All locked on you. Change your life.

after Rilke

FOUND, FOR MY BROTHER

Here in my dream of Uncle Grant's shack,
Grubbing (for what?) in the packed fawn
Clay—alone, no human or bird to watch—
I find your old red square sand-shovel.
Neither of us can have seen it for thirty-odd years;
And surely it has either dissolved where you lost it
Or survived reforging for an interim war
(Dissolute atoms in the schist of Korea;
The thickets southward, your Vietnam).
It had leached anyhow from my consciousness.
I've longed occasionally for toys of my own—
The Seven-Dwarf set of castile soap,
The pillbox of dried mud from Hitler's Mercedes,
The boy-sized Charlie McCarthy with hinged lips—
But hardly for yours. Yours were weapons—
A footlocker-armory of realistic guns:
Colts, Lugers, Flash Gordons;
And you miles gentler than the Dalai Lama,
Despite your party renditions, age four,
Of "Don't Fence Me In!" with cap-
Pistol chorus (piano by me)—
Yet here my hands uncover this peaceful
Implement, realistic and real. I stroke it,
Quick to recall; then reinter it,
Certain it will constitute treasure for you—
Another true self endured and found.

Awake, tomorrow, I bring you here—
Actual site (the house long gone)—
We crouch by the oak, my fingers hunt
Unerringly.
                    You own it again.

TO MY NIECE—OUR PHOTOGRAPH IN A HAMMOCK

No one thinks you are mine.
I could have bought you from gypsies
Or—desperate, if solitude had left me desperate—
From a defrocked doctor who bootlegs at night,
With abortions and morphine, a sideline of babies:
Derelict blond blue-eyed bastard
In my Black-Welsh arms.

They're wrong. You are.
At eighteen months—a day, a moment—
You are my remains, my physical remains;
And you hoard already, little banker (no choice),
Every egg you will ever pay out on speculation,
Four hundred maybe in your fertile years.
Each one, of thousands—you're chocked for safety;
Roed like a shad against loneliness, extinction—
Guards already in final form, unknown as your death,
Some of the instructions I might have passed to Man.

Man may yet do without them.
If our picture is omen, you may seal your vaults,
Say the monthly No to the monthly hope,
Balk every try at blind continuance;
For though, in the frame, my hands strain to hold you,
You struggle to escape—me, your volunteering life
That swells each instant in you, presses every wall—
And you laugh, not with me but elsewhere, outward.
I know in retrospect that you laugh at the sky
Northwest of my roof, but what decked the sky
For you that day?—that evening, evening light.
What vision? What clear shaft opening to joy?
Like a white baby-seal—a dugong calf!—
You paddle the June air around us toward freedom.

I am laughing for the cameraman (your laughing father)
So I do not notice and wouldn't mind.

Here, I have you safely—my arms vs. yours—
And if, in years, your struggles wrench you loose,
Award you solitude, sterility, space,
The world will return you in hunger or duty
(It has brought me to you; I am choosing to hold you);
Trap you, raving, gnashing: feed you its diet.

Look. Neither of us noticed the news of that day—
You rapt in babyhood, I in pleasure—
The bedrock above which we hung and giggled.
Our picture, pitiless monitor, preserves it:
Even the hammock we swing in is a net.

I SAY OF ANY MAN

I say of any man, when he is good
  And wise, what does he need? Will some things
    Feed his soul? Is there an ear of corn,
      A secret vineyard ripening in the earth

To nourish him? Here is the truth of that—
  A friend may be the loved one, art is
    Much. Dear friend, here is the truth of you—
      Daedalus' ghost is yours, the summer woods'.

after Hölderlin

AURORA

Is it unacceptably
Self-absorbed
To ask if tonight's
Colossal veil
Of ascendant light
In the boreal sky
(First aurora
Visible to me
And displayed precisely
Twenty-four hours
Beyond the line
We drew beneath
Two perfect days)
Is admonition,
Responsive glory,
Or ions stunned
In our conjunction
And fleeing north?
The record can
At least confirm
That colors shifted
Steadily through
The ten cold minutes
I stood to watch,
Faced opposite your south—
No two alike,
All tinctures of blood.

A RAINBOW AND A DAY-OLD CALF

Four months of straining
To burn each other to the ground,
Strew the ashes; and here we agree
To a sunset walk in the greening field—
Day after April Fool, dry breeze—and
Are met by a rainbow in shameless stride
And a day-old calf who thinks it's hid
In two strands of honeysuckle,
Plain as a blaze.
                                I note the single omen
They make—arc and hider—
Read it for hope.

MAN AND FAUN

MAN This narrow stream pours to a waterfall;
And—what is that, a hairy shank which hangs
From dark moss cushioned onto dripping rocks?
The thicket of its head mats round a horn.
In my long hunting—woods, distant hills—
I have not yet seen this: no, do not move!
I bar all paths, shelter. Stand, face me.
Calming ripples lap a split goat's hoof.
FAUN We neither will be glad you found me here.
MAN I knew of beasts like you from ancient books,
Not that such useless things survived, ran free.
FAUN When—as you will—you drive me to depart,
Starved you'll thrash your woods for worthy prey—
Your only plunder: rodents, blind worms, slugs—
And when you've hacked your path through every thorn,
All your wells will dry into the sand.
MAN Warn me, huddled freak?—I who have killed
Giants, hydras, gorgons, glimpsed the basilisk;
Cleared wilderness, forced wilderness to yield?
Where black swamps smoked, grain ripens in the light;
Cattle safely pasture my green hills,
Farms flourish, cities rise, gardens gleam,
And woods enough survive for stag and doe.
My treasures I have dredged from sea and earth—
Stones themselves concede my victory;
Light and order strengthen in my tracks.
State your purpose, relic of chaos.
FAUN You are one man and where your vision fails,
My eyes burn on. You recognize no brink
Till you plunge to its pit—broken, torn.
When your grain ripens, when your cattle thrive,
When trees bend to you with their oil and grapes,
You call these recompense for labor, craft.
But earths that breathed beneath this crust still breathe,
Have never died, are welded in a chain
That will flail mad the hour one link is breached.

This was the day allotted for your rule.
Now surrender—you have seen the faun.
Doom begins. The cunning able mind,
Your light and guide, softens as you stand.
Your bond with beast and dirt also dissolves.
Revulsion, lust, tumult, monotony,
Dust and flare and death and origin—
Your grip upon the buried chain is broke.
MAN Who told you this? Gods provide for me.
FAUN Gods have their day like men. You were, you died,
And never knew your secret name.
MAN Blank raving!
FAUN Fall and pray to me that blankly raves.
MAN Bitter monster—twisted spine and mouth—
I see in you, ruined mirror, my old face.
In pity I delay my fatal spear.
FAUN No beast knows shame; no man knows gratitude.
All your craft, and you have never learned
The precious thing. Yet I have dumbly served.
Hear final warning—kill me, kill yourself.
Where my fur brushed, milk gathered, warm milk gushed.
Where my hoof did not press, no stalk saw light.
Were your mind all you'd had—ages since,
Your kind, your hectic business had stopped;
Woods had blackened, seedbeds burned to ash.
I was the water at the roots of life.

after Stefan George

TOWN CREEK

Two hours from home
(My home), we climb a mound
Heaped *circa* 1480 by the Creeks—
Tidily refurbished for the grade schools,
Idle adults scouting savagery.

On top, a box mud temple
To the god—sole faithful Sun.
Inside, pole benches—one a vacant altar.
Straw roof, pierced by a smoke hole, still transmits
His daily visit to the dugout hearth.

We edge into an unrequited glare;
You lean to touch the fuel
(Four pine logs). None here but us,
Five hundred years too late.

Whoever else embraced by this dead fire?

DIVINE PROPOSITIONS

That the animals love us.
That horses the size of granite bluffs
Will lay their huge hearts beside us
At night and sleep till we wake.
That wolves who gnash down stags in air
Will nursc our lost young,
Return them whole.

That you have laid your hawk head here
In my room (strange as the ocean floor),
Borne twenty nights' danger,
Returned each dusk.

YOUR ELEMENT

Earth, Air, Water, Fire—
The four meet in you
But your element is Silence,
The hard clear ether in which
You advance—

As last night,
Scraping dishes alone,
I caught at the window
A wash of lights,
The car they guided,
Your silent upright body
Through leaves,
Bent against me
The whole cool night:
A speechless shield.

BLACK WATER

Black water runs
Down in that ditch.
My love for you
Has locked my tongue.

But you talk love,
Talk loyalty.
A lie grates under
Every word.

So if I speak
My love ten times
And you still lie,
I'll go for good.

I thank you for
The time we had
And wish you luck
In days ahead.

after a German folksong

MEMORANDA

TOWARD JUNCTION

No map can show how—through the world—
Ample in power, clean in aim,
You move toward me. Incredibly, you do.
Certain the route is no print-out
From an odds machine, I wonder *Who?*
Some one or thing is sending you.
I suspect an intercession, a dead
But potent witness who has caught a burst
Of my gentlemanly thirty-year-long
Bellow and throws the switches that shunt
You here. Candidates narrow
To my mother or father, a bachelor cousin,
And Wystan Auden—not because he's starred
On James Merrill's Ouija or because
I'm reading the new biography he'd rightly
Have loathed (obtuse as a mirror) but because,
Despite his cold-douche kindness,
He's the one of the numerous familiar
Dead who'd have sought the post:
Yard-master of lines for lives he'd touched.
See him at the console, straining at lights
(All green for him), ears peeled
For groans, beaming again and sure
For once he can meet the task.
                                        You're
Not here yet. Proceed respectfully,
Observe timetables, augment the prayer:
Wystan—whoever, whatever—clear
The rails.

MEMORANDUM 1

At the first revelation of your body in the room—
Shabby dark of a family motel,
Ocean beside us (your first sight of it:
You asked "Will it keep on all through our sleep?"),
My eyes averted to grant you air
You did not require—
You called my name, compelling my look;
And though the body was calm, unflaunted,
Its ample secret flared, your gift,
And you said "None of my clothes are good enough for this."

May never be.

MEMORANDUM 2

You asked him to bless the cross you'd picked
From his narrow room of featherweight rosaries,
Saints' lives bound in frogskin vinyl.
He could no longer stand, and he'd welcomed us in whispers—
"Fifty years here but I come from Tipperary."
He found in his lap the frayed magic band,
Slowly hung it round his neck,
And for maybe a minute whispered to your cross
As he stroked its cellophane wrapper with earnest crosses
Secreted by his own wide hand.
Then from the shelf eight inches to his left,
He took an old eyewash-bottle and squeezed
A drop on the wrapper—more whispers, crosses
Till he offered it to you, potent for use.
When he told us the monks would gather in the chapel
"In five minutes now to sing for ten minutes,"
I asked would he go (we could help him go).
"I've hurt meself. I'll stay here an hour."
His noble skull was glazed cancer-yellow,
His tan hair fallen in saucer clumps,
Only the smile was straining to last.

The blessing undoubtedly endured our night.

MEMORANDUM 3

You are so dark I misapprehend you,
Seizing dry hair when I reach for a hand—
Where are lips, the guarded rims of eyes,
The intact message you promised in daylight?
Mute, you patiently recite yourself;
And slowly I reconstruct you in Braille—
Word of reprieve—then devour you.

No stranger, here or ever, shall read.

MEMORANDUM 4

This famous lake
In its famous hills
Is shut for the winter—
Not a bed to rent,
Canine grouches
In fake-fur
Coats at every dock—
So we stay on wheels
And you reel me past
A sizable gift
In sloped yellow light:
The woods you combed
Ten years ago,
Empty of all but
Your memory now,
A slow hand in them,
Probing for—there—
The ordinary tree
By which (stunned with patience)
You'd wait in hope
Some girl might pop
A strap, flash bare,
You know the last secret.

MEMORANDUM 5

On the nubby teal spread
(Veteran of maybe ten years
Of afternoons silent as this),
You are one compact swagged
Calligraph in phosphorus,
Still but transmitting—
You have earned this
Today. Can you keep it?
I grin my Yes; your eyes take it,
Grave. For the third time
I bolt you down in gobbets—
Strengthening horse-meat,
Rank haunch of bear.

THE FIELD

Isn't this the field where the lodestone is hid?
Hasn't the intact chart to its grave been confided to us?
Aren't we sufficient in breath and limb to walk from here
To the shifting rim of its sovereign draw?
Won't the palms of our bare hands home to the core?
Can't we break inward, hunting, locked but fed?

CUMAEAN SONG

Now last fruit of Cumaean song—
Great wheel of ages, youthful, turns again;
Virgin restored, Saturn's reign restored,
New child sent upon us from high heaven.
Pure Lucina, nod on newborn boy
So with him Iron generations end,
Gold men rise again across the earth,
So your own Apollo reign at last.
And in your consulate, yours Pollio,
Splendor begins, abundant months proceed—
You guiding, remnants of our wickedness
Be canceled, earth be freed her ancient dread.
Godly life awaits him. He will see
Heroes ranged with gods, be seen by them;
Will steer a world placated by his father.
Wandering ivy random with foxglove,
Acanthus smiling mixed with colocasia—
These, Boy, presents poured by untilled earth.
Goats uncalled bring udders bursting milk,
No ox fears lion however huge his power,
Even your cradle blossoms to enfold you,
Serpents perish, perish deadly weeds,
Syrian balsam springs up everywhere.
Later when you've read heroic glories,
Father's deeds, and know what manhood is,
Slowly plains will gild with waving corn,
Purple grapes droop clustered from wild thorn,
Honeydew distill from hard heart-oak.
Still traces of old fraud will wait in stealth,
Lure men out to try the sea in ships,
Lock towns in walls, divide the earth with plows.
Then again will come a second Tiphys,
Second Argo bearing chosen heroes,
Even war—second war will come,
Hard Achilles sent again to Troy.
But when strength of time makes man of you,

Merchant seamen will forsake their routes,
Piney ships swap nothing—all be full—
Land not suffer harrow, vine no hook,
Robust plowhand free his team from yoke,
Wool no more learn counterfeiting colors,
Ram himself in pasture change his fleece
Now to blushing purple, now to crocus,
Scarlet ringlets sprout on grazing lambs.
"Speed the day!" Fates have cried to spindles,
Unison fixed will of destiny.
Enter—almost time—on your vast honors,
Dear child of gods, strong increment of Jove.
Look—world arcing under heavy dome,
Earth and tracts of sea and heaven's depth.
Look—all jubilate in time at hand.
O last days of long life lengthen for me,
Breath come steady so I tell your deeds;
Neither Thracian Orpheus nor Linus
Ever then could vanquish me in song,
Though one should bring his mother, one his father—
Orpheus, Calliope; Linus, grand Apollo,
Even Pan, if Arcady would judge,
Even Pan would grant my victory.
Begin, small Boy, to know your mother, smiling—
Ten long months have left her pale and weak.
Begin, small Boy—who does not smile for parents
No god feeds at table, no goddess beds.

after Vergil

FOR LEONTYNE PRICE AFTER ARIADNE

. . . ein Ding wächst
So leicht ins andere. . . .
Wie schaffst du die Verwandlung?
HOFMANNSTHAL

Things easily change to other things
If a goddess speaks—men to trustworthy
Gods, trees to merciful hands.

Find her first. There's only one.
She comes in single relays through time,
Required to live apart in rocks
By water—long nights—surrounding
A solitude deep as her power, its cause
And food.
There, stand at her door.
Dare her name—*Tall Lioness.*
Beg grace, beg voice. She's forced to yield.

She'll rise unsmiling, speak your hope.
The speech is song. Try to bear it—
Audible light. Eventually
She sings your name. If you last to hear,
The change begins—you're godly then;
Trees bend toward you with loyal love
Till she's still again or memory dies.

It will not die.

THE ANNUAL HERON

December 27th, down for breakfast,
Profoundly fondued from the previous night,
I raise the blinds on panes broadcasting
Cold, a signal—clear sky, sun,
Pond still liquid though thickening
At the rim, and the annual heron
Fifty yards beyond me in rigid profile,
Four feet high, slate gray,
One flat eye, cocked in every cell
(Neck out, legs locked), hunting again:
Fish or me?

His tenth year with me—the fish or me.
I know because when I saw him first,
I wrote him down in my first novel
Which was ending then. He still stands
There, page 169, proffered oasis
For a couple too gorged on mutual
Misery to take his option—consolation *in situ*
Or an emblem of flight, contented self-service.
Hungrier then myself, I wondered;
And now, nine visits later,
Hollow as a whistle, I press this annual
Appearance for a meaning beyond the obvious—
Migration.

After three, four years of two-day visits,
The message seemed identical with Yeats's wild swans'—
Mortality, mine; that chances were fair
A bird as fragile as a cuckoo clock might
(Despite yearly odysseys through air thick
With threat, toward waters jelled with poison)
Outlast iron me, revisit this pond
In my total absence. Or even the reverse—
Yeats again, *Lapis Lazuli*:
"Over them flies a long-legged bird,

A symbol of longevity."
—Bird's or mine though?

A year ago it seemed suddenly mine.
He arrived late—mid-January—
One day ahead of a hard cold wave
(Clanging air, foot of snow, pond dense as ingots)
And stood on the surface, staring at fish
Safe as houses from what I assumed was
Desperate need. Or took slow
Aimless steps, maladroit as
A nineteenth-century German child's
Toy, all gears and contingency—
First *this*, then *that*. And wouldn't leave—
Waited four, five days as the weather screwed down:
Zero for the first time in my life here.
Mornings I'd come down to see him there,
Condensed a notch farther by night, famine
But hunting still—fish roared in joy,
Their own only enemies. By then his plight
Seemed roughly mine—vital provisions
In clean showcases, permanently sealed—
So I tried to let him at them: coated, booted
Myself and fumbled with a log to stave
A usable hole in the ice. Sealed
Also. All I managed was scaring him
Out of sight (slow agonized ascent,
Unlikely, ludicrous as the doomed Ornithopter).
Two brief consolations—that mere exercise might
Warm him a little; that maybe
He was gone on finally, roused by my impotence
From some odd equinoctial daze—
Fish under glass!—and packed off to Georgia
Or the Everglades.

No. Next morning (sixth day of the freeze)
He was not on view, but when I got home
At five o'clock—light nearly dead—he was
There on thicker ice, stiffer, shrunk,
Bitter as a cast-iron flamingo,

Facing me. Seeing what?
Transmitting what signal? *Hunger to death.*

Plea or command?
Plea I decided and took from my freezer
A twenty-inch trout (gift from a friend's
Weekend in the Smokies), stiff as cordwood,
And thawed it in the oven—instant stench
Which the furniture blotted for slow release.
Then I suited up again and moved down toward him
Gingerly (my normal mode though
I'm awful at it, scare a number of targets—
Was he here to teach that? a hunter's
Tread?). He seemed to watch me head-on
From the center where he stood suspended over
Twelve feet of water; but if he saw,
He'd abandoned fear as a luxury—
Better to risk this absurd approach
Than exert one calorie of life on flight.
I stopped at the edge though the water would have borne
Me as easily as him, stooped and slid
The trout toward him, bowled it perfectly
A foot from his feet, then gingerly left—
Not looking back on my charity, his gratitude
Till indoors again behind my own glass.
He was there, unmoved, facing the trout but
Blind or stupefied or too weak
To eat or had to have water
To lubricate a swallow or didn't like trout.
I watched long enough to register nightfall—
I could stand another ten minutes,
Watch him folded in darkness
Or fix my own supper (less desirable than trout)
Or take quilts out to bundle him up,
Force-feed him before his own supper
Froze again.

I ate, watched the news; and by early
Morning he was still out of sight,
No sign of the trout though—hopeful omen—

Yet after coffee I went down to check.
From my end of the snowy ice to where he'd
Last stood were crowded dog tracks
And, on his site, a small handful
Of lilac-gray feathers. No beak, no bone
Of bird or trout. I'd only succeeded
In luring the neighborhood clutch of hyenas,
Standard lethal suburban equipment.
I knelt for a feather—strong wing
Vane—and thought if that was the meaning,
The message straining through years for delivery,
Then it came as no news, cliché oily
As an oleograph moonrise. Why should nature labor
Through staggering waste to state in mammoth
Semaphore the conclusion any
Baby draws once it's cleared the sphincter
Vaginalis?—*We tear what we touch.*
I dropped the feather and climbed home,
Satisfied.

A normal year passed—normal quota of reminders
That the sentence held (some devious
And eloquent, all wasteful as
The heron episode).

He rises from death. Here anyhow
He stands, eleven months later
In the shallows at my end, facing
Me plainly. What am I meant
To do with my first exposure
To resurrection, at year's dead end,
Before my breakfast? (I manage to recall
That resurrections, like natural births,
Have a habit of dawning in the pre-breakfast
Deserts, roses aghast.) First,
I tell myself it's an accident—
A similar bird on the same flight-path.
That holds me long enough to boil a kettle,
But then I remember a way of establishing
Whether I'm confronted by chance or worse—

By a serious note sounded on air
Clear enough to bear it straight at my eyes,
When I've twiddled these chinking metaphors
(Mortality, Immortality) ten years.
My old heron had something wrong with
His knee (is it called a knee? elbow?
Wrist?)—a knot or tumor
Size of a walnut, stained darker
Than the leg. I decide not to check
Precipitously. In fact, I don't
Look out again. I have my breakfast,
Then carefully search *Britannica*
For firm ground to stand on—
Life span of the great blue heron,
Migration. There's ample word on plumage,
Distribution, abundance ("Herons are the most
Cosmopolitan family"), relations with man
("Members of this order are considered to be
Either beneficial or neutral in respect
To the human economy"), feeding habits,
Vocalization ("Many of the ciconiiforms
Are rather silent," which comes as relief—
The chance mine may speak has seemed
At least even); but no help
At all on maximum age, senility
Or the wintering routes of Atlantic
Seaboard members of the family. What is
Unexpected is the constant reference to
Family—"An outstanding feature
In ciconiiform behaviour is gregariousness.
Even when the mode of obtaining food
Necessitates solitude . . . the tendency is
For reassembly at the end of day"
Though mine, or the long succession of mine,
Stays through nights however arctic:
Loyal, alone, next to me.

Hatted and scarfed, I finally look—
He hasn't moved a visible atom
In forty-five minutes. And doesn't move as

The door slams shut and I start
Toward him. But he's watching me,
Not water or the road—unless he's blind
Or some flawless decoy or angel
Or demon or symptom of lunacy; mine,
At last. I walk to within twenty yards
Of the pond—normal racket of dry leaves,
Sticks. At the noise, I know I'm volunteering,
Offering myself for whatever's next
(Which later will sound like symptom number-two
But then—in bristling winter light
By four still acres of cold
Brown water ringed with chalk-
White bones of sycamores,
Sepulchral cedars—was the rational course).
I walk on. He has the knot on his right
Knee. It's grown—size of an oak
Gall now; is it killing him?
With a speed, calm as perfect, his head
Leaves me, flings out from its coil,
Pierces water silently and rises with
A five-inch brim, lets it quiver
In my sight an instant, eats it.
So I step forward another five yards;
And he bears the nearness for maybe four seconds,
Profile to me. Credible angel—
He gives a first wide fan of wings;
Then rises, trailing legs like crutches.
Till he's half-gone, I hear his oaring
Like lashes—*hrr, hrr:* no pain
Ensues.

So left with that—actual phoenix
At the edge of my yard, possessed of new
Grace since his nocturnal skirmish with
The local dingoes; entirely acceptable
Minister of silence—I climb to the otherwise
Empty house and make for myself
An oracle from his mute persistence
Through volumes of air, corrosive years—

Endurance is fed: here, in time.
Therefore endure. Then make another—
You hope in vain. The heart is fed
Only where I go when I leave you here.
Follow me.

II

THE LAWS OF ICE

(1986)

PRAISE

Holy flame
By any name—
Creator, Terminator,
  Hand—

Receive this praise,
The due of days
Of hobbled terror, healing:
  Thanks.

Your muffled light,
Its comrade night
Swept outward, forward, farther
  Home.

ONE

AMBROSIA

The hard part, I grant, in being a god is standing
Still to bear the worship—enduring the leach
Of dilate eyes, incessant frisk of adoring
Hands: meals of the blind.
                                        In defense, most gods
Extrude some cast of themselves as durable adequate
Receptacles of awe—a seal on the air of one
Patently suitable place from the unplumbed
Intaglio absence of their force:
                                                chryselephantine Zeus
At Olympia, dog-dugged Artemis at Ephesus—freeing
Their essences to vagabond the landscape, debauching briny
Island lads or booming the birthrate in crossroad hamlets
(Six glorious girls and a brackish well),
Triggering outbreaks of scabies or earthquakes or six months'
Boreal splendors at sunset or sulks on their tripods
At final subjection to dread bronze Necessity.

Of you, when the live body takes its furloughs,
There is just this thickening sheaf of photographs
(Coaxed by me, peeled off your presence) and this one
Cranium's smoky memorial corroborations
Of the radiant claims incredible in monochrome—
The days during years in which for hours there would settle
Upon you or burn from within a packed imperative
I am goal and terminus, first and last. What
In the world shines or refuses is chargeable to me,
All thanks all blame. Choose which, kneel here, enact
Your choice.
                    In the body's vicinity, its transpirations,
My prompt enactments have mostly seemed thanks (though you've
Suggested the occasional oblation was clandestine management,
Puppetry)—the thanks of, say, a mature self-
Possessed English setter at dusk who swabs
The master's nutritious hand in transports of service
Pure as the moon's sucking gaze at the sea and rapt

As the heart of stalwart Gabriel in rainbow gear
Lobbing pitch-perfect glories at the Thunder Throne.

—Which raises the unbrushed but omnipresent
God above Necessity, ireful desert
Yahweh, El Shaddai, who's made a long
Point of vouchsafing no image and whose
High shrine was an unlit cubicle empty
Of all but a wood box holding two rock
Slabs with rules for fleeing Egypt
(And maybe the conduct of stationary lives throughout
Our universe till Hell reopens as an ice-skating rink)—
The second rule forbidding surmise at his face,
Other efficacious organs.
Yet—
This is crucial—recall we're built
Precisely "in his image, after his likeness." Assume
We are. Then each is an ample portable altar
For any other's holocaust;
and what I silently
Say to you—presence not pictures
Though they may yet serve—in hour-long veneration
Bouts (when, thoughtless as a sponge, I roam you minutely
Companioned by orts of pleasure in a voice I take
On faith to be yours transforming) is my best
Equation of the offering earned by palpable data.
I choose you again. Vulnerable ramparts—
Blood, oil, water, effulgent crowns
Of crackling hair, ten local odors distinct
As dialects—sufficient idol of absolute
Stillness, motion, making, annihilation.

So, at ease. Enjoy each instant of this. Never think
You're alone. I'm also Adam and thus another
Mold however botched of the Convex Love that monitors black
Holes, cheerleader contests, the footwork of quarks,
Famines in the Punjab. With logic and full right
I incorporate for a hundredth time the excess
You yield—copious sacrament, feast of gods,
Which I turn to good.

WHAT IS GODLY

What is godly
This moment
Is the sight of you,
Promise of indelible memory
Of the sight—
Motionless heave
Of vertical body
On bone-white wall
In October light, slant
But gilding—
                    what has been
Godly ten unquestioned years.

GOOD PLACES

1. WARM SPRINGS

We think we've come here to start
A life or that figure of life
Neither of us has drawn: closed
Circle, live circuit.
Initial trials have suggested
Feasibility (quick congruences
In your house and mine);
So we take us on the road through July
Mountains to this enormous
Round pool in a valley, warm
As we, for the first attempt
On public ground.

Jefferson bathed here, R. E. Lee;
Centuries of Indians, vatic lustrations;
Protestant dynasties of hearts,
Livers, reins.
We strip, descend, and water
Receives us—no Tantalus-flight—
Enlisting to serve, plating
Our entire pelts with air:
A zillion beads of adhesive buoyance.
We may levitate!—glide
The ridge on thermals till night,
Nude as eggs.

Why then do you whisper "Watch this,"
Exhale and sink—white
Plummet—to the green cobble
Floor, untouchable corpse
Twitched by currents gentler than my hand?

And why do you rise?

2. RINCÓN 1

You wake each dawn and silently leave
Me in our dank room beside an ocean
Calm as custard and drive our rented
Car through a village posing for the start
Of a John Huston movie—louche
Alleys, cantinas with one-eyed cats.
In two green miles you reach the north
Cape, the squat-globe *planta nuclear*—
Effluent warming the warm Caribbean
To a half-mile shark-cafeteria,
Waves the best in the hemisphere
For your present purpose. You launch your board
And paddle to the break a hundred yards
Out where eight baked blankface
Earlybirds from the hippie surfer colony
That camps in the hills all winter refuse
You—glares meaningless as toads'.
                                        I sleep
And dream houses, a child hunting
Houses.
            You plane in, roll after roll, perfect
Rider in the element that grants
You triumph—sentient sea.

On the beach a fatboy hometown
Liberationist in Che Guevara tam
Dreams of slicing you down with automatic fire.
Failing that, he watches. You are not unseen.

3. RINCÓN 2

Christmas eve afternoon in the hot toy
Plaza, beer—me learning
Lycidas, you coaching my lines,
We apparently invisible: no passer,
Woman or child, concedes us.

Dinner on the cliff by the suicide curve,
Tropical lobster (all tail),
Men's room with a ripped-off basin
Trembling on its pipes. Vast sight
Of the sea, calm lid on "the bottom
Of the monstrous world"; outrageous stars.

Our first midnight mass since Vatican II
In the glum beige church swarmed
Solid—steady jolts: no syllable
Of Latin, dignified slab-altar hung
In carcinogenic colors, whiskered
Ladies at ease in the chancel
Machine-gunning dialect scripture
Grim as death lists.
                                        A summit
When a prepubescent boy and girl
Advance in white, kneel, embed
The shocking-pink Child in actual
Straw as a man in azure leisure-
Suit squats to flip a loud switch—red
Lights wink antiphonal relays on the stable
Roof.
            We think it's over now; our eyes
Think *Sleep*. Our neighbors in the crush,
Men with horn farmer-necks, spread
Barrel arms and seize us; you laugh

"We're mugged!" Dry kisses at our ears;
Then standoff faces again, quarter-smiles,
Intermittent tan teeth; their hardwon salutation
Spent on tall pale strangers.

Well, we bear its health back
And sustain it three days.

4. CHEROKEE

For my day on the roads
In your direction
(Last two hours
On wounded-snake
Blue Ridge ascents,
Eating lilac monoxide
From not-quite-stalled
Road-crazed oldtimers
In campers equipped
For Armageddon),
You offer this—

Half-hour warmup
Before the show;
Dancers worked
Like puppets in oil
By Tchaikovsky's *Serenade*
For Strings, such grave
Jubilation; you
Unhurried on the dim
Periphery, trainee
Mover:

Dazzling enactment,
Crystal grown
By the music's glut,
Its durable reward
And mine, six years.

5. LIGHTHOUSE, MOSQUITO INLET

If we'd stood here in this upthrust lantern
Eighty-six years ago, staring east through eyes
As officious as these we've turned on each other, we'd have seen
The steamer *Commodore* (out of Jacksonville
With guns for Cuba) sink just there, a tidy
Knot in the hectic juncture of water, sky; then an all but
Phantom spot start toward us at the rate of roots
In basalt—Stephen Crane and four men in a ten-foot
Dinghy yearning toward us, this light at least,
What they can see of a shore craved ardently as heart's ease
At sunset (the sun will desert them on its compulsive chore,
The lid of the known world lock on their faces,
Lips eat frigid salt a whole night
From unseen whelms—January 1897).
None of them knows the color of the sky.

Our day, a late November noon, is likewise
A woodcut in gray and gray—though (safe in the glass
At the close of a jaunt distinguished, I feel, for torpid
Bliss; posing you against a sea glum
As a rattler in a roadside cage) I hardly guess
We are also scuttled by the silent insatiable bit
Of your fear: dread precisely of proximate safety,
Harmless salvage. In an hour you're to fly north,
Weapon stowed in a skull Etruscan in numinous vapidity.
The strength of its seams invisibly compressing a craze
More urgent than your plane's for flight. My adjacent blindness
Is the noon's chief glow—rays from a hope perennial
As sleet, sufficient to stoke me and blaze strangers on.
Flee in it, well-lit (a final gift), your shadow
Flung forward, no backward stain.
You at least know the color of the sky—
Ashen for waste, jaundice for lies.

6. HAWK HILL

August dusk. We rest on the green porch,
Yellowjackets and ants at our knees—
You in from work, ready to cook
The dinner I can't; I three-fourths through
The eightieth sick-day, weaker still;
We cheering a milestone with smooth Glenlivet:
Eleven years of peace and war,
Our squalls and calms. The hidden thrush
In the big beech behind us pauses to plan
His billionth variation on the five notes
Stamped in his throat.
                                        You face me and say
"*Real time*," then add with customary
Unbarked candor "Whether you make it
Or not, these days were real time"—
Twelve days in which you've fed me squarely,
Dried my bedsore, each night stripped
My slack legs for baby-sleep (that sound and brief):
No word or sign of balk or grievance,
The flawless service dreamed by kings.

Whether I make it or not, old struggler
(Treasured as any, with all our scars),
Feel it hereafter as all real time—
All one linked try to tread one void.
We pay for it now.

The Sons of God saw that women were lovely and took wives for themselves.
GENESIS 6:2

BEFORE THE FLOOD

1. HER CHOICE

My sisters and I were climbing from the spring,
So we moved slow and upright—no drop wasted.
The ground had been dry but cool when we went;
Now it blistered with each careful step but I
Couldn't stop. I was leading, the tallest.
The Earth herself was famished, begging mercy.
I thought we might each splash a few drops.
He
Rose in the path, a silent shout—from earth
Or air itself, I never saw. I lurched enough
To spill a whole drink; my sisters managed
To save their pitchers but fell and hid
Their eyes.
His face was the single face I'd
Dreamed. The eyes, the brown space between
And beneath them, were a whole world I'd mapped
And prowled at night. His body was dense and
Lean as a bench, entirely bare. Where a man's
Sex is, he grew a third hand—long clean
Fingers with thick ivory nails. It reached
Upward on him but was still as the light.

It was why I went to him, why I gave him
My whole firm body to rummage like a strong
Blind beggar for what seemed life. His
Eyes never shut.

2. HIS DISCOVERY

What I found up in her—
Not the fluid complicity
Of celestial hydraulics,
Grave conjugation
Of stainless souls
But a nubby palpable
Compact relief-map
(Canyons and foothills;
A tan savanna)
Of a county with rough
Tongues and hardy scrub timber;
Chinked huts at intervals
To slow an enemy
And children at low doors
In stairsteps of age:
Brown, oiled,
And skittish in
A dark that baited,
Welcomed, eased
Me more than
Guaranteed endless
Silent billows
Of curative shine.

DROWNED

The hour strikes and staves our hull.
Crack of night, fate founders,
Famished storm whelms flesh and wine.
And I (all man) groan, calculate.
My mind's too keen, too fit to watch
Time's brittle hourglass destroyed.
The deep and I are one machine
For scrounging littered memories—
Mother, my china cups, the whore
Greased and throbbing on the lurid sill,
And Christ! See Christ there lashed to the mast
Jigging to death in pitchdark salt.
His bloody eye flares one last sign—
A *great ship perished, all hands drowned.*

after Valéry

When David returned from the slaughter of the Philistine, Abner took him and brought him before Saul with the Philistine's head in his hand.

Saul said to him "Whose son are you?"

David answered "I'm the son of your servant Jesse the Bethlehemite."

It happened when he'd finished speaking to Saul that Jonathan's soul was knit with David's soul. Jonathan loved him like his own soul. 1 SAMUEL 17:57–18:1

JONATHAN'S LAMENT FOR DAVID

You young in the bronze day, gore to the wrists,
Coarse hair kinked in the cold sweat of triumph,
Thrusting the startled head at Father
(Pumpkin-huge with turquoise earbobs,
Chinking bells), you rank with the first wild
Stench of manhood roasting your fork—
It happened I loved you, watched my heart
Fling thin cords past the grinning giant
And bind you in; watched yours bind me:
Safe in the first and strongest bond.

You were fourteen, herdboy still.
I was nineteen, prince and heir.
I'd prided myself on self-possession.
In the wheedling murderous alleys of court,
I'd owned my own soul, long-thewed body—
No man's boy to fetch and carry,
No milky girl's to trap and tame.
A love to outrun love of girls—

We only flourished, fed by glare
Of priests' eyes—king's and cringing slaves'—
The packed hot floors of muffled rooms,
Cool caves, dry bivouac beds on rock.
The first taut cords of meeting eyes
Became twined legs and hands, locked lips,
Pooled opal seed we planted deep—
Buried to bloom in secret night,
Public deeds of sunstruck valor.
Love past woman's love or God's

*

And proved through daily fierce onslaught—
Palace, tent, every hand,
Father's envy, Samuel's rage,
Our blank despair at shrinking ground
On which to join and feed again
This single-stalked bent desert tree
We bred to last on air and night.
Love past every human love

Till now you rise in gilding light
And stretch your brown blunt victor's arms;
Assume the bleached dense marriage-shirt
To take my sister, your first bride—
Grinning head thrust ruddy toward me,
Swapping me for one pale girl
(My nursery-mate, your throneward path).

This love—gazelle to bound all crags—
Breaks, gored, on thorns of our killed tree.

DAVID'S LAMENT FOR SAUL AND JONATHAN

Gazelle of Israel slain on the heights
The mighty fallen

Conceal it in Gath and Ashkelon's alleys
Or the daughters of the Philistine rejoice
Daughters of the vile uncut exult

Hills in Gilboa no dew no rain no harvest fields
The shield of the mighty grimed with dust
The shield of Saul stained unready

From gore of the slain from warrior fat
The bow of Jonathan turned not back
Sword of Saul returned not hungry

Saul and Jonathan loved and lovely
Unparted in life in death unparted
Past eagles swift past lions strong

Daughters of Israel weep for Saul
Who decked you in crimson hung you with gold
The mighty fallen in midst of war

Jonathan slain upright on the heights
I mourn you brother too dear for me
Your love fell on me spring of wonder
Past all women's love and wonder

The mighty fallen
The arms of war

after David

PORTA NIGRA

Why wake me to watch you rule the world?—
I who watched the grandest days of Treves,
Paired in fame with her one sister Rome.
These eyes have burned with flare of clattering legions,
Blond Franks bled by lions in the sand,
Trumpets at the palace and the god
Augustus purple in his golden car;
Have rested happy in my river home
(Ringed by shouts as grapes were pulped to wine)
On girls who lifted jars tumid with life.
   And now you rouse me to blank rubble fields,
Shards of walls nightly licked by fog,
Sacred statues blasphemed in their graves
By what you dig above them—slews for swine.
   Only my lovely gate stands undefiled.
Hung with black swags of time, it still flings scorn
On your squat roofs, squat backs, from every hole;
On princes, vassals, priests—each in his mask
(Alike, jowls bloated, flaccid grin, blind stare)—
On women my drunk slaves would not gang-rape.
   What diet do you drain from breasts of junk?
The only precious thing has fled you—blood.
We shadows still remember streaming fire.
   "Live corpses!" laughs the boy Manlius;
"I would not rule such men even with this rod
That hooked my bread when—oiled with Persian musk—
Each night I prowled our dim triumphal gate;
Sold my lean self to Caesar's own bought men."

after Stefan George

LAST CONVERSATION

FOR JOEL JACKSON
1945–1980

One of the comfort-stops
In my adolescence, grim
As the War of the Spanish Succession
And some years longer,
Was the laughing home your parents
Made—you the readiest
Laugher. At three or four
You sang me "Little Oyster,"
Eight-second song
That became our rune.

Little Oyster went to school.
He couldn't learn the Golden Rule.

Had you made it up?
Or heard it right?—the leakage,
The stench! Was it maybe "Oscar"?
"Oyster" it stayed, though,
The rest of your life;
My name for you.

The week you died, I sat by your bed—
Noon July murk, fresh
Tacos in the yard, muttering friends,
You and I alone, you
A flung sack of bones, mind
Burning unpredictably in and
Out of service. I strained to think
What to ask if you looked up again
And knew my face—something
Idle enough to spare you work
But earn me credit for a visit
Than which I'd have rather drunk slugs
Of battery acid. In minutes your eyes goggled
Round, me the target. I said

"Whyever did I call you 'Little Oyster'?"
And thought I knew the answer. You could no
Longer smile, only groan "Goddamn"
To signal surprise; so your answer was slow
But Delphic in closure—"You used
To say the world was my oyster."

Did I? I recall no prophecy,
Though the far skirts of doom are among
My bigger lines. The world
Anyhow took five more days
To eat you.
            Is the pearl of that
Long transaction swelling
Now?

REMEMBERING GOLDEN BELLS

Disgraced and sick, a man age forty.
Oblivious and straight, a girl age three—
Not a son but enough to ease odd moments,
The occasional kiss. Then they lured her ghost
Who knows where?
                    Remembering how,
The week she died, she groped for words
To tell me news, I learned that gambles
On flesh only win me desolation.
Thinking to times before her though,
I sealed out pain.
                    Three years now
Since my heart froze, each day of three winters.
This morning—spring—the grief ran free.
On the warm street I met her old nurse.

after Po Chu-i

DEAD MAN, DYING GIRL

FOR ROBERT KENNEDY
1925–1968

In England—bored one Sunday, '61—
I spent two minutes staring at your face,
Photograph cast up in that day's news.
Staring because you seemed (baffling then,
Two years pre-Dallas) trapped in silent woe;
And just two minutes, what it took to see
The principle of line that signaled pain.
Your eyes, not straight, rushed downward from your nose;
Watershed beneath a simian brow—
Eyes of my friend Kaufman, Lew Hoad's eyes,
Petrified dumb masks of Greece and Rome,
Stock-in-trade of subsequent cartoons:
Lines sloping downward indicate real pain.

But seven years farther in—you freshly killed—
I see your eyes, no continental ridge
Or open sockets drilled in howling mask,
And see they tie you to another head—
The Boston Museum's marble girl of Chios.
She works to smile but fails. Now I know why.
Face still trembles pure, three thousand years;
Skull remains unfinished, sides rush down—
To bear a mantle, all the guidebooks say;
Cloth to roof her beauty, name her fate:
Bride in white led out to meet a life
Or thistle wool to warm a colder way.
She waits on there in Boston your raw home,
Not yet quite living—needy, bare, no mantle.

Yours has descended, spared at least the wait.

SLEEPER IN THE VALLEY

A green hole in the hills, a river sings
Clutching a path through weeds like torn drowned silver.
Blank noon sun takes steady aim and flings;
Spent rays converge here, arrows in a quiver.

A soldier—young, mouth open, naked head,
Bathing his hair in fresh blue watercress—
Stretches at ease beneath pale roofing cloud,
Bedded in raining glare on deep green grass.

His feet are in sword flowers, across his nap
A sick child's smile is creased. Rocked in earth's lap,
Pelted by warming light, still he is cold

And flares no answer to the heavy scent
Of day. He sleeps, one hand in silent fold
Of chest. Two red holes in his side. Here on the right.

after Rimbaud

A HEAVEN FOR ELIZABETH RODWELL, MY MOTHER

Each morning her mother does not die.
It is always August; she's eleven years old,
Her father comes toward her in the far bedroom
Which is already shuttered against a sun dry
As a fired brick-kiln. She's clean,
Dressed, ready, seated on her bed, and has prayed
He will not come—that someway the room
Will answer the sucking light, tear free, and rush
(She's been nowhere, can think of no refuge—
Sky bottomless sky?). Her father reaches
The mat by the bed and touches a spot
On the crown of her scalp that has been sore six years—
She fell backward, laughing at a joke
Of the cook's, from a kitchen window and tore a short
Mouth in the fishbelly-skin round which
Coarse hair already darkened. Now he says
"Your mother needs to speak to you." Elizabeth
Rises, sustaining his palm, a helmet on her brain;
And says *"Is she going to die today?"*
Her father nods and leads her through the only house
She's lived in—Jack Rodwell, matrix
Of her dark eyes and hair; his own hair stiff
As hemp, still mostly raven. The front
Bedroom is bright but cool; her brothers have sent
For two huge blocks of ice—they melt
In galvanized tubs by unscreened windows. There are three
Brothers, all grown, by the bed—
Three older sisters—a clutch of inlaws, a Negro
Nurse, the young useless doctor.
They make a slow aisle; and her father draws
Her down it, damp miles to the bed.
It is white iron and high, the mattress butts
Her windpipe, her eyes—mottled bronze—
Are in a thin plane with her mother's hip.
Her mother—Lizzie—stout for years,
Is bloating unstoppably instant by instant with the refuse

Of a short hard jocular life,
An early good marriage, eight children (one
Dead), and forty-eight years: now
Bright's disease, ruined kidneys, poison
Lapping at her eyes. But she can still
See. She faces Elizabeth, a skewed right
Angle; and though she does not intend it,
Grins in the sodden pleats of a mouth that was sweet
As wings days ago. Then she says "*I meant*
To see you through. You're the one I'll miss." Boots,
The sissy brother, blubs. Elizabeth
Nods once, sips ammoniac air, and bites down
Gently on a fold of sheeting, the nearest
Refuge. A thought speaks, keen in her head as a blade—
This is making me an orphan. This is all against
Me. Her father takes her left wrist,
Awkwardly turns her. She staggers away,
Mute as she came, to lie on her own bed—
Far too big—and wait for a life
If a life volunteers. Then her mother does not die.
The cook bears the message, tall Mary Green—
Mopping her own eyes with sugar-sack apron
And hands like leather primeval birds—
"*Your mother all right. Or going to be. She*
Last till you stop needing her.
Get up and run." Elizabeth believes it (Mary Green
Is one thing here that's never lied)
And stands like a cold pony loath to work,
Then strides into this new life I provide—
Full August noon, an endless furnace,
That does her no harm.

Each afternoon her husband takes her,
Standing on the beige tile floor of his toilet
In Rex Hospital where he waits for tomorrow
When they'll split his huge chest in search of tumors
That may be the murk scumbled over
His X-rays, blundering hands. Not hers—
Hers by their silent presence, still
As objects, on his cold bedsheet have summoned this rite
For survival in a body hefty as a grown

Tree, bone-tan and precious in her mind more than half
Her life till now; cause of food,
Two sons, a stillborn daughter, the customary
Rages, all the safety and recompense she's known
To this day. February 16th, a day
Like a broad glass pane onto nothing but
Cold; she turned forty-nine nine
Days ago. She cooperates to the bounds
Of her still perdurable strength as she's done (barring
Helpless failures by her body) for twenty-
Seven years since their first night, bare
In the rickety dark of a Pullman grinding
To Tampa Bay for their one sustained stretch
Of unblocked access before quick thickets
Of tollgates descended between their flesh and where
It aimed to go—entire conjunction,
Inseparable compound of self in self, companioned
Only by grateful laughter and the requisite
Mercies toward whatever ambient life might prowl
The nutrient glow of their steadfast blaze.
William—still Will, eyes still
Hot as brands though gray as his hair:
He's half a head taller and must buckle to root
His broad way into the place he never
Thinks about—warm as his mother, more dreamless than sleep.
Bucking on his long calves, he does not
Think but rests for maybe the final time. She
Braces and thinks *This will kill me too.*
In a minute I'll flood with cancer. She sees it—chalk
White and fitted with irresistible
Baby-claws that will score their way to her heart
By spring. Yet she keeps strict time
With her own strong hips, assisting him deeper
Into fragile shelters he's never found
Before. He asks "*Is it right?*" for the four thousandth
Time, she moans at his neck, he floods
In apparently endless gouts—scrubbing her forehead
With a sharkhide chin. Now he always
Thanks her, she waits, he's silent. She thinks
He knows he's infected me. She thinks
I cannot bear to hear him beg pardon;

So she stops him by saying her own lucid
"*Thank you*" and pulling back, free. Only then—
Slow as finding home in a nightmare
And richer in joy—she sees it's cured him; she's
Cured him: her sad compliant skin.
In the glint of his new health, his first face
(Simple and stunning as a hill in cloudless
Outrage of sun), she forgets her own doom,
Saying as she grins and joins him again
"*You'll outlast me. Dress. We're leaving here.*"
He thanks her at last.

Each night she dies under expert watch—
Intensive Care—in Wake County Hospital;
Surprisingly eager to quit this course
She's run sixty years, ravenous hunt
Through familiar ground—occasional ambush,
Uncharted voids: no halt for pain.
The right carotid artery behind
Her eyes ruptured at five o'clock; and she
Was brought here, unable to speak,
Apparently senseless, her brain already so crushed
By blood as to be past all known help
But witness. The breathing proximity she lent me through dozens
Of childhood nights (barking croup, dreams
Of flight) is now repaid in a single sum,
Ruinous speed. But shutdown though
She appallingly seems, she files my presence; makes
It the token to trip mired cogs
Of easement; they grind this last lean wish—
Her first son (me) will leave now,
Freeing her to end among strangers: brusque dry
Mercy on white rubber soles,
Prowling her border, an arm's reach away
If the arm could reach (her only other
Son is becalmed on a Navy scow
Off bristling Cuba). I accept then and stand,
A last obedience but hedged with scruples, imperfect
Service. I have this last chance
To lay up sights to see me through maybe
Four more decades of memory. Do I want

An album of angles on a stout lady swamping
Silently beneath a weak glow?
The only relief, an uncurtained window
On a May-night storm, air itself
Gorged on its own warm sap. Then I see the change that,
Stunned, I've missed—she's somehow flying.
The gullies of her shut face are leveled, swept
Back by a rush down something, toward
Something. The goal is stripping years off her,
Stale padding. She will soon be
Her first self, the girl before me;
Not dreaming of me; not subject
To sons, husband, parents, a life. I have this
Last chance she speeds to deny me.
I take three quick steps into chill
Light, she's almost arrived, her wake is
Diaphanous. I touch the mattress, lift a seersucker spread,
A leaden sheet, and find her blue
Hand—startling and expected like teeth
In a dig, wire-thin platinum wedding-ring
On the prescribed finger. With my nail I nick it—
Chip-diamonds, half-lost; little black mouths of absence.
It wobbles to my touch, loose on its knuckle.
I remove it easily. She knows, thinks *No*, imagines
She's said it. I slip it on the outside finger
Of my left hand, firm safe fit.
She thinks *Yes. Go.*

EPITAPHS FROM THE GREEK ANTHOLOGY

1. You gaze at stars, my star—that I were skies,
   To gaze at you with endless billion eyes.

after Plato

2. I'm dead. For all I care
   The world can melt. I smile.

Anonymous

3. All of Zosima that slaved
   Was her body. That's free.

after Damascius the Philosopher

4. I lie under this now—
   The famous woman who lay for one man.

Anonymous

5. This is where Philippus buried
   His twelve-year-old son Nicoteles, his hope.

after Callimachus

THE LAWS OF ICE

Ice has laws
(Oxygen, fire,
Lord Gravity
Have laws) but loose—
A mother's call.

Human life
(Yours, mine)
Will glide down decades
Free as oil;

Then seize on the instant,
Rigid form—
Your statue, mine,
Perfected ice:

Random pose,
Appalling laws.

TWO

DAYS AND NIGHTS

A JOURNAL

On 13 February 1984 I began a notebook in which I meant to write short poems that sketched actual events of my days and nights (events that are often invisible—thoughts, reflexes, dreams; the dreams here are plain transcriptions).

From the first I attempted a tone that was brisk and supple, sufficiently Horatian to permit both the minutiae of a diary and more sizable concerns. Always I aimed to walk the charged line that divides the territories of poetry and prose, with only the requisite tacks to right or left—the flat-lit grasslands of prose, the jagged uplands of verse.

The fact that many of the impulses came in sonnet forms was a surprise and, for me, the confirmation of an old suspicion—that the shape of the sonnet participates in a near-metabolic unity with the western mind's rate of experience and reflection.

When I began I had no expectation of the catastrophe that would announce itself on 2 June, but subliminal warnings sound as early as number 21 (3 April). The remaining entries confront the aftermath, through 14 February 1985.

Here are all the attempts of that year. None was retouched after the day or two in which it was still malleable, though in deference to a friend's privacy, I have altered two words.

DAYS AND NIGHTS

1. SALAMANDER

Sun—in the belly of February—and through
The hot pane, a motorized tiller eats
The old garden: basil stalks, wet gourds,
Hulls of our summer like rented Heaven:
Maybe six harsh words (all mine).
                                                  A week ago,
Snow; and I led you out eighteen miles of ice
Through cars abandoned like tanks to an airport
Crazy as Lisbon 1940 and left you
To slice your own lean way to new summer—lions!
The meat-chocked plains.
                                        Have you yet faced west?—northwest
Toward here? Next time, remember to face the ground.
Concede the earth's curve. I might be in Hell.
You might be, from where I face down here.

Grin back. Adore the flame.

2. FLOOD

Full moon in three days, and last night black rain
In deafening sheets all round whatever sleep I got.
Through it, rags of dream—each a flash of you:
Outside, unshielded, upright in the roar
On the dam of the pond in phosphorous glare,
Both arms at your sides, palms curled toward me
(Strontium chunks), face blank as bread but fixed
On mine with lidless eyes.
                                        This morning, calm—
Pond at bankful, the creek a torrent—
I grope toward day, stunned as any drowned rock.
No way to know if I've prophesied, *seen,* or staged
The millionth tableau of punitive dread—
Me flailing me for excess joy
In my old toy theater, endless night-court.

3. COOL

The tenants fire-up their burglar alarm, then rush
To a party—forgetting the antique dog's indoors.
Ten minutes later she trips the siren. Its Gestapo
Wow-wow bursts on my dinner. Pillaged at random
Five times myself, I creep out into the dark
Muddy field in bedroom slippers and watch their windows—
Just out of pistol range. Every chink is lit
Though shaded. *Who's there?*
                                        Mired to the ankles,
I may be watching one more loved body gutted
From the heart out, ravenous jaws.
                                                Despite the premature
Fug on the night, I stay the coolest object—
Stroked by the nine-tenths moon breaking treeline:
A menopausal diva, gone in the slats.
Splinter every board. I can watch.

4. HMMMM

Famed as you are for your trick of snoozing through direct
Two-or-more megaton strikes on your actual bed
(Or rampant prowls by me, the Dawn Unicorn), I doubt
You're fazed by tonight's moon—fulfilled, size
Of a radioactive sterling washtub hung on my chimney
And frying *me*, prone sleepless as a Wall Street ticker at noon.
   I and several billion sensitive-plants worldwide
(Including all oceans, all tectonic plates, pigs, bird-egg yolks)
Are rung tonight like tuning forks, a lunatic
Barbershop trillionet.
                                        I beam my helpless tone
Your way, not knowing your way—Masai corrals
(Lapping bloodlaced milk), tawny sedge veldt, or diamond shaft
So deep in rock as to be past even this silvery suck?
   Hear my one note though, sleep refreshed.

5. LUNA

Why has no one, in no country ever, contended
You were male? The Man in the Moon was
Never you but in you, on you—idiot leer.

You want us back in you? Is that the famine
You burgeon through four weeks to glut; then phut out
Empty again, futile mensis?

—But maybe me. I've been a sentient target
Since birth. Mother's landlocked meer
Surely neaped and ebbed to your mute pull.

I still dream at least of treading in womb dark,
Dreading your draw through Mother's pink hide—
Slack-webbed to save me but bound to lose.

Vast pitiful gorgeous toothless mouth at the east pond-window,
Vast Hole Mother—this son yields finally. Now feed deep.

6. LETTER MAN

Saturday—the best in this lifeline of warm days
Flung at our heads—I was indoors of course, stripping
For a nap, when some force blammed the frontdoor glass.
Songbirds regularly dash their paper skulls
On its simulacrum of trees, berries, bugs.
So I assumed, say, one dead bluebird and
Fell on the bed. A second hit and "*Mr.*
Price" bellowed in a desperate strange voice.

Through the glass he looks like the Pale Avenger—black-
Headed, short, in a rose plaid shirt, with grainy skin,
A bowed shrunk right arm, and blank laser
Eyes.
        Helpless, reckless, I open the door.
He says "Mr. Price, can I fish your pond?" I say
"Where do you live?" (odd—not "Who are you?").
He fights a hard tremor; the dwarf arm shakes
South toward my dense woods—"That trailer
In yonder." I say "It's fished out."
He says "No it ain't."
                                        I've already offered my throat,
The lush baggage of my life strewn behind me. What's
Left but "Yes"? I add "Just you." Smiles
Are not in his power, but he tackles one—tormented wrench.

He's halfway gone in the throat of the woods when I see
The sign he always makes—upright spine,
Bent arm at his side: a trembling P
In the I's of the trees.
                                        Wracked mascot, fish for me!

7. RELIC

Your first card's here—eleven days in transit—
And you're not after all nailed to the mulchy
Swarming floor of a third-world jail, being
Flayed in elegant unbroken strips,
But are tented in candlelight thirty yards
From lions and hyenas chuckling at their feed
And have already witnessed a circumcision
In a Masai village.
                                        Look, six days ago
Here I guessed you might be feeding
On warm Masai cow's-milk streaked
With warmer red.
                                        Did they circumcise a boy or
Girl? What age and how? Who saved the blood?
Short of being speared-down in the ring by braves,
Could you have caught it in a clean white rag?

8. PRAISE ON YOUR BIRTHDAY

Edible flesh,
A leavened bread.

Eyes to watch
Your flood consume
Me, match my smile.

Mind reckless, fragrant,
Open-handed—
Alexander

By the green Hydaspes:
Elephant charge!

9. HECATOMB

Dave, a gale's slamming through from the west;
And you're at another stand, reading your high hot
Grave-eyed poems to another room of eyes.
I'm beached back here in the dim house alone,
Stove-up from our night of talk—word-oblations,
Big shoulders of each life slabbed on a communal
Altar in midair above the teak table's
Ashtrays and books: propitiations?
Rewards? Raw fuel.
                                        Your son—weed-high
With a sooty lip to forecast beard—
Sat (an angle to our line, watchful as a nauga);
Then smiled my way and claimed "I've never
Seen him like this." What had we shown
Him but unendable hunger?

10. WARNED

Christmas, I gave myself a set of runes—
A softedged California guru's guess
At the lost Norse code of divination.

This morning, packing for our plan to meet
(Eight p.m., Eastern Airlines, cold Milwaukee),
I sheepishly consult the old-new signs—

Blindly drawing three from the leather pouch,
Spreading them facedown, one by one
Confronting their bleak promise, silent threat:

Signals reversed, Constraint, Movement reversed.
Crouched, I proceed as though the toys are charged—
Urim and Thummim, eyeslots onto time.

Milwaukee eight hours later, no surprise.
You fail our meeting, swear you'll come tomorrow.

11. A POLAR SIMPLE

Six times in precisely forty-eight hours
Together, half-dark, we descended the shaft
Lined with no eyes but ours; and there on the flat,
On firm yielding ground, concurred in the earnest
Minutes of strife that always end
In blinding glare of absolute joy—
Each thanking each for gifts dense
As pitchblende, discoveries startling as the polar
Crocus (eight leaves locked round
A rank flamboyant pistil) from which
Today these crucials are derived:
An imbrication for the fear of dreams,
Heartsease in ampules small as seed,
A dauntless fulminant for hope.

12. RIDDLE

Stalk that blooms in total night,
No need of eyes.

Astonishment that powders rock,
Silent as fur.

13. THE AIM

We rise from these days and walk west and east
Into thriving separate worlds blank-ignorant
Of what we've swapped on this clean bed—

Your hidden essence, tapped by pleasure;
My circling hunger to consume but spare;
Our silent pact to man this circuit

For lasting service, warming both lives
(Their adjacent towns) and lighting the acts
Of creatures undreamed of here but implicit:

Red droves of children at play on hills,
A woman sworn to tend you always,
Whatever calm stranger shuts my eyes.

The secret of fire was our main aim.
Surely we turn in its fierce candor now.

14. SAME ROAD

Twenty-five years ago—me dark and lean—
This road was only the hyphen between us,
Five hours of concrete I could roll tight
Till we joined again in roomy Georgetown,
A brick village still, you gold and gleaming.
  The highway's wallowed, devouring oaks
And crossroad stores with handmade signs
(If you believe in credit, lend me $5.00);
And Georgetown's crammed with clerks young enough
To be our sons, each hazed with hope
Of bone-on-bone, adhesive flesh,
Yips of joy in rooms cramped as milk cartons.
  Like us—then, now. But what we made!
Utter trust, safe decades, past shoals of thieves.

15. LATE

There are three of us, yes; but why
At the end of this courteous night
Are we posted still at three angles
Of a table by cold scraped bowls
When—huge at the window—an avid
Moon pumps white demand
To rise, dowse lights, and hoop
Our limbs on bed or floor:
Joint enactment of her
Lone unity, streaming gift?

16. EELS

From the first full letter,
This falls, first-pop;
And is thus my first sight
In five weeks, of you
—On an Afrikaans beach,
Encased in French models
(Worn as brogans,
Nude wilting tits),
You wear black trunks
You wore the day
We bobbed the Dead Sea's
Mucilage-slit
In the earth's main cleft.
All grin at the lens,
None at you.
    But me. I watch
From a Tennessee hill
Ten thousand miles off—
You clad in bodies
Raw as eels.
Why ask me to face
Their shame; your modesty,
Your hedged consent?

17. FOR VIVIEN LEIGH

I was the show, reading the murder-suicide
From my novel-in-progress and my heron poem
Whose gaunt last chill mostly rivets the rows
At these odd inexplicable rallies of ears.
(Tonight a radiologist sleeps till peppered
By applause, then bolts up to swear he's heard
Every word—all soothing).
                                        At the after-party
I haunt the kitchen, leashing the ego
That—uncurbed now—will howl till dawn.
Slowly the room fills. Again I'm the act,
At a round worktable gnawing tuna and cheese.
A bald man asks me to tell my tale
Of autograph hunting by mail in the 40s.
I run through the early easy successes—
MacArthur in the Philippines; Eisenhower weaving
The Norman invasion, a shirt of fire;
Toscanini, Barbara Stanwyck on her own stationery
With a skywriting plane inscribing her name
In blue at the top.
                                A woman suddenly
Says your name—hadn't I met you?—
And I give them the story that holds them closer
Than my own read-words: the three times in New York,
Stratford, London when you let the black-haired
Boy I was (and am, seeing you)
Come backstage and stand two feet away,
Having kissed your hand, and see, just *see*
Your burning face (we spoke ten minutes
But no word survives).
                                    The short years before,
The long years since, no other face moves
In the world yours ceaselessly generates—
Radium lily, slant eyes fixed
On mine (green limpets).
                                        I knew
You were half-mad, knew you were flung
Like a rag real-child off high rock
Walls into real rock gulfs time

After time and rose like this; knew you'd
Blessed me forever—these eyes to thank
In lucid memory each day since:
Perfect, utterly informed, no glint of blame.
  Now a whole new room, twelve still Tennesseans,
  Has watched the gift.

18. SECRET

Any room you entered thirty years ago
Rang for me with the high white pitch
That cows maddogs, guides bats through briars.

Noon today I passed you at St. Patrick's—
You in your old brisk trudge, forcing air;
Jaw still firm—rampart I never took.

I called your name silently, the waves lapped short,
You never broke stride or veered an inch
But pressed on south—home, a new daughter:

One more thing you'll never hear from me.

19. FOR LEONTYNE PRICE (*La Forza del Destino*, 1984)

At the end of the convent scene, act one,
When you'd begged the Virgin to cloak your sin
(In a voice that still might wring quick pardon
From rabid jaws) and were bound for your cave—
Hermit's bell, wretched bread—the abbot handed you
An earnest cross: no toy, nine tall feet
Of staggering wood. You held it upright
A long half-minute as the monks concluded
Their rousing send-off; then you walked it away—
Curtain, cheers.
                I sat still long enough
To fix the sight, knowing I'd seen you
Enact your emblem—ravishing prayer
At shut iron gates, silent assent,
The whole weight borne.

20. CAUGHT

The past three nights were long hot comas,
Requisite maintenance for two jarred weeks
On the road by air. But plainly more.
Beneath the hectic signal of dream
(Last night a fast hour in forced pursuit
Of an old landlady's slick covered trail—
Adulteries bucked-out in wet back alleys),
I know I'm cocked for one right word
That's already flung my way from the source,
Will pass any instant at the speed of black light,
And, lost, will not be beamed again.
  Selfless chemicals I hear toward dawn—
Truth seized and held in juddering eyes,
Final secret of sexual love.

21. CAW

Splayed face-down on the last pool of sleep,
I'm gaffed by *caw-caw* from one distant crow.
What Roman would rise to face this day?

Half an hour later I loom at the pond window,
Glum while my two globes of barnyard cholesterol
Gurgle behind me in salt-free fat

To the tune of the radio voice of Charles Simic
Who suddenly flings out a cold crow poem.
What human would join me to face this day?

22. TRANSATLANTIC

This voice—light-tenor
Ghost of your body—
Hunts me ten thousand miles,
Burns down from its satellite,
And halts me here
(Precisely its laugh)
On the last long step
Into loss of your six smells,
Burr of your neck,
Eyes still by day
As famished stoats
But adrift by night
Like well-fed fishers
Borne toward me.

23. A LIFE IN DREAMS

I'm proud second-fiddle today to Eudora's
Seventy-fifth, a sideline smiler, when
A man walks up in the crowded hall—
I met him once, two minutes, years ago
(Classicist, teacher, opera librettist)—
And says he dreamed a new novel by me:
Plot and characters vague but the tone strong as music,
Late Rilke to Schoenberg's *Transfigured Night*;
Each figure guarded and drawn through the maze
By a single angel, gleaming and apt.
He says "I even dreamed the title—
Actual Presences."
"Perfect," I say.
"Now write it for me please"; then know I have,
Five times in two decades and mean to again.

24. REST

Day calm and gray as a pewter plate,
Chartreuse new leaves in billows at the glass;
Broody wrens commanding the eaves
With a purpose pure as the laws of ice;

And me—laid-up from the frantic last days
Of a term of students famished as sand,
Winning as fawns (their smoky ordnance
At Milton and God still litters my floor).

Rest. The promise of a week like silt
In a sweetwater delta, stirred only by minnows
And the mutter of each slow skin of nacre
As it welds to the pearl of a somnolent oyster—

Mindless companion while I too mutter
Round my gritty core, this ruined glad life.

25. FOR JAMES DEAN

Twelve months ago we sat here dark,
Apart on the sofa, and watched James Dean
Burn through *East of Eden* like the universal solvent,
Unquenchably craving all bodies, all eyes—
And he underground these twenty-eight years
That silvered my head (two years his junior)
And brought your parents, through whole states of pain,
Together on a late-May bed, starting you.
 We gave him eyes two hours, barely blinking.
The bodies waited another five weeks;
Then fueled by him but balked at the sealed
Dry cleft of his absence, took one another—
Same dark room: a thanks launched deep
Toward his mute head, and running still.

26. THE CLAIM

Since you agreed to live in my house
And sleep like a chloroformed rock through a hundred-
Fifty nights six yards from my hand
(No balks between us), I took this liberty
Throughout your drowned nights; and while I'm still
Unbowed by guilt, I nonetheless feel
At the rim of my mind—like a child's fist tapping
In awe or thirst—this present duty
To full confession, months too late.
   I covered you, every cell of your hide,
With my potent name.
                    Potent, I say
Since from age five or six I'd seek lone stretches,
Stare at blank sky, and rattle those thirteen
Letters (three syllables) high and fast
Till they stopped being me and fused into one
Selfless senseless mantra on which I skimmed
More gulfs and peaks in planing light
Than on any other wing—right into pubescence:
That burning air-net, feverish toy.
   You look and see nothing?—follicles, hair,
Moles familiar as dreams of falling
Or maps of home. The sun's too strong.
Stand there in shade by the cleanest mirror.
Gently press the thinnest skin
North of your left eye, bone of your brow.
Step quickly back and focus fine.
See the blood flush in and, for this red instant,
My whole name. Only there on that frail
Supraorbital scrim will it yield to force;
And only there is it boldly legible
As letters, words.
                  Elsewhere, from absolute
Crown to sole, you are calligraphed
Invisibly in an endless trail
That is both my name and the framing outline
Of ten thousand pictures, perfect memories
(In universal code of human mime)
Of those two-thousand-two-hundred-fifty minutes

When—merged in mutual angelic maintenance,
Consuming each other like buttered carp—
We earned our vast short seamless luck.
There are scenes in the strongest light on earth
By the deepest sea; scenes in absolute night
By God's hometown, black walls of his house—
You in thriftshop rags and lion head;
Me gimp-kneed, silver, game as you
For the million figures joy can twine
When fearless, fed, and bound to end:
No single mean or ugly turn,
No public sight. You're a shut museum,
No eyes but ours.
                    Caution though—
My lips are sealed; still there's one hard fact
You must bear in mind. My inks are invisible
In normal use—normal pain, daily love.
They'll even hide through quick convulsions
To purge the wells or a conflagration
To clear the scrub. Foxfire however—
Cool constant gleam (blanked by day
But patient to eat whole woods and cliffs)—
Will print you plain as a satellite photo
Of Russian tank-maneuvers toward Texas:
Every tread and finger, thicket and stream.
Any second burn approaching ours
In radiance, stamina, silent roar—
And you'll stand manifest, claimed for life;
Indelible track of the first real name
To vow you all and keep the vow,
Your true best days beneath this hand.

27. TV

At five p.m., grim as Charon's punt,
The neurologist finds me on my stretcher by the door
Of the radiological torture-tank
In which four searchers kind as children
Have found the fault—"A ten-inch tumor
On your spinal cord."
                                        Now at nine
I lie here alone, flanked by chatter and howls,
And watch TV—a flabby endless
Documentary, "Portrait of Giselle,"
Starring Anton Dolin with clips of Markova,
Alonso, Makarova: each her own
Absurd self blazed by white elation,
Cause of the helpless joy I sport
In this hot stale proliferating dark.

28. NEIGHBORS

My name is *Edward Reynolds Price,*
So here on the ward I'm *Edward Price.*

Last night I looked at my new neighbor's door.
He's *Edward Reynolds,* plain as ink.

Which one of us is the other's *doppelgänger*?
Scapegoat? Porter of an alternate fate?

29. PEARS

Perfect pears no bigger than hen eggs;
Gold, spotted brown, one mouthful even
For me a boy. My father's brought them
Home from a trip; and I devour
Them in one long evening, then sleep
Black dreamless night till he shakes me—Sunday,
His day.
                    Forty-six years pass. Home
From surgery (tumor still in me), I wake
At dawn and taste that cool flesh;
Hear his waking voice.

30. VISION

I'm sleeping with Jesus and his twelve disciples
On the vacant east shore of Lake Kinnereth—
The Sea of Galilee—near where he exorcised
The demon Legion. We're flat on the ground,
Cocooned in clothes. Mine are light street clothes
(Apparently modern, theirs are classic robes);
And I wake early, well before dawn—
Hour of the worm that desolates hope.
I give it long minutes to line another tunnel
With eggs that will yield the next white wave
Of ravenous heirs.
                                        Then I roll to my right side
And see in the frail dark that Jesus has somehow
Moved nearer toward me. I listen to hear
If he sleeps or wakes.
                                        Then we stand in the lake,
Both bare to the waist. Light creeps out toward us
From the hills behind; the water's warm.
I see us both as if from a height.
My spine is scored by a twelve-inch incision,
Bracketed now by gentian-purple
Ink that's the map for X-ray therapy
Due in two days. Jesus's beard
Is short and dry, though with both broad hands
He lifts clear water and pours it down
My neck and scar.
                                        Then we climb toward shore.
I get there first and wait on the stones—
We're still the only two awake.
Behind me he says "Your sins are forgiven."
I think "That's good but not why I came."
I turn and say "Am I also cured?"
He comes close but looks down. He says "That too,"
Then wades strong past me and touches land.

31. THE DREAM OF REFUSAL

I've come on foot through dark dense as fur
(Clean, dry but pressed to my mouth)
To find my mother's father's house
In Macon, N.C. I know he's been dead
Since she was a girl, but—stronger—I know
A secret's here I must face to live.

At the end of seventy miles I see it,
Though the dark's unbroken and no light shows
From any tall window or the open door.
I pull myself through the rooms by hand—
All dead, empty, no stick or thread,
Not the house I loved in childhood

And no more hint of a vital secret
Than noon sun stamps on a working hand.
I forget my life is staked on this hunt,
That these walls store dried acts or words
To kill or save precisely me who pass
Fool-fearless and out again—the yard, lighter dark.

I'm leaving the place and have reached the thicket
Of shrubs near the road. I step through the last
Clear space that can still be called my goal—
My mother's father's home in Macon.
I lift my foot to enter freedom
(And death? I no longer think of death).

Behind me I feel a quick condensation—
Sizable presence barely humming
In furious motion. Fear thrusts up me
Like rammed pack-ice. But I know again
Why I'm here at all, and slowly I turn
Onto whatever deadly shadow waits.

What seems a small man—blackhaired, young—
Crouches in yellow glow he makes,
A smoke from his skin. I know at once
His motion is dance; that he dances every

Instant he breathes, huddled ecstatic.
His hands are empty. He beckons me.

I know he will make his thrust any moment;
I cannot guess what aim it will take.
Then as—appalled—I watch him quiver,
He says "Now you must learn the bat dance."
I know he has struck. It is why I came.
In one long silent step, I refuse and turn toward home.

I will walk all night. I will not die of cancer.
Nothing will make me dance in that dark.

32. OCTOBER SUN

Long silence here—six weeks of days
When numbness climbed my body: this chimney
With ample footholds, a shuddering fire.
But now as dead leaves stroke the house
And crazed squirrels race to hide (from themselves)
The deluge of beech- and hickory-nuts,
I warm again to the heat of life—
A promised stretch of upright time.
The vision of cure in Kinnereth;
The calm white-hot assurance
From six sane friends that I'll survive
In human, useful, usable form
Are credible again.
                                        And these words boil up
Sure, unhedged as a year-old boy's
Blue gold-edged eyes.

33. MOTHER

Dear girl, dead twenty years
But hot as new blood,
You're eighty today.

Do you see me here—
Stove-up at fifty-two,
Numb as a plate?

Can you beg for help?
Will your own starved lips
Move once to save me?

34. TURN

Eight months since surgery, six since radiation
(Twenty-seven daily trips to Hiroshima),
I sit in my bedroom, its prisoner,

When my long hope was to hold some other
Inmate, glad to wear my yoke
And smiling not one hand's breadth from my face.

35. LATE VISIT

February 10th, 9:10 a.m.,
Bright icy Sunday—Jeff Anderson phones:
"Look out your window. The heron's on the pond."

Indisputably he is, and frozen out again—
Barred from his breakfast but preening the thousand
Blues of his wings, clearly assuaged.

Seven weeks late for his yearly stop,
Thrown maybe by the crazed local weather
(Coldest month in a hundred years)

Or detained to alter his former message—
Endurance or death. What news today?

THREE

LINES OF LIFE

Various as roads, the lines life takes—
Twisting like the boundaries of lakes.
What we lack here, some god can there increase
With harmonies, amends, enduring peace.

after Hölderlin

Now Joseph, being a man of principle, and not wishing to make a spectacle of Mary, decided to dismiss her secretly. MATTHEW 1:19

THREE SECRETS

1. JOSEPH

That's way too strict a version of the truth.
The principle was—*I'd never seen her like,*
Not in fifty years (and I'd seen a few).
My first wife had died the previous winter;
And once we had her cold underground,
My boys gave skittish signs of dread—
The aged parent, unobligingly hale,
To stuff and josh through centuries more.
Without my knowledge, they set up a hunt—
Some well-fixed widow or crosseyed girl
Who might not gag at stringy hams,
The treacherous tool that let me down
More times than not those last years.
They came back dry and said as much—
"Take it from here; our hands are full."
"—Of the trade I taught you," I thought but didn't say
And turned back to minding my own cot and pots.
Still they'd set me off, and the itch gnawed steady.
So I made my own hunt—dignified, cunning,
Best foot forward—with no better luck;
Then resigned myself to space and peace
(A big, not entirely unwelcome surprise).
Toward spring, however, an old local girl
Moved back up here. She'd married well—
A Temple priest—and lived in the City
Till he keeled over one day, slaughtering doves.
I'd cavorted with her before she got grand
And wondered now what jig was left.
None at all, not a skip—she let me know
On my first visit (and I'd washed my beard).
The daughter though—the blinding girl.
I hardly watched her serving our tea;

My eyes would skid off her face like ice
Or live wood-coals. She looked that rare.
Whatever her mother had had, long since
(Good eyes, straight teeth), whatever the priest—
All boiled in her and changed to skin
Rich as goat's cream, eyes
Deep enough to hold the world.
She never spoke. But as I left
Anne seized my arm and said "Protect her."
I thought she'd gone off her rocker in town;
Baffled, I bowed and scuttled out.
Protect her from what up here?—the odd snake.
   But I dreamed about her the next three nights
And then went back to ask Anne's meaning.
She meant what happened, a marriage deal.
And though I faced a hail of jokes,
I kept my bargain and married the girl—
Even with a belly slung on her by then,
A wen gorging hour by hour on blood.
   Why? Not principle. Not manly kindness
And—God knew then—not second sight
(The way I saw it, some City boy'd ruined her).
I was glad enough to take people's pity,
Nod my thanks when they said "bighearted."
My heart's big as yours, a small man's fist.
   The principle was *her*—all skin and eyes,
Lank horsehair bound at her strong-stalked neck,
The covered promise of undreamed more.
   My secret till now (and it scalds to tell)
Is the one fact no one's guessed at yet—
I saw her just once, the whole bare her.
Wracked in dry straw, sweating great clots
Of absolute dread, her bloody thighs
Swung boneless out and blue with agony
To make clear room for that huge head—
Her first live boy, a ten-pound wedge.
The ox-team bent down nearer than I.
   Years after, back home (the nine years left me),
I never begged more. A younger man
Might have barged through risk to claim that glory—

Even one short night, succeeded by her death.
Not I. I slept at a good arm's length,
Though in reach of her breath—the musk of milk—
Till I died, still stunned.

The angel said to her "The Holy Spirit will come over you, and the Highest Power will darken you." LUKE 1:35

2. MARY

It did, no question.
My hands worked to save me;
The dark was so deep
They couldn't find my body.
My skirt had melted away
In the glare (I felt that much),
And the wind scorched my legs—
The scars are still there,
Though no one's seen them since Bethlehem.
Mother begged to see, any shred
Of proof for the cock-and-bull story
I had to tell—a girl
Flung down by the Last Resort,
His hot seed blown
Into her green womb: a country
Girl, never asked to write
So much as her name, now asked
To gouge it plain enough to read—
An ordinary name in the dome of creation.
I stood and wrote, apparently
Right—the word still echoes,
A million mouths, each instant
Each year. Who was I, fifteen,
To say flat No?
Twelve thousand days later—
Toothless, hunched, at his raw
Red feet—I knew my answer
And mouthed it toward him. I doubt
He heard; he was screaming by then.
So I've held it in, two thousand
Years, and see no cause to speak
It now.

"There are eunuchs who were born that way from their mother's womb. There are eunuchs made eunuchs by men, and there are eunuchs who made themselves eunuchs for the kingdom of heaven." MATTHEW 19:12

3. JESUS

I said as much to test their edge
And waited for the question *Which are you?*
—Sweaty silence. I'd lost them again
To the nearest sight: two amorous dogs
And a peg-legged girl. When would I learn?
I was not meant to be heard but seen,
The final emblem.
It was near the end;
I was all but hungry for the final round.
So I let it rest on the humming air
And turned toward blood, thick sheets of blood—
All I had.
The question waits though,
Three-pronged riddle any man must solve
For himself or choke—*Who cut my roots?*
The lines to power, and why, and so what?
My premise plainly was *Power is flesh.*
Man's power—woman's—maybe God's,
Flesh as it yokes with alien flesh
In single relays, bearing the charge
Till flesh burns out and is someway replaced.
Me? I came here fully equipped,
All requisite organs, members, glands;
All ticking dimly at the human rate—
A fresh bud here, a wilting there,
Crisp hair and eighteen separate scents:
All triggered also by natural time.
At fourteen no boy anywhere near me
(Where we swam in the quarry) showed more than I—
A convex exhibit of Ready Boy,
The height of the climb, my splendid noon.
All wasted, unspent? All slashed and hurled
In the rank dog's-bowl?
Never, no.

The loyal women who watched me nailed,
Hung high to drip, know I died intact—
A youngish man still fit to stamp
His face on countless scores of souls
As yet blank, dumb, in the waiting line.
Even soldiers flung up cheers
At my pelvic gear.
So yes, I chose;
It was not specified in my commission.
I made myself this dead-end road
I walked to the end, this low Skull Hill.
I vowed it at twelve when my fork took life,
And twenty-one years I kept the vow
With no more ease than a healthy stallion
Tethered in a field of fragrant mares.
More nights and dawns than any friend knew,
I gnawed the heel of my hard right hand
To purple pulp to balk my yen
To know the common sweetness of skin.
Why? I knew I'd need clear gaze,
No flickering others at the rim of sight,
No colored glass between me and day.
I was the prism, sole translator
Of this whole world that poured through me
Toward God's own mind—the stroke of dark,
Light, jackal-crunch of teeth in bone,
Human eyes so swamped by pain
I'd have howled and run except for the choice.
Every conscious moment, I stopped my arm
On the near edge of touch. Healing, scourging,
Anointing, yes; never the melding
That brings frank joy, knowledge and joy—
Likewise shackles, blinders, gags.
That was the cost. *I was always free.*
I could speak any syllable that creased my mind
(No family glares)—sleep in the dirt
Where I happened to tire—raise a cold corpse
Without its permission and then walk out.
Few ever saw me twice, except the twelve pupils.
They were close-by daily, huddled close at night;
But they were who I touched least of all—

Once when I tapped them to follow me;
Second, that last time as they sat bolting
Down broiled perch to numb their betrayal
And I stepped through the shut door—live!
They had to touch me to prove their fear.
   He meant all he said. This country eunuch
With a two-edged tongue, a babymaker
In mint condition (never unwrapped),
This silvery bore died in the pain
That splits black granite in the hearts of hills
And stands *here now, skin pierced but closing—*
Reach here in the side, know a new brand of flesh.
   I managed, just, to bear their touch—
One by one, eleven in line;
And then the three women, diehard loyals
From the earliest days. I thought I'd shrink,
That the flesh itself would flee their hands
As it always had.
                                    But no, it held
In place for all three (Magdalen last).
And as they rushed out to scrounge me a bowl,
Salvage some scraps—I must be starved—
I suddenly saw a changed new world,
Sight strange to me as my face to this room,
What my vow had forbade my knowing till now.
Each particle linked, perpetual chain:
Yoking, binding, bonding in glee
These fourteen before me, old companions,
Now newly born, more welcome than rain—
Bumping and jostling to dry my hair,
Guiding my elbow on to the bench
They'd cleared to bear me, crouching round,
Hand joined to hand at the white core of space
Where they'd been from the start,
The lovely tread of lean and hold
—Which I knew in an instant I now must flee.
I wept hot tears to learn so late.

ROAD

Dead vine on dead tree, evening light, one crow,
Low bridge, streaming water, empty house,
Old road (the Road), cold wind, a starving horse.
Sun falls on broken man at edge of day.

after Ma Chih Yuan

THREE VISITS

1. DIONYSOS

A god stopped in at the house last night,
Claiming to be a Jehovah's Witness
Peddling tracts and offering to expound
John's Apocalypse—what it meant for me.
I pierced his mask at once—two mistakes.
I lied at the door and claimed to be Catholic
(A claim that always halts true Witnesses);
But he never flinched so I let him in,
Asked him to sit, and awaited his purpose.
Then as he bent to sip a cup of water
(All he'd accept from my profuse bar),
I saw a two-inch edge of leopard skin
Otherwise hid by his white Arrow shirt—
Hot and spotted at his tawny neck,
The formal dress of Semele's son.
We bumbled through numb amenities—
The glorious day, rags of a staggering
Fall aurora north of my door
(He took clear family pride in that).
I felt we were warming, felt I'd won his trust,
That now we'd surely proceed to his secret
On some straight beneficial path.
And his next few gambits seemed propitious—
What did I feel about his eyes?
Did he have some major unfilled need?—
But once he'd drained the glass, he dozed—
Lounging slack in the deep plush chair,
Gold eyes blank as aluminum washers,
The short dense body melting till it formed
A lithe live-model of the seat and arms,
The finest slipcover this side Elysium.
The transformation took ten minutes
But felt like a geologic era—
A casual dozen million years.

Watching it from my new wheelchair
(The first improvement in invalid gear
Since the Crimean War), I helplessly underwent
Conversion—conforming like liquid to my seat
And wheels, agreeing to this crouched rolling
Life as endless, my mere fate
On earth and under, a likable mode.
Poured out, dumb, we both lay on
Just past an hour (my digital watch
Chimed cheerful eight and his hide shuddered).
Then slowly still his essence gathered;
Limbs, trunk, head throbbed, coalesced—
A second prolonged transformation.
The glare consumed his peddler's mask
Till he sat up near my face, then rose—
Himself revealed, incendiary core,
A megatonnage unforeseen
By any computer or institute:
Precisely the grandest male I'd found,
Exhaling from every pore of a skin
Dusted with a pelt of slant tan hair
The constant ground-bass of majesty.
Scared, I hunkered through the long bombardment,
Guessing I'd scorch to a charcoal crackling
Like his dimwit mother in the throes of Zeus.
I didn't, though I heard my eyebrows singe.
Eventually I could nod and I spoke his name—
Syllabic thunder, in school-Greek.
It must have been the test; I passed.
His right arm moved out toward me then;
In its field of force, I also grew—
Firmed and steadied till I rose to meet him,
Irresistibly drawn onto legs
Again as apt as a working boy's
In a field of furrows of standing grain:
Not the filleted flippers I've lately worn.
Then entered me—the god himself.
Or I entered him (it was all his plan,
I knew, his purpose). Either way we melded
Through the next calm epoch into one discrete
Bounded body of a grace and spangle

I'd only guessed in pornographic moments
Of boyhood, rapt at Father's fogged pierglass—
I devouring gouts of his power,
Undying springs of riot and calm;
He absorbing my new skill,
Invented, patented by mortal man
(The means of thriving on a void salt prairie,
At the entire mercy of all that moves
On foot, segmented belly, or wing:
Gnats, chilled vipers, the odd escaped arsonist
Or neighbor-punk with knucks and shiv).
   Then separated, again slowly as leaves eat light.
What he was by then assisted me back
Cross the steerhide rug to my patient chair
Which seemed, in his hands, tolerable home.
Silent, he brought me cool tapwater
In the cup he'd drunk from (my good silver).
As I bent to sip, he gripped my skull
In a force I knew was bound to kill
(Calmest thought of the past two years).
But then relented; met my eyes
A final time with his (not blank now,
Plunging slow through infinite mind);
And left the way he'd come—off east
Up Cornwallis Road toward the upright, town:
The shifting lights of the crazed-for-motion,
Jolt of willed contingency.
   Whoever else detected him
On his gleaming way, I've yet to hear—
Outrage or praise, death-rattle or glee.
   I even wondered most of the night
At my own answer—rage or thanks?—
Till dawn when I woke in the same brass bed
I can no longer roll in and rolled my tongue
On the tart astringence of early grapes,
Then raised and saw my sensible threatened
Working arms woven in tender
Young green vines: tendrils reaching
Toward my heart,
                    Which pines for touch.

2. APHRODITE

The spring I was fourteen we lived in a house
That had been a recent massacre-scene,
Greek in volume—a Mr. Young
Locked himself and his wife in a bedroom
And beat her hard. A grown son pounded
The door in rescue. The father fired
Through the wood, killed the son;
Then killed the wife and, neatly, himself.
When we moved in, the door was patched
With plastic wood; but the sheetrock ceiling
Bore two neat holes (superfluous shots).
My family'd never known the Youngs.
Still we kept the scene as our spare bedroom;
And Mother thumped my younger brother
When he'd tell guests they had the "Bullet Room."
I conspired in the secret but kept the room
As a sulking chamber for afternoon pouts
(I was crawling, appalled, through my own hail—
A puberty stern as trench warfare
With poison gas).
One Sunday in June
I shut myself in and turned the key—
Ferocious self-service succeeded by a doze
And scraps of stolen satiate dream.
When I woke sun was broiling the blinds
In orange fire; and a full-grown woman
Stood by the bed, naked as any
Forced magnolia—that white, flamboyant,
Stupefyingly rank.
The face was nearly
My mother's—familiar in humming vibrance—
But the hair was long and bound at the neck
With amber pins, a few strays gleaming;
And the belly bore no scar like Mother's
(Aftermath of a burst appendix).
Elsewhere she managed to cantilever
A magnanimity of flesh that poised
On the razor-edge of corpulence—
An endless clearly magical No

To gravity and its train of bylaws.
   I'd dreamed such luck for three, four years
And pictured it frankly in my locked diary.
This was plainly no dream—dreams flaunt no odor—
And when my left hand stretched to try her,
The hair in her fork was sufficiently charged
To halt a herd of yearling bulls.
I drew back, burned, and sucked my finger.
   She smiled, begged pardon—"I always forget"—
Stood a moment to damp her voltage,
Then folded in pliant glory beside me.
   I'd known so little joy till then
(All solitary, all mainly outdoors—
Childish transports, though truer than adult
Beatific unions with angel thighs,
Cherubic darts pumping flame),
I froze in blue paralysis,
Cowlick to crotch, and expected death.
No Methodist boy could butt through this
Not stamped on the brow with a black-scabbed *L*
For goatish lust, passport to the Pit.
   She understood, stroked my rigid belly,
And murmured a word I heard as *Cyprus.*
   I'd finished the eighth grade, studied myths,
And understood she'd named her birthplace—
The sea off Cyprus, wind-blown foam,
Pregnant scallop-crib of ardor.
The knowledge freed me. I grinned wide as Kansas,
And blood crept out from my clenched heart
To my locked limbs, chiefly my third leg
(The sturdy friend that'd seen me through).
But I knew no way to enact the force
Beyond the handy grip of palms,
The knowing permanent portable socket
I'd found ten years ago and trained
To the fleet dispatch of consoling perfection.
   She seized control and in the next hour—
To muffled sounds behind the patched door
(Father's day-off shuffle, my brother at the keyboard
Hellbent to bang out *Adeste Fidelis*
In the Bombay-day)—she endowed on me

A Himalayan glide toward snow-saddled heights
Of corporal joy I accepted with helpless
Copious tears of dumb amazement
And the inexhaustible readiness of boyhood
But also the certainty that never, with no one
Less than she in the maybe sixty years
That lay before me, would I stride so high
On so bright a ridge in blinding light
That deigned not to blind but aimed my eyes
To a piercing keenness that laid back skin
And peeled the ample spine of pleasure
That waits unimplorable, unforeseen
In the will of God, gods, their hapless consorts.
   Both ways I was right—I made the climb,
I bear the scars (concealed red stripes,
Authentic as the oozing wounds of Francis),
I've sought their mate in a hundred bodies:
All lovely, most human, some demi-divine
(She'd left when I roused from a ten-second stun;
The house was more than naturally still,
Dozing in its own grateful lustration).
   No subsequent match (though a few proximations
For which I burn the lamp of thanks);
So I live as the human—only one I know—
Who flowered on the low near-sill of life:
Young as a Rebel drummer at Shiloh,
Now an aging vet, grateful, grinning
And fueled by hope of a second bloom
But privately hunched for the downhill path
Torched by memory, dimming daily.

3. HERMES PSYCHOPOMPOS

Sit with me, utterly still at dusk. Look there
To the left of the big beechtree (always askance;
He's prevented or shied by a direct stare—more than glances,
Flicks at scraps of his face). Hold still; the hour
Of the hawk's at hand.
There, sweeping toward us cross
The field—the redtailed hawk who rules
The beech (though daily contested by wrens). There,
It's seized the roosting bough at the crotch of the trunk;
It knows we're here but conserves its grandeur, the iron
Eyes by a pure disdain that all but deletes us.
The sky falls now, light years per instant. In four
More seconds he'll take his place—the man in question
(If he's on tonight; three nights each lunar month
He's off, though I've yet to succeed in cracking his code,
Whatever schedule dictates the vigil.)
Now. *There*—
Cut an eye quick to the low leafpile: his bare
Feet (no, no heel wings). Now up the runner's legs,
Long waist, strong neck to the wide gray eyes—
Lucid gray of frozen dawn and locked
On me from here till sleep. Enough. Rest.
That—in jeans and chambray workshirt—is almost
Surely the high gods' messenger, guide of souls
Through death to life (whatever life waits, there
On the extreme verge of breath—recompense,
Tonic lines of the fugue we'll play till time resolves,
Or near-starvation like Odysseus' mother when he finds
Her in Hades—so desperate she laps hot blood from a ditch
When her son dispatches a ram to save her). *Hermes*
Psychopompos there in my yard where
He's waited more than twenty years—for who else
But me, sole resident?
First he came
As a string of beasts, all but perfectly transformed
Scouts—a great blue heron recurring each Christmas,
A more than normally watchful redfox,
A small herd of three unflappable deer
At my study window, a pale uncanny near-fetal

Cat that stalked my terrace the day Mother died
And one more day years later when I sat
Laughing with two friends, recalling the cat; and there
It was on the windowledge pressed to the pane
Intent on me (both witnesses are live, sane, ready
To testify); possibly a very peculiar blacksnake,
Also recurrent and able to speak.
                                        But human,
In that form there tonight—he's only come thus
Since the day I finished five weeks' radiation
(Twenty-nine thirty-second trips to Hiroshima, ground-zero,
Blast). At first I thought it was my new neighbor;
Then a peeping Tom (sorry, no flasher). Then
As the held-off astonished baked nerves in my spinal cord
Began to die (they never revive in human
Tissue) and my hips and legs became boiled noodles,
Then wet rags, I'd search his evening manifestations
For some plain sign he was more than he seemed.
                                                        I never
Found more than what's there now, by the beech before us—
A young man barefoot in all grades of swelter, rain,
And ice; black-haired, gray-eyed, low-browed: he never
Looks down but locks on my face fiercely
As a satellite circling Russia on a missile-
Hunt through frozen tundra and sleepless armies
Of golden elk or clouds of gray geese steered
By the moon, magnets buried in the thrumming earth,
And patterned stars.
                              Soon he'll face me and bear
My gaze. Then you'll know I've named him right.
He's come for me. Or waits. He flies no sign
Of impatience, though it's more than a year
And though I've strengthened nicely again—
From waist to brain.
                              Is he Hermes then in another
Aspect?—god of fraud, deceit, good luck,
God of dice, wealth, body games? Am I soon
To be the first gimp billionaire, first gimp wheeler
Of a four-minute mile, first wheelchair-spy (compromising
Star Wars and avoiding jail as a privileged minority)?
  Is he Hermes at all or, more, Apollo—god

Of healing, light, streaming music? Apollo, dark,
Enduring nights in a Tarheel winter, iced limbs
Crashing round his head till day, famished squirrels
Gnawing his toes?
                         Hermes surely. Should I call him
In? Roll out to meet him, ask for his papers,
Offer him cocoa, the evening news?
                                                    I jest. I know.
I've seen his staff. Notice there at the base
Of the tree—the peeled stick propped and bound with what
Seem vines or rope? They're two dark serpents, often
Live but rigid now, though I've watched them writhe.
He granted me that much the night he first arrived
As himself (or his familiar guise). When my eyes caught
Him standing, he gravely brandished the staff
Before him; serpents both faced me and writhed.
(The best texts claim they were given Hermes by Lord
Apollo who'd sanctified the snake to healing
Because of its gift of renovation—its trick
Of shedding last year's skin, even the surface
Cells of eyes. Snakes though were also sacred
To Pluto, god of death, for the pure efficiency
Of venom and grip.)
                         So. I'm finally resolved
To stand. Or sit, awaiting his patient will.
He's all but too fine to stay there posted behind
Thick glass; but calling him in would force his hand—
Entire healing (new life, erect) or condescension
(The broad initial step to entire dark and death).
  Not, after all, the first god—gorgeous as life
And death—I've left outside in night and rain,
Though he offered care.

YOUR BLOOD

You boast of your day's freedom, wisdom, mercy
And call the times before you wild and dark.
They crawled at least through torture, murder, dread;
Through grimace, error, frenzy to a god.
The first crime of your age was—kill the god,
Hack out an idol nothing like His face,
Pet him with names gruesome as no other's;
And fling the best you have, meat for his jaws.
You call it *our* way and will not stand calm,
Racing in drunken fury till—alike,
Cowards and vendors—not red blood of God
But idol's pus gutters through your veins.

after Stefan George

HELIX

This dense lactescence—pattern to repeat
The blank unprecedented fact of you
(Smallest gasping valve that drains a heart,
Southward arc of coarse hair down a brow,
Cheerful jack to pump the spiral plan)—
Is uncracked cipher, flung to waste on me?
   Pause at its drying glaze across my eyes,
Tongue still ruminating its command;
Consider thick potential tribes of children—
Astonished, feeble hands slack at blue thighs—
Hanging in belly-dark for one white word
To strengthen, stride, gesticulate in light:
Deeds of kindness, poems of fate and grace.
   Thrust again. Endow these endless heirs.

I AM TRANSMUTING

I am transmuting. Since you touch my heart,
It gilds inside me. Look, I turn to gold.
Stone I carve, plaster that I paint
Assumes new worth—warnings, praises, glories.
So since your face scored target on my eyes
And I still live, pocked by your barrage,
I move in armor, forged by incantation;
Halt for nothing, nothing harms me now.
I walk on water, walk unscorched through flame;
I kindle light in beggars blind from birth,
And my warm spit sucks poison from hot sores.

after Michelangelo

A TOMB FOR WILL PRICE

A serious visit demands at least three hours of your life,
Preferably starting on a summer evening and stretching till dark
When you're shown the secret. Any quicker tour will deny you the secret,
And no initiate is permitted to tell you. Applications are
Made in personal script, with two unaltered recent
Photographs, to me as guide. I choose and respond the day
Received with either the stiff white dated ticket—no fee
Is charged—or courteous refusal, no explanation.

You come alone a little past seven, clear high evening,
Crisp new moon declaring herself on the hip of the sky.
I meet you at the gate, offer you water from the ordinary fountain
With a worn foot-pedal, indicate the shed half-banked in holly
(Your only toilet). Then while I walk you on toward the mouth,
I recite the few facts you can use to start; the rest are comprehensible
Only inside, in the ultimate light—
"The rooms preserve and honor the builder's memory
Of his father's life in eastern and piedmont North Carolina.
The builder is I, his elder son (no surviving daughters)—
Sole *builder. I've had nor wanted no other help.*
The aim is to guide you back through the life, to a sense of its actual
Weight and refraction, the consequence of an actual quest
For radiant virtue by a traveling salesman of freezers and stoves.
It's all underground, dug out by hand—my hands, as I said—
And braced with beams. It may never be finished. We can enter now."

The first room's largest and entirely finished; it contains the museum—
Based on the old brand of roadside farrago he could never resist:
Some aging rattletrap's cases of bird eggs, blown and mislabeled;
Some veteran Rough Rider's curling postcards of Cuban canebrakes
And veiled señoritas, a lock of black hair bound with red twine,
And a withered arm still hung on the vet, a hook for a hand.
I display only relics of his life before me, my ill-timed birth
At his lowest ebb. Amazingly few were found to survive;
Our gypsy years had deleted his youth—only this pair
Of *pince nez* glasses I never saw him wear, copied from his idol,

Woodrow Wilson; an autographed letter from Wilson himself
Thanking my father (nineteen years old) for his manly support
Of the threatened League; the fossilized bones of a fried-chicken dinner
His mother cooked him to eat on the train toward National Guard
Camp in Morehead City; the pink invoice for a string
Of pearls he gave my mother at their engagement; the box
Of talcum in which he stored a single birthcontrol
Device in Depression years when penury ruled even boyish
Lust; a travel diary with his sales reports for 1929
(Penniless year); a letter from the pastor who dredged him howling
Through alcoholism; the draft of a poem to greet his first child,
Should she prove a daughter: "*Loved long before your eyes appeared,*
I love you more now you lie in my hand."
Second, an unfinished
Replica of the space he was born in—a dim attic dormer, barely
Headroom to stand. If I last, I'll hunt out the deep brown bed,
The stained mezzotint of "A Shepherd's Kiss," the actual air
He recalled till his death—gold light, dust motes, the salt scent
Of blood. His mother's hair, two chestnut strands coiled loose
On the pillow. His father's revolver—clean, loaded—on the mantel.
All exist somewhere; no matter is lost. I must simply hunt.
The atoms spin at our ears this instant, yearning to converge
In their old shapes—the forms they filled to cradle him.
Pause here to listen, a wiry cry at the threshold of sound.
I watch to see if you truly hear. You plainly do.
Now we are dark. Night falls at our feet. So I read the prelude
To mystery, my final disclosure. *Next room, the secret—*
Core of the tomb and demonstration of all he meant.
Expect no danger, no threat to your eyes. Only the fact
His quest discovered, opulent bloom on the utmost branch
Of the single limb he managed to grow in fifty-four years.
Move in silence one step behind me, hand on my shoulder.
I turn the key. Open your eyes.

The man before you
In the overstuffed chair is no real man but a risen body.
It passed through agonized life and death in the common way
And is now changed flesh, changed bone and hair. My dedication,
Your need to see, have earned it leave to come back here
And wait for you—proof of the soul, perpetual life;
Risen flesh in the form it will hold till all time ends.

Note the eyeglasses, apparent bifocals, thin gold frames—
The eyes behind them, clear steel-gray; the speckled hands
Mottled with age. Note the wide lips, parted to speak,
Moist with yearning to call your name. No words come;
He's lost your language, knows only the nine chief angel tongues
Unknown on earth. Even I'm unable to hear his message.
But look, he'll smile. He's resigned to smile, his one plain message.
It aims at you. Nod your acceptance. You may touch him once—
I suggest the right cheek, flushed with strength.
                                        Now he'll sleep upright;
The visits tire him; he requires long rest. In his sleep a music
Spins at the crown of his head. We won't stay to hear.

Finished. You're free. Find the long way home; hold the secret safe.
It may not be conveyed, as I warned—can't be. Urge friends and kin
To come on their own; it must be their choice, their need and courage.
I'll greet and serve them as I've served you, in simple joy.
Urge them to hurry; I've strained to my limit and may not last—
No guarantee of the sight if I fail. No heir to my work
If I cannot finish. No servant to tend this eternal father.
Will a soul at the white-heat need my tending, miss my presence?
I can only affirm he has never faced me, never smiled toward me
As toward all others.
                        Ignore my fears, they are my last secret;
A burden I never foresaw but must take (what burden's foreseen?).
Say only, I offer the sole exhibit on this earth now of the final
Hunger—a visible soul.
                        As you leave, climb slowly. The path's
Lit only by your new light. You may not return.

MIDNIGHT

At midnight, half-unwilling, I would walk—
A boy, lonely boy—past that churchyard,
Past Father's house, the pastor's; star on star,
Each separate, burned beautiful and clear
  At midnight.

Then when later in my distant life
I ran to meet my darling where she lay,
Stars and aurora struggled overhead—
I going, coming, breathing happiness—
  At midnight.

Until at last the full moon's radiance
Pierced my darkness cleanly, absolutely;
And my mind—willing, knowing—rushed to twine
With past and future waiting where they lay
  At midnight.

after Goethe

HOUSE SNAKE

All summer it seemed a fair exchange—
Black snake on the lot, better mouser
Than a cat (the previous winter I'd lost
Eighty pages of Marcus Aurelius and a Phaidon
Michelangelo to squads of mouse teeth).
He could prowl the crawl space
Round furnace and pump, have whatever
Life was separate from me—frogs,
Baby birds, chipmunks, scuttling mice,
The chance copperhead wandered up
From the pond. I'd receive the service
Of his plunder and pay only rarely
In frigid instants of seeing him—
Breakfasting, sapped by bliss, on the porch;
Turned by the chime of a silent signal
To find him embossed on the beechtree
Above me, string of hot tar
Ready to pour *(does he see me?)*
Or thrust down, rigid as a cane,
From the gutter, devouring raw wren-
Hatchlings in the house I'd suspended on wire
To miss his reach.
                                        I learned to take
That much—and with measured pride:
One of my early templates was Mowgli,
An agreeably imitable brunet boy
Whom large beasts loved or anyhow
Addressed in lucid warnings and thanks
For service; so his tolerance in admitting
My presence was a parched hard honor
I mentioned to no one, though aloud
I thanked him one late August morning
As he elevated his bullet head
And ten inches of neck from unmown
Grass at the utmost limit of the neutral
Zone where fear began—mine

And his, I'd thought; the line of our agreement,
Real on the ground as a chain of voltage.
I watched him, still as he; then smeared
A palm on intervening air,
Set down my coffee, and said "Thanks,
Nero"—naming him as Adam
Named the stock of Eden, spontaneously,
Straight homage to his essence: clandestine, pure
Black. I turned to eat again and by
The time I remembered him, he'd soundlessly dissolved.
That afternoon I needed a book
From the dining room (semi-basement,
Drowned in must). I was wearing shorts
And no form of shoes; the room was shuttered,
Slotted dark. I was down—six feet
Toward the dimmest core—before a voice,
Clear as airport advice, said
"You should have worn shoes this far
Underground." I stopped, midstride,
And solicited my feet. It took a long
Moment for eyes to gape the stagnant
Murk—two beige feet, flat
As buckwheat cakes (apparently mine)
And one crooked yard of black snake
Watching, a step to the right.
Nijinsky at his zenith never equaled
The leap I launched on the instant.
I swallowed a lobe of my heart, sorted
Options—fetch the shovel, chop him up
(And the rug) or pin his head, lift him;
And restore him to his beat, his larger half
Of the premises: nature. He made no feint
As I padded to the stairs, seized the stout-
Handled broom, and (ignoring my bare legs)
Descended to snare him—every nerve by now
Worming through my pores to cling aghast
To the upright hairs of neck, arms, calves.
He'd waited, so still that—a light switched on—
I wondered for the first time if he might
Be dead. He was not merely flat
From nose to tail but deflated,

Merging with the rug, seeping down.
I extended the blond broomstick,
Brushed his neck.
Ignition.
He flung two-thirds of his length up and back,
Parabolic stake in the new
Usurpation, and defied my intent.
Frozen at the marrow, I at once took
The dare and thrust the first stroke
For my demesne—floor, walls, roof;
Hope of unscathed nights, companioned
By my own taste in guests. *I'll take him;*
Expel him, alive and whole, to the zone
Conceded.
He fenced, live leather,
Through dazzling changes—hydra, basilisk,
Devouring rod.
I steadily assured
Myself he was harmless—baby-
Teeth and no venom sacs—as I
Parried his lunges, resplendent in power
And perfect in aim: strike after strike
He gummed the broomstick, sparing me
(I assumed I was spared).
After maybe two
Minutes of torrid duel, he betrayed
Exhaustion—a shudder at the pitch of his grandiose
Lash. In thirty more seconds,
I pressed him to the rug and, before I could climb
A new rung of fear, bent
And firmly clamped his neck in thumb
And forefinger. I paused for his answer,
More than half-expecting a last transformation
To steal him from me;
but he
Bore our juncture, my victory,
Pressing on me nothing worse than skin
With the dry packed vigor of slate.
He was straight as Aaron's magic staff,
Unmoving.
So in that clutch, poised

Between grip and strangulation, I rose;
He streamed down viscid from my fist;
I stepped toward the yard door—
One, two strides.
He threw
A lightning coil round my wrist;
Then as I halted, astonished, threw
Bracelets toward the hinge of my arm,
His whole present self consumed
In the work. Constriction began—uniform
Clasp of a bloodpressure sleeve
Pumped toward implosion.
I knew he could do
No serious harm; but stalled at the door,
I thought of one sure way
To shed him—chop my arm off.
We moved into tons of sunlight,
I at least glad to be back in his
Place. At the edge of trees, I raised
My captive-capturing hand and faced
His face—no face: machined
Consumers of sight, smell, prey.
The black tongue stroked at air
For my plan—death or release. I
Asked him his. No more answer from that
Ensemble of obsidian curves and plates
Than from my own species at similar bay.
But I knew a way out. Had he thrilled
That toward me through thickening light?—light
Was stacking round us, too humid
To speed.
With my left hand I took
The blunt tip-end of his tail
From my right armpit and, holding
The garlanded arm out—caduceus!—
From my body, I slowly untwined in broad
Safe loops. He barely resisted.
When I had him (straight as he'd ever been)
Before me, I extended him westward;
Then realized I'd generated one more
Vatic pose—hierophant

In some unmanageable rain-forest,
Placating night as it eats another
Day. I'd seen a last problem—
How to set him down. If I dropped him at my feet,
He could launch a final bite. With arms
Still out and up, his undulance between
Them, I threw him broadside.
He landed
In undergrowth three steps beyond,
Calm gelid S, monogram
Of something. He was not watching me
Or the walls of my house nor was he fleeing;
And only a hardened anthropomorphist
Could entertain the thought that he thought of me;
Remembered me even now, a moment
Apart.
I reminded him "Out *here*."
If the sounds ever reached him,
He didn't budge. I turned
And went in, lit the downstairs
Room to stadium brilliance, and searched
The floor—clean as a surgical scrub-brush,
No cast skin, no tail. I headed
For the sink and scoured my own hide;
And within half an hour was mostly
My self, altered only by the burr
Of one new fact—*He knows*
The way in, a secret
Way. The whole next morning
I roamed my perimeters, chinking holes,
Blocking grills; and for two weeks
After, I never saw him once—
Though the number of times I told the tale
Of our congregation might have lured the shyest
Monster back for a second go
At the battle bard.
Then an ordinary night
(Nearer four a.m., heat a steady
Hand at my mouth), I woke on my back,
Aware of company. Dazed, I shuffled
Candidates—visitors longed-for, two

Or three dreaded. I turned my head
Right and kissed the spare pillow, cool,
Unburdened. My arms swept slow half-
Circles at my sides, unrewarded.
I was three-fourths gone again before my left
Hand on its own recognizance slid
From the one sheet and scouted my chest,
Belly, thighs, groin—usual
Automatic meaningless tumescence,
Concomitant of dreams erotic as knitting.
Below the compact bulse of scrotum,
Fingers encountered another coiled
Mass that—stroked on the grain—was fishskin
Rough and remarkably cool in the ambient
Swelter. I suspected it was he; no fear
Arrived, fast or slow. I was somehow
Resigned or, truer, curious.
He apparently
Reciprocated. A minute to read the coded
Data of my sluggish blood; then he calmly
Rose through unresisting hands
(My right hand had joined him); through
Genitals, belly, breast to my neck.
My hands trailed his abandoned wake
Of body that seemed more an odor
Than palpable presence, rank not putrid—
Another staked claim to be
Here, safe. His tongue lapped
The stubble point of my chin, fed
There by whatever mineral scurf or exhalation
He'd hunted out. My hands felt
Wrenching swallows down his sides—
A nourishment urgent as the wolf-found
Boy's, drunk on death, and slow
As the parting of tectonic plates—
But he didn't grow. Some poised stasis
Was eventually achieved, entire annexation
In which I concurred. I assumed he rested,
Converting what he'd skimmed off me
Into the strength he needed most.
I frisked my body for depredation

And found no change—same moderately well-
Formed limbs, going slack (no fault
Of his). In hopes of guessing his purpose
Here, I searched his length again—firm
As old bread but warmer, stiller:
No rigor of anger, vengeance, or famine
(Benevolent incubus—succubus—both),
And no detectable tick of intent.
So I lay suspended in active patience—
Tired but not fearful so much as alert,
Passively watchful like any gripped creature
And fending off rags and flares of dream,
The traps onto sleep.
He spoke at last
Or managed to speak; had he tried from the start?
Had our transaction awarded him power
To say his piece? There was nothing a monitoring
Instrument could have caught; yet I heard it as voice—
The lean andante clarification
Native to youthful baritone humans
But flat inhuman, like nothing born
Of woman since the picnic grounds of the Olduvai
Gorge were discontinued. His head
Was somewhere below my left ear,
Not touching skin. His tail still
Looped at evident random in my now-
Cool groin where my right thumb
Flicked the free rim of scales;
So the voice may have transpired by bone
Osmosis—an uncanny sympathy
Of all-night companions, however
Bizarre. I affirm this true report:
"They watch you with interest
After so many years.
One of us has sampled
You at least each year
For the hours prescribed
Of sleep and day,
Employing the usual
Sounding procedures;
Instructed till now

To avoid detection.
I alone failed
But, since you spared me,
Am sent back
On sufferance
To meet your mercy
With payment rendered—
The essence we know,
Having known you entirely
(Your private titles,
Precise destination,
Balance to date).
I require permission,
However; you are free
To refuse receipt."
I at once
Refused—who would bear his sentence an instant
Early or from any mouth but the Certified
Horse's Himself, enraged, and attended
By seraphs congested with ire, not a renegade
Egg-thief's, terror of wrens? And of all
Things, I dozed then, drugged
On awe.
Dawn—rare work-bound
Cars on the road, my own mouth slimed—
I woke alone. Hands affirmed
His absence; eyes gauged the room.
Unaltered, spared—all but memory,
Me. I replayed the theophany in fine
Particular; and while I again weighed
The chance that what I'd endured was retrograde
Delusion (legacy of childhood days
Bogged in Poe), the certainty of earnest
Visitation outweighed. I'd balked at revelation.
Who else in the record of Israel and Christendom
Had flat said No to a visible, audible,
Graspable deputy of Central Wisdom
With news at his lips?—my secret name,
Point of my life, debit or gain.
First I bathed (no punitive scouring now);
Then searched the house—nothing—

Then chose a slow breakfast on the porch
As my sign of regret and proffered submission.
A ragged parade of other beasts passed—
Spiders drugged with expectance, strolling ants;
Sixty feet downhill, the spinster muskrat
Endlessly nesting in the pond's clay dam
For broods that methodically decline to appear,
An obese cock-robin of startling eloquence—
Till I'd also sunk in dumb blind patience.
There.
            Two yards northeast of my seat,
Conformed to white creek-rocks in the ditch,
He'd materialized (how long ago?)—
Right eye toward me. I wiped
One hand, slow, between us in air
Much cooler than the night. I said "Permission."
He moved—or managed to advance two lengths
From rocks to ground (I saw no motion,
Only registered change). On the brilliant moss
Of my acid soil, he was his precise
Self again—common yard-dragon,
Wholly unearthly. I sat, assuming he
Posed for me (his head was barely
Up, immobile; no sign of the tongue).
Then I saw beyond him a condensed brown
Toad, appalled in his glare. The three of us
Froze—a garden-group, mixed media:
"Permutations of the Hunt." Toad and I
Had mutely yielded to what seemed
A hunger ferocious as dwarf stars'—
The bungholes of space, cold ravening.
It would not take us.
                              Never turning to me
Again, he broke his stare at the toad; dropped
His head through minute fractions of space,
Joined the ground in all his length, and moved—
Hauling on through dead leaves, the spindly azalea,
With languid sidelong flings of the spine
Till I'd lost his wake.
                              The toad gave no sigh
Of gratitude, relief, only kept its place

With the ponderous contentment that implies complicity.
Had my refusal of the daunting message
Demoted the messenger to predator now?
Had I been his chance at ascent on any
Ladder he climbed? I rose to find him;
The toad flinched (a heartening proof
Of my weight). He'd left no discernible trail
Or trace—not even the customary belly-
Sweeps of a doomed ground-dweller.
On the chill face of evidence, I could
Say he vanished a handspan beyond
The desolate peachtree I'd planted years
Before that failed to thrive—it stood on
Gamely, limber as a buggy whip, one lateral
Branch with six tender leaves
And the thickening knuckles of premature age.
Even there, in real sun, I clearly thought
"Will I now be host to botanical marvels?"
And recalled the hapless bush flamed
For Moses, the fig cursed by Jesus,
The thorn in Lourdes creaking into diffident
Bloom for Bernadette through mountain frost.
Was I in for armloads of luscious peaches
Or a pocket-display of selective blight,
The innocent switch smoked to jerky by sunset?
And how would I read either wondrous pole?
Would fruit mean *Praise. Continue as now?*
Would blight be the tangible verdict for *Turn*
Or *Wrong. Too late. Prepare to pay?*
How would I answer? Who would I tell?
A baffled week later I drove to the garden
Shop and chose the makings of a small
Commemoration—three dozen
Of the homeliest plants known to science,
All succulents: stonecrop, echeveria,
Aloes, sempervivums. The troll-woman
Ringing my purchases said "You're not
Expecting flowers from these?"
I said "Flowers
Never meant much to me."

"Me
Either," she whispered, "but that's a trade-
Secret."
I promised silence and she warned me not
To eat them, "though they look good enough."
Home, I half-stripped; scooped
A bowl in the unnourished earth
By the peach, and set the green flesh
Of thirty-six low and blind-
Faced lives at the mercy of the site of his exit.

They've flourished, yes, but nothing prodigious—
Within two years under light care
From me, they'd filled their bed: huddled
And plump. Guests remark their oddness,
Their sturdy pluck in prospering on ground
Hospitable as sulfur. I offer no homily
On their local meaning, and no one's asked
For usable cuttings. The peachtree's holding
Its desperate own; I went once to move it
But stopped myself—if it means anything, it means
It *in place* (like ninety-eight percent of anything
Radiant). Since I live by a pond and its draining
Creek, I've met other snakes fairly often
In the time. Mostly harmless—red ratsnakes,
Kingsnakes, garters—they're asking only for sunning-
Space athwart my drive and the excess
Lesser reptilia to eat. Two weeks
Ago, I came on a large king
Resting at the chore of consuming a slightly
Thinner king—four inches of the vanquished
Neck were still free, apparently
Serene as a griddled saint—but the few
Black snakes are smaller than my visitant
And keep a skittish distance from the human
Zone. If his sons or avatars, they're plainly
Branded with the serpent curse, not spies
Or receptacles of my daily failure.
Me?—I poison my mice and harvest
Their frozen corpses from the crawl space before
They ripen. I work long days in near-

Solitude, am praised for my trick of making
The ecstasy of oneness look princely,
And sleep less each year—no dreams
I care to recall on rising.
                                        I'm simply
The one happy man I know,
Assured of witness and judgment entirely
Beyond my power to guess or change—
Absent proprietor of gardens unthinkable
For beauty or pain.

WATCHMAN. TOWER. MIDNIGHT.

Twelve begins her frozen lucid chime
And in it each night's question—Do I stay?
Am I required to man the striking time?

(Nineteen thousand shifts since thrust out free
From Mother's hot embalming rose blind dark,
Upright here alone and meant to see

The convex world pressed green beyond this glass,
The dazzling open faces bent my way
And balked by height, excluded, forced to pass

With only muffled calls, my signing hand
As earnest of a craving crater-stark:
A desert tower on the fruitful land.)

Silence. Midnight then. The instant gone.
Blood still floods these fingers, eyes still stare.
Agreed. And seated now, I hunt the dawn.

III

THE USE OF FIRE

(1990)

ONE

UNBEATEN PLAY

FOR ROSS QUAINTANCE
1957–1985

The night before you die, you wake at four—
Dredged by fear from sleep and forced to thread
A tunnel narrower than Mother's pelvis
(The straits you breeched to win your short good life).
   Arms and legs pinned helpless to your sides,
Your putty skull compressed by bony walls—
Red glow, furred bats, avid scorpions
Line the bore and prise your parching lips.
You warn yourself you've got long years for this
Nocturnal useless hateful self-corrosion,
Visions of a likely private future.
   Twenty fierce uninterrupted minutes
And then you halt. Same appalling goal
You reach each time you slide the airless mine—
The fate that pulverized your neck last week
Returning from a camping trip in Canada,
Crossing a murderous drunk in a hurtling truck:
You're quadriplegic now and twenty-seven.
   You lie balked in hushed officious dark,
No human face at hand but desert time
And tenor mumbles from the neighbor bed,
"Jesus Christ, I'm hurting bad as You."
   Guessing the pain of three hours' crucifixion—
Spiked through the flesh to crossed rough-hewn beams,
Mother and toothless female friends for witness
While cell by cell the rusty blood swags down
A flogged and foul disjointed naked body
In April sun toward winter-famished dirt—
You lay the guess beside your situation,
Know you understand Christ's final scream,
Corroborate the neighbor's grisly claim.
   So in your mind judicious howls bloom,
Each silent as the pulped nerves in your spine.
You let them swarm the ceiling, walls, stone floor.
Then, drained for now, you nap—a jittery mercy.

*

Here and nowhere else, my care might serve.
If I knew of your wreck, your whereabouts,
I could attempt to press a gentle dream—
Short but true shared ancient memory—
Against the thousand miles and touch your mind
Till intervening sleep might cool the hours
That throng from here till death pervades the room.
You're three years old, summer of 1960,
Coastal South Carolina, Pawleys Island.
You, your parents, Kathryn your one sister,
Andrew (a friend) and I have come to buy
A slow week here surrendered to the sun,
Broiled seafood, surf—its ceaseless light-and-dark
Combine of chores: washing, soothing, dissolution,
Death (the night we check in, one creased local codger
Tells of a neat tall German washed up here
In 1942 from a depth-charged sub
With, in his pocket, one soaked canceled ticket
From two nights earlier—a Charleston movie).
I swim with you, your guard, each sunstruck day
Knowing I couldn't save you from this friend,
This mother-warm embracing buoyant sea
Ready to be the sudden father-throat
Grinding you to death, its other chore.
I even warn you, young as you are now,
Not to trust me—guard yourself, guard me.
So that day on, you laugh and cluck your warning,
"Reynolds, watch your knees! *They're getting wet!"*
Or "Reynolds, help, my ears *are sinking fast!"*
And our minds loosen, mine at least, lean back
Through that whole blessed arc of restful days;
Smile at a sky unblemished far as Asia
And slowly learn to trust each other's claims
(That we're sufficient guards—me, you; you me)
When all we ever manage to become
Is loving, happy, lying in our teeth.

That's my memory anyhow, pressed toward you—
That and my own deck of images

Which might be added to the wishful dream:
   The night I watch your willing harassed father
Herd you toward bed, "Ross, it's time to pee."
You hold out, pounding through the hot apartment
Naked as any newt in spastic glee
Till he exasperates "If you don't hurry,
I'll flush myself down this john and drown."
You still refuse. He flushes, gurgles loudly.
You hurry to the toilet, search the bowl—
Your grinning father in plain sight beside us—
Then look to me and grimly nod "He did it!"

Even in babyhood you generated,
Instead of other babies' farce and yells,
A mainly steady field of dignity.
A strong boy basted brown, your golden hair
Towed by a sun that tormented my hide,
The legs that later thrust you through all sports
Already firming in the slumbrous thighs—
You handed us each day your demonstration:
   Children grand as you are oracles,
Speaking (before they speak) of their grand sender
And His specific will to bless our eyes—
Maker, molder, keeper, sun of all,
Lord of surf and hemlocks, drunks in trucks,
Lord Who this week clubbed you to the Earth
Efficiently as any tortured madman.

Had I known where you lay, had I succeeded
In my dumb hope to lighten your close dark
And press those childish laughing memories
Against your boiling present—any help?

Forgive the living their least helpful dream,
Our craving to rig smiles on failing lips
And win a merit for the clownish service—
Another soul winged off, wreathed in grins.
   You in your knowing smile can now afford
To free me from this hook and condescend
Majestic thanks toward my shamed regret.

*

I never saw you in the pitch of manhood,
Heard of your death from distant friends too late
To tell your family my useless sorrow,
So what's this speech but an earnest tardy try
At my own demonstration?—*You endure.*
   Here in these lines, my mind that generates them,
Your brief life burns, will burn through time
And past the eye of time's own frying end.
The vaster mind that sent these lines sent you,
Sent me to know you at the gleaming start
And cut your image deep in human words—
That mind has you forever safe in hand.

Confide me then one sight however quick
Of that new home and your perpetual work.
Return in this world's voice and let us glimpse
The harbor carved in bliss for you and us.
Your old shed pain is only ours now—
Watching your vacant figure in our rooms,
Concave statues of you in dim corners;
Betting on endless day, your new address

—*"In glory, gorgeous fair unbeaten play*
On emerald lawns (the game of stellar love)
Where I in spotless uniform fire teams
Of souls like mine, last seen in agony."

Thanks from now until our boundless meeting.

SOCRATES AND ALCIBIADES

"Such steady worship, sainted Socrates,
  For one young man? Surely you know better?
    Why these ardent gazes,
      Fit for gods?"

Who thinks deepest loves the liveliest,
  Who looks farthest ascertains the heights—
    Sages often bend
      At last to beauty.

after Hölderlin

THREE DEAD VOICES

1. DIRECTOR

Sudden Night was my last play—one cocky
Boy, one spunky girl spar for two hours;
Then force themselves to bend and bear each other's
Fate till death breaks every human vow.
I was hardly into my fourth decade; so *Death*
And *Vow* were words on stage, not earnest monsters
In my room.
                I'd spent ten years in eager service—
Charming the calmer upper senses of ticket-
Holders with my invisible puppeteer-hands,
Galvanizing actors' bodies in flattering
Light and, in off-moments, galvanizing
My own frail bones with every jolt of male
Voltage I could scrounge or beg (I never bought).
   The final list of names of every man
I knew went past three hundred—not to speak
Of the humpy mob of nameless faceless flat-
Forgot men hotter than light, one or more
Of whom passed me the death I then passed round
In murderous oblivion.
                                Vows? Two years before
I died, I found one sane magnanimous man.
We vowed—one life from there till night, the final
Dark so far ahead it loomed no bigger
Than a lone starved bat on the evening sky.
   No one did what I did better.
Few were smarter, saw the world clearer,
Laughed any kinder.
                              Stand here please—
No closer, *there*—and hope with me
I have not also blindly killed
The same unfailing man I vowed
To keep and guard.

2. PHOTOGRAPHER

I was the prince of thieves of faces in my
Short time, my wallowing city.

The gold and silver, nickel and lead poets,
Novelists, dramatists, dancers

Came for metamorphosis—I
Only, in my time

And country, wielded the precise arcana,
Spells and charms to lure

Scared souls from their black lairs to harmless day—
Outrageous blooms of the covert

Self: this grove of orchids I abandoned,
Grown from simple light.

By night I lurked stock-still, disguised as one
More satyr in the groaning wood

And lured down on me hordes of souls, likewise
Concealed in horns and hooves,

Who ended me. What blinded my two piercing
Eyes that meant to see?

3. TEACHER

My gray eyes frisked your Earth for three things only—
The lean bodies of smart young men, true poems,
Sunlight.
My body lived for bountiful meals
(Larded but zesty), reliable booze and the glide
Of my fingers on willing skin—those lean boys
Poised in the blocks of manhood: hungry to start
As I to touch, as godly as smart.
I dreamed
They watched in self-possessed thanks while my
Soft hands repaid their patient condescension
With skittish but, most nights, foolproof speed.
Three
Lay back; all but one of them watched in what I dreamed
Was mild forbearance, courtesy at least.
One
Of the watchers left my bed and blew his brains
Out five hours later. The other two ate my hearty
Cooking, drank my wine, graduated
And never looked back—not at me.

So I took
My hope to the fountainhead—Greek islands burnt
By a sun that gilds the occasional goatherd into one more
Snack for Phoebus, Zeus Himself, men wise
As Socrates: boys rare enough to carve and worship
Till stone, and the human race, dissolve.
Somewhere
Aging still above ground, my stack of dog-eared
Polaroids bears witness to what precisely I got
For the odd cigarette-lighter, cufflinks, dinner—these swart
Ephebes (goatherds turned sailor turned soldier, barely
Able to say the word *thanks,* if thanks had dawned
In heads as blank as their marble kin),
The dull percussion of honey-brown flanks on my
White ass and the sweet delusion of hearing the sear

Of their rank seed hurl into my waste. I never
Heard

        But ricocheted home in the nick of time
To pitch my slack white skin at the moil of a quick
Decade of risky dreamers, famished as me
And stripped to feed—more teachers, truckers, husbands,
Sailors, felons, horse-hung saints.
                                        In white
Tile baths, I huddled on my hands and knees
While upwards of a hundred starvelings
Sowed their tribes of nonexistent sons
And daughters up my bore; then sowed my death—
A wilder famine, baby-new and cruel
As any madman's prayer.
                                From here at last
I see a fact I overlooked. *In fifty-*
Five ravenous years on Earth, no one I dreamed
Or touched or housed in my hot vent—no god
Or poet, man or boy—exceeded me
In the unstanched offer of an ample soul, full
Of unspent love as your average dad with silent
Woe. Neither death nor the fuming pit itself
Has canceled such a boundless gift, still
Unclaimed.
            Can any man I dreamed or pleasured—
Any boy I led into the steady sun—Art's
Courtly games of calm attention, perfect
Service, journey's ease—will any dare
This thick dark now and thank my barren burning
Hand?

HALF OF LIFE

With yellow pears
And full of wild roses,
The land hangs to the lake—
Auspicious swans—
And drunk on kisses
You dip your head
In holy sobering water.

But where shall I take, when
It's winter, the flowers and where
The sunshine
And shadows of Earth?
The walls stand
Speechless and cold; in wind
Cocks clatter.

after Hölderlin

THE EEL

1. 25 JULY 1984

Mother, the name of this thing is the eel.
It is one foot long, thick as a pencil
And lives in the upper half of my spine—
Ambitious now to grow all ways.
Every atom of me it turns to it
Is me consumed.
                                        Yet it's been here always,
Original part—which is my first news
For you in years. It came in the first
Two cells of me, a gift therefore
From you or Father—my secret twin
Through those hard years that threatened desolation
But found rescue in dumb resort
To inner company, a final friend
Concealed at the core on which I'd press
Companionship, brief cries for help.

It helped. My purple baby convulsions
That got more notice than a four-car wreck,
Weak arms that balked a playground career
And kept me in for books and art,
Toilet mishaps, occasional blanks—
Tidy gifts to aim and guide me.
I steadily thanked it and on we came,
Paired for service fifty years.

Now it means to be me. And has made huge gains.
I'm numb as brass over one and a half legs,
All my upper back, groin, now my scalp;
Both arms are cringing weaker today,
And I walk like a stove-up hobo at dawn.
What broke the bond, the life-in-life
That saw us both through so much good?

*

Mother of us both, you left here
Nineteen years ago—your own brain
Drowning itself, eager blood—
And prayers to the dead are not my line;
But a question then: have you learned a way,
There where you watch, to help me kill
This first wombmate; strangle, fire out
Every trace of one more heirloom
Grinding jaws? Do you choose me to live?

Struggle to tell.

2. 26 JULY 1984

Mother, this man is now all eel.
Each morning he's hauled upright to a chair
And sits all day by a window near trees.
Pale leafshine honors the green of his skin,
The black-bead eyes. He wants no more;
His final triumph stokes him with permanent
Fuel for the years of wait, twitched
Only by drafts, damp rubs by his nurse
Or mild waves of gravity flushing the compact
Waste from his bore.
He does not know you
Nor the twin he ate. He could not name
The taste of joy, but he licks it slowly
In his bone hook-jaws. He thinks only "Me.
I became all me."

3. 26–30 JULY 1984

Mother, this man will stay a man.
He knows it three ways. First, he's watched
A credible vision—no dream rigged for comfort
But a visible act in a palpable place
Where Jesus washed and healed his wound,
The old eel sluiced out harmless in the lake.
   Then a woman he trusts like a high stone wall
Phoned to say "You will not die.
You'll live and work to a ripe old age"—
And quoted Psalm 91's reckless vow,
He will give his angels charge over you
To guard you in all your ways.
   Then he knows what a weight of goods rests in him,
The stocked warehouses of fifty-one years—
Waiting for export, barter, gift:
Lucid poems of fate and grace,
Novels like patient hands through the maze,
Honest memories of his own ruins and pleasures
(All human, though many blind and cruel).

Years more to teach the famished children
Rising each spring like throats of flowers,
Asking for proof that life is literally
Viable in time.
                    Long years more
To use what I think I finally glimpse—
The steady means of daily love
In daily life: the patience, trust,
Suspended fear, to choose one soul
And stand nearby and say "Be you.
Be near but *you*."
                    And thereby praise,
Thank, recompense the mind of God
That sent me, Mother, through straits of your
Own hectic womb and into life
To fight this hardest battle now—
A man upright and free to give,
In desperate need.

SIX CONSOLATIONS

1. AUGUST 1939

You drift on the creaky green porch swing and count
Dim water stains on the ceiling. They've dried themselves
Into maps of countries, shapes of organs—kidneys,
Hearts, Bolivia, lungs. The woman you
Trust best on Earth is snoozing not four feet
Away; you think her dream concerns your eyes,
Though you know she tried to kill herself two years
Ago—she has you now and means to stay
And said as much in ten plain words an hour
Ago. In another minute you'll think her name—
Not speak, think. Slow, the thought will lift
Her head. She'll turn your way and yawn and ask
"A brown-sugar sandwich or a cold fresh orange?—say which.
Quick, *say*." You mull the choice and think your entire
Drift, here out, will move this slow.

2. JULY 1946

Your mind has been continuous each step of the way,
Each day of more than four thousand days
Since you saw day. It keeps the sight of every
Gift you've won, each dread. Time was, it hauled
Dreads up by night to balk your rest. But here
Below, unbroken downward from that mind,
Your old child's body undergoes the greening
Upward flush of spring until one dusk
You understand your mind has built you one
Stupendous pleasure palace—stocked and humming,
Ready, free. You close your door and open
Both the windows on an evening lit
By fireflies burning their own substance, lone
As you. You shed your cotton summer clothes,
Lie full-length on the ample bed and wait.

3. JULY 1956

Midsummer late in Stockholm, hot, we hear
The birds complain—ingrates, barred from sleep
This near midnight by a radium glow: the sun
Half-tucked beneath that line of hemlocks, itching
To rise in four quick hours on town, lagoon,
The sea, the luckless herring, our rented room
Not half a mile from Garbo's grim birthplace.
We're not a minute past our own refusal
Of the world's raw gaze, our try at melding bodies
Fired by this uncanny light to pour.
I think *I'll take this moment, clear, to my grave*
And turn to give a penny for your thought;
But one more time you give it recklessly,
I doubt we'll spend this short a night again.
You sleep. I'll wait for day. Cool now, we wait.

4. SEPTEMBER 1961

You've had a long lunch at the Lamb and Flag with your old
Teacher and laughed full-tilt through everything
From British naval slang and trench warfare
(He fought in France, whiffed mustard gas) to the eerie
Chords of late Shakespeare—lost daughters found,
Cold wounds annealed. You've both skirted the week's
Bad news—Khrushchev's H-bombs stacked to your right
In split Berlin; Kennedy's glistening lockjawed
Moxie, cocked to lunge. You're still theoretically
Draftable, if America lasts to crank a draft.
Christ Church Meadow, your slow route home in glare
And shade, has never looked calmer, splodged with late flowers
And a tall girl singing in Gaelic to the sky.
You think *Any instant, this vaporizes.* Your teacher
Says "It's far too fine to vanish—say so."

5. OCTOBER 1976

We've weathered that *tsunami* of a day I still
Recall as my main day—the riverrun, a late
Long juncture—and here, next afternoon, we climb
The perpendicular laurel shag of the nearest
Peak, hospitable Hokum with her promised look
(In such pure air) right round the globe to at least
Japan: Kyoto, the flammable Gold Pavilion,
Black sand scored for meditation and a single
Fading bass gong tone. There—intact,
Though bushed and dazed—we only see the curved
Pacific, placid as silver every way
And not one other soul in view, even
On the beach a quarter-mile down. I say "I wish
We two survived alone in a planet painlessly
Cleared." You take your time and say "We do."

6. NOVEMBER 1989

Brown leaves gag the plucky creek. A last
Flamboyant lotus hangs, neck wrung by frost
This dawn—first kill. Fall, your next-least welcome
Stretch, stalking horse for curt black weeks,
The mind's black dog. But sun, this sudden ladder
Thrown across my legs and outward, one
Hot fling to the pond. Then crows, three gangsters strut
Through the ailing beech they've seized. And quick, I know
The only news of this dry day, the ending
Year—I'm needless. Bare. In which case, earnest
Bows to the day, in lieu of thanks to the unmoved
Mover that rolled me here, end-time, and left
Me needing food, light, water (*substances,*
Not symbols for the tawn of skin, understanding,
Purity). Needless, trapped and dying glad.

INITIATION

Whoever you are, walk from your room,
Which you now know, into evening.
Your house is the last before space,
   Whoever you are.
Raise tired eyes from your worn threshold
And slowly set a single black tree
Against the sky—slender, alone.
   You have made the world.
Huge, it ripens in silence like a word.
Then when your will has comprehended essence,
Shut your eyes. Gratefully abandon it.

after Rilke

MORTAL SEVEN

1. PRIDE AND SLOTH: 1985

Man of sorrows, grief's companion—
I am the man that suffers and am here,
No instant free of agony sufficient
To crystallize black coal to quartz.

Step closer now. I welcome touch.
This youthful skin—apparent standard
Human gear—muffles a steady
Feral moan, pain's harmony.

See, no fear. I welcome a chance
To spread my wound again, for you—
The single show of pure forbearance:
A man assailed to death but *here*

By his brute force, his will to serve.
Thrust in this slit. A pounding heart.

2. ENVY AND COVETOUSNESS: 1952

All you had that I wanted was you,
Not to taste your body but be it.
Wanted? There were maybe twenty nights
When I hid in shrubs beneath your window,
Hearing you laugh with your freshman roommate—
Baritone joy that made me not only
Dream (lurid color) of being you but
Crave it, waking, with a metal roar.

Did you ever guess? Did I fly one clue?
That summer we spent three nights together
Watching two dozen undoubted mammals
Prance for the crown of State Beauty Queen.
Who there saw how, dark at your left side,
I burned—corroded—to be mild you?

3. ANGER: 1985

None, a thoroughly puzzling lack.
Doctors, friends, commend it to me—
Excavate this smothered rage;
Bawl at the ludicrous rubber legs.

I've dug a long year—no glistening seam
Of anthracite to stoke the wail.

No diamond either, no joy in the dig.
Amazement maybe. A bystander's transfixed
Gaze at the debris, pride in a skill
I'd never suspected—models of the U.S.
Capitol dome in dry toothpicks,
No drop of glue: freak labor
In the yellow grin of death. But anger?
None. I'm entertained.

4. LUST AND GREED: 1962

We stroke through dry woods to this hid clearing,
Silently stand—eyes locked on eyes—
And strip to the last discardable layer,
Two hides laced with potable blood.

I break at the knees—a hinged boy-puppet—
And grazing your shins, begin to eat
You in hot red gobbets. You
Beg the service, yield with moans

Of responsive joy till—an hour of peeping
Birds overhead, the reservoir chuckling
Unseen beyond us—I pause and lean
To see you gone, consumed, *in me.*

Now I must stand, find the house, your wife;
Explain our lateness, disgorge your parts.

WINTER

Emblems of fall—vanishing, then vanished:
Fallen, rotten, locked in crystal cold.
The field is blank; the tree that once stood bold
Is torn by wind, though calmed at night by rain.

As I am calmed who rest now at the close,
Hearing the year's last question to the sky,
Hearing no answer to the rising Why?
Trusting an answer when spring's coming shows.

after Hölderlin

TWO SONGS FOR JAMES TAYLOR

1. HYMN

Source of all we hope or dread—
Sheepdog, jackal, rattler, swan—
We hunt your face and long to trust
That your hid mouth will say again
"Let there be light," a new clear day.

But when we thirst in this dry night,
We drink from hot wells poisoned with
The blood of children. And when we strain
To hear a steady homing beam,
Our ears are balked by stifled moans
And howls of desolation from
The throats of sisters, brothers, wild men
Clawing at the gates for bread.

Even our own feeble hands
Ache to seize the crown you wear
And work our private havoc through
The known and unknown lands of space.

Absolute in flame beyond us—
Seed and source of dark and day—
Maker whom we beg to be
Our mother, father, comrade, mate
Till our few atoms blow to dust
Or form again in wiser lives
Or find your face and hear our names
In your calm voice, the end of dark
If dark may end.

Wellspring, goal
Of dark and day—be here, be now.

2. DAWN (JOHN 21)

After he died that dreadful way,
His friends gave up, went home to stay—
Wives and children, boats and fish,
Any way on Earth to drown the wish
To see his burning face again
And hear his voice flame through a night
That has them drifting now, half-lost
On a lake they fished the whole slow time
Till he walked by three years ago
And hauled them up to light and life,
Then bled in public view and died
That dreadful way—strip-naked,
Pierced: head, hands, feet, side.

Dead—darkest hour of any night,
When daylight stalls below the brink.
Seven friends in a bantam boat
Taste each other's hopeless hope.

Then light, serene, a fragile glow
Beyond them on the narrow strand—
A man upright in clothes so white
They race the sun to crow the day.

The man looks their way, cups both hands
And begs for food—"Boys, what to eat?"
When one shouts "Nothing, not one fish,"
He points to starboard—"Cast again."

They cast and haul the biggest catch
Of their whole lives; and then they search
The shadowed face of their new guide,
But one—the youngest boy, named John—
Sees the feet beyond them on
The narrow strand: naked, pierced,
Rusty, cold. John dares to cry
His hopeless hope—"Lord, Lord, Lord,
It's him again!"
Sick with glee.

Old crazy Peter hits the lake
And swims for land.
The others sail
A final hundred yards and beach
The teeming net, then edge ahead
To where the man waits, Peter gasping
At his feet.
They do not dare
To call his name. They do not touch
His rusty hands. But all their hearts
Are hot as if they'd feasted on
Warm new-baked bread and sweet young fish.

Then they smell his own big catch,
Broiling on a well-laid fire.
He's been here, waiting out the night—
For them, for them, they dare to hope.

With that whole teeming net behind them—
Food for all their kids and wives—
They hunker down in cool spring dawn,
No single word in all their mouths,
And wait again round this same man
Who claimed to love them from the start
And now has cut a way back here
With ruined hands through agony—
And three days dead—to prove his word
And feed them fish and bread again:
New bread from Heaven, fish from God.

DREAM ELEPHANTS

Huger than dreadnoughts, battleship gray,
Wise as the tallest evergreen
And mild as all my gentle kin—
Though incontestable overlords
Of me and the low-slung world I watched—
They roamed my life from the year I was three
When Father took us to a two-ring circus;
And one old female lugged herself
With solemn patience and the will to please
Through a tired set of stunts: for me
As fresh as love on sight.
                                        Before
She shuffled back to peanuts, straw
And ludicrous leg-irons, in a silent chime
I knew I'd met a needless soul
For that last room in my mind, crammed
With hungry parents, nameless fears.
   After the show we found her feeding,
And my hand stroked her crusty hide.
Her long-lashed right eye drank me in;
I watched her store me and knew I'd stay—
Instant inexplicable obsession.

With plentiful orphan dogs in town,
Rabbits, tidy snakes and goldfish,
Why choose the least convenient mammal,
Insatiable as forest fires and chancy
To tame?
              Gone as I was,
From that glad night, I drew and painted them,
Shelved their statues in herds by the bed
And gathered reams of textbook facts
(Their trunks can find a lost straight-pin
On a moonless night or uproot oaks;
Their minds are endless vaults for what
They see or feel, endure or love).

Their place in me was the calmest place,
The room to visit in wordless sorrow
Or the private joy of lonely days,
Tramping the local fields and pines
In mute refuge from the other two
I loved as much—the bottomless hearts
Of Father, Mother, watchful as spies.

Free at six to leave the house
On my own rounds, I haunted movies—
Elephant Boy, The Jungle Book.
At nine or ten I began nightly prayers,
Steady and stubborn as howls for food,
That someway I come to at dawn
Faced with all I'd ever need—
Free in the backyard, one grown elephant
Waiting for me.
                    By then I partly
Knew what for—for me to worship,
My choice of a single godly outcrop
On the swarming world, a worthy magnet
For my awe and praise and, best,
A heart to comprehend the burning
Daily news I'd bring in a secret
Language we two shared: blank code
To others, a soothing cure for her
And me as we grew into one enormous
Mind that bridged our former solitudes
And drugged our pain.
                    I was broiled in puberty
Before I quit the epic dreams
Of me and an august elephant steed—
My guide to every useful craft
And risky dare, the bravery
To wade through fools and traitors till
Heavy with deeds, we died together,
Which would be far off.
                    Long years after—
Past shoals of human guides and losers,
Shielded by nothing harder than hope—
A glimpse of elephants came like grace:

No question they are our tall masters,
Bound to graze their tan savannas
Ages past our dying out.

Now, and me hacked off
At the waist, they roam me night by night again.
In dreams as pure as our first love,
They find my bed—slow single-file,
Changed worse than me—and call me in our
Old dark tongue to turn their doom:
Stampeded, killed, chain-sawed and left
To rot beside their panicked young.
In every dream my same right hand
Goes out to meet that dense familiar
Skin, now fragile as my palm;
And my grown voice warms to sing
The healing bass harmonic arc
They taught me when my mind was smooth.
But night by night before I end
The vital phrase, my ruined partner
Groans, staggers, pitches down
And, soundless at my frozen feet,
Shrinks to a dusty handsized carcass—
A pygmy toy for that tame herd
Of statues lined above my bed,
Trunk coiled in final agony
That even I, their truest living
Human kin, can meet with nothing
Stronger than a speechless vow:
Loved a lifetime, thanked each day,
Die in this cold certain solace—
Starving vengeance stalks my race
That, crazed, obliterated you—
In blood and dung for common greed—
Who willed us nothing worse than peace.

NOON REST, BEST DAY

Eagles common as cones in the trees,
Water hectic and plaited beneath us—
Water in Leonardo's notes:
Single medium of making, ruin.

Sovereign sunlight ladled on legs
Ample then to bear you all
A long fall night toward our accomplished
Joint in midair, shedding joy.

Sun on eight unknown companions
(Sapped as we on adjacent rocks)
Of our dawn mail-run up the wild Rogue
Nine years ago—you asleep at my hand,

Cocooned in trust; I weighing the day
On this dry tongue, a full life's best.

TWO

DAYS AND NIGHTS 2

A JOURNAL

In *The Laws of Ice* I published the first year's work from a journal of poems, 13 February 1984 to 14 February 1985. From the start, my purpose was to save a few of the arresting encounters, memories and thoughts that otherwise vanish through the mind's wide slats. I set myself three main conditions—each poem must be as true as possible to its stimulus (no lies and even the dreams are faithful transcriptions), each must be as taut and lucid as I could make it, and none could be significantly changed past the day or two of its arrival. I was not conscious that in June, midway through the first year, I'd be ambushed by a physical devastation, though in retrospect it's clear that the poems knew it.

They kept a grim pace with the early months; then the impulse broke and most of 1985 went unrecorded. The present stretch started on 14 October 1985 and ran till 13 February 1990, six years past the first impulse. The early poems here inevitably fix on that private internal combat. If a reader perseveres through the self-absorption, rescue comes, then a gradual outward look again at the world and other creatures, many of whom recur from Part One.

As before, the lines are determined by stress, most often the old English count of four accents to the line, with an indefinite number of unaccented syllables. And again many poems volunteered as sonnets. Apparently no other common shape fosters the range of voices I need—from easy conversation to a trim elevation, no space for dead noise.

DAYS AND NIGHTS

1. PRAISE

This stands for praise—
A book of days
Of frozen terror,
Scalded nights,
The horn of healing,
Tethered flights
To follow that
Tall muffled light:
Whatever name
It wills to bear.

2. AGAIN

Praise?—this mountain bursting my back,
Blundering out toward day and light
Through me, the space I've fought to hold—
Clear of pain, secure for rest:
One evening glide toward tranquil night?

Pain. Labor. The birth-throes of death—
Mine, for me. Selected by what
Or whom? Sent why?

The source and socket
Of end and start.

What else? *Praise.*

3. REX

Fourteen days at a dismal junction,
Forty-two meals at the All-You-Can-Eat
Buffet and Grill (obese Gold Agers
Burdened with platters of strangled catfish),
No liquor, no unblotched skin to touch—

Yet I leave, reluctant. Your actual face,
Frank miracle, your pillared throat—
Ample abutment to bear a mind
That in dark eyes burns steady,
Grave, extending gifts: constant you.

4. THE DREAM OF SALT

I'm waiting for Jesus in a room built of salt,
I have an appointment; he's bound to appear.
But I stand now, studying the white walls round me—
Twenty feet high from a circular floor
And sheered in perfect hard-lined planes.
No one waits with me; I'm forced to stand
(No bench in sight). I'm calm, convinced
My wait will yield uncounted good.
I think one thought continually—
"Don't weep. One tear would melt this room."
Happiness floods me and I pour great tears.

5. NOCTURNE FOR A WEDDING, 26 OCTOBER 1985

Let there be night,
Your night at last—
Sworn man and wife.

Let silence be
Your single sheet—
The rest be flesh.

Let joy commence—
Grave rush between you—
Now for good,

Hallowed two—
Watched, loved by me.

6. THE DREAM OF FALLING

No jeweled hummingbird, no angel
Equals (much less passes) me.
I hang midair in a dim cathedral,
Poring slowly down faces of windows
Lit by setting sun outside—
Enormous roses, apostles, crowns;
A thousand tints of violet, green;
Then the face of God.
                    I prowl its hair,
Planes of a forehead prairie-wide;
Then dip past the cataract nose and lip.

The mouth springs open, an endless hole
That swallows me—the grandest bird.
I plunge down a throat more gorgeous than glass,
A luge-run paved in Byzantine mosaic,
Billion translucent gilded tiles—
All joy till I comprehend the goal,
Terminus waiting at Time's own end:
The heart of God, God's belly and vent.
Whelmed, doomed, I pray to stop.

No answer. *On.*

7. BEN LONG'S DRAWING OF ME

This face, serene as an anchorite's,
Is apparently mine—all friends name it.
Have I won nirvana unbeknownst?

At the least I've transmigrated you—
Broadcast these intrinsic lines
Behind your eyes, through the mind, down arms

To five blunt fingers that print me here:
The Long translation of my long text.

8. 31 DECEMBER 1985 (TO R.L.C.)

Even a sane man staggers to points where
The smallest grain may suddenly blast out
Promise or threat—the wrong birdcall,
The rate of sunlight prowling a face,
The day's first word. Today, butt-end
Of an endless year, you tumble me
From chair to car in chill sunlight
And then yell "Whoa!" I crouch in the plush,
Expecting blood—cut forehead, cut foot
(The practical hemophilia of the numb).

You've found, at your own safe feet in leaves,
My grandmother's wide gold wedding-band,
Century-old companion of her life
From marriage at sixteen to death at forty-eight
(Eight children, a flagging fame for laughter)—
Lost from my left hand days ago,
Despaired of till now. I seize it, cold,
And warm it fast on a stout right finger
Blasted by luck—a year redeemed,
Her fame renewed, her gift of time.

9. THICKET

Gone a week, your memory
Hardens in odd dim corners
Till a small assembly of statues
Halts where you once moved—
Thicket of perfect likenesses
Made merely from empty air,
Your force (eyes, mainly eyes),
And these two molding hands:
Brute longing, wild regret.

10. SAMUEL BARBER (1910–1981)

Sam, meaner than a lovelorn yellowjacket,
Twice as toxic—fanning me on
That first summer of my drunk first success
To climb a body given you in trust;
A barely human soul built of light
And foul him, claw him, burn him to his knees—

You're safe years dead and I'm bound safe
In this bolt-upright cripple's chair
To hear you out these twenty minutes.
First Symphony, one breathless reach,
You young as the me I let you spoil—
An angel's sunset amble through pines
Toward pure blind union, God's bald face,
Your just deserts.

11. STEPHEN SPENDER

Stephen, assailed at your new height,
Wreathed in hair like Everest's banner
Or the Jungfrau's struck by ice at dawn—
Remember this in this new storm:

Fifty-three years of kin, friends, loves
Have swept through, under, and past me—gone.
You've stayed, unblinking as my two eyes
And thanked in words more constant than we.

12. VALENTINE. HERON.

Mid-February, pond laced at the rim;
You chime one more year frozen shut,
Locked behind us—
                    lilac heron
Old as the pines that shade your shallows,
My famished grateful counting eyes.

13. NEAR A MILESTONE (FIFTY-THIRD BIRTHDAY)

Time is clearly no concern of the Great Watchmaker—
Keats, Mozart, Schubert, Anne Frank, James Dean;

My father strangled at a hale fifty-four,
Still working the ground at his feet (sweet laughter);

Me jackhammering my slow path, micron by micron
Toward my own dread: his early ghastly howling end.

14. PAID

Ten nights ago in a hospital bed
More like a pine box than most human constructs,
I lay in unblinking glare of pain
At four a.m. and asked if agony—
A late surprise—was worth donating
Toward our retirement of Christ's
Big loan, that hungry debt?

15. GOOD FRIDAY

Or gift. Is pain an outright gift?
Is he so far gone (three-quarter million days)
That pain sufficient to polish steel
Is his one memory of human form?—
Three hours of a stormy spring afternoon,
Spiked up in a reeking suburban landfill
To drain in sight of his toothless mother,
Her younger friends: clear in his mind
Still and wished back on us, last possible link?

16. EASTER SUNDAY 1986 (TO E.R.)

Permitted to write on this one Sunday
Of all the year, I roll these two
Uncertain hands (cold, twitching)
Into flat frank sun, face east and draw
The day's best sight—concave planes,
Hid valleys, hot wells (two walnut eyes):
Your resting face, consuming light.

17. BACK

A whole quarter's silence—
Flesh-colored tunnel with sanguine walls,
No time to speak of pain or fear,
No extra breath (and no real
Fear: fear is the luxury
Two years behind me,
A bourgeois comfort like overstuffed chairs
Or flannel sheets and pain
More nearly a bore today
Than the acid agony that blanked all March).
So *life*, an apparent road ahead
With what seem trees and sky for walls
And natural light. So work. So this.

18. AT SEA (TO E.R.P.)

Mother, this sea—narrow wedge
Of south Atlantic (gray sand, gray breakers)
And you born inland (red hills, black pines)—
Was your best element all your days.
Your face, ready smiler, beamed outrageous
At the whiff of brine twenty miles up the road.
But here—in shorts, heels on the rail
Of the southward porch, nothing between you
And white Antarctica but brine, brine—
You burned a grin fit to toast all penguins
Otherwise frozen in their crisp opera suits.

19. SKY, DARK (TO E.R.P.)

This sun, that raised your entire skin
To the winey pitch of Cordovan hides,
Would flatten me with papules, welts
(Skin loathsome as any scapegoat's driven
Dead Seaward with pustular welts and boils).

Now you wait out your twenty-second year
In tepid velvet grave-deep dark—
Your leather lips still curled in a rictus—
And I still huddle up here, surviving
In the safe cool shade of memory and eaves.

20. TWO CAVES, A HOUSE, A GARDEN, A TOMB (MEMORIES OF ISRAEL AND THE WEST BANK WITH J.C.A., 1980)

1. *Nazareth, Mary's house*

This mid-sized hill town, then a crossroads hamlet,
Has two sites of interest to show—a spring
From which all ancient residents drank and a cave
Covered by a vast bizarre modern church.
For a Westerner, caves are strange but proper here—
Emblem of woman: dim convex force.

This one's Mary's house and has been so honored
Since at least the second century—small, low, shallow
With a marble altar saying *Here the Word Was Made Flesh,*
That hilarious unthinkable moment when virgin God
Merely boarded a spotless likely-teenaged girl
And spoke some sound, known only to her (she'd already
Agreed), and thereby flooded her darkest space
With scalding light—her eventual death, our torturing shine.

2. *Bethlehem, birthplace*

The birth cave of Jesus, plated in Byzantine glory
By Constantine, stands in the cliff-edge of this old village—
Birthplace of David a thousand years back. So no one
Can prove that the silver star—*Here Jesus Christ*
Was Born of the Virgin Mary—doesn't hang in air
Above David's birthplace or circumcision site
Or the very spot where Samuel stood, anointing
David (Jesse's baby boy) as Yahweh's choice,
Israel's next king and heart's delight:
For he was ruddy and had beautiful eyes.
So
David bowed to Samuel's oil and drove Saul wild
To be surpassed by a shepherd boy born here,
Let's say, maybe ten feet down from a subsequent crib
Which by then was the stable of a packed-out inn.

3. *Capernaum, Peter's house*

At our feet fairly certainly, Simon Peter's house—
A basalt ground-plan smaller than a burnt-out trailer,
Three cramped rooms in which Peter the Rock
(Dumb and lunging and a lot less faithful than a wet
Retriever), Peter's wife, her mother, maybe their children
Offered their mud-and-wattle roof to a man
From the next county west through the Horns of Hattin,
Deep notch clove in the lilac hills,
Because the man extended plain hope: "a fisher
For men!" when lately Peter and Andrew his brother
Had netted far more water than perch, the Peter's
Perch we ate that night, so fine, at our inn
Ten miles south—Tiberias, where Salome danced.

Here dozens of sick were met head on and entirely healed.

4. *Gethsemane, garden*

This urgent land
Is one huge rock—

Exultant rock,
Cold black terror:

David dancing nude by the Ark,
Christ sweating blood to dodge his fate,

All on this one rough-hewn slab
Extruded here, altar of one more sheltering church

Where Jesus, abandoned in dark, face down
Begged to live a human life

Not gashed, stove, pierced
And drained blue-white

But sustained upright with hope and voice.
Midday tomorrow he'll die—bald agony.

5. *Jerusalem, Jesus' sepulcher*

This warm cube, size of a diva's steamer trunk,
Has triggered Crusader and Saracen bloodbaths
The equal of several dozen Vietnamese tunnel-hives and canebrakes,
Though now is mopped dry and buffed by hungry hands
To a mirror gleam—my own slim face stares back
From the shelf that bore dead Jesus Friday dusk
To Sunday dawn:
                        my face and neck in plea
For hope, life, long years of time when
Here I also bring my own big riddle—
Death, life, naked incalculable wait between.
   Hid in the three-foot cord of my spine
Is a foot-long tumor (*astrocytoma,* dark
Slick eel there with me from birth).
                                        One spasm
Now in this hot cube might kill me on the floor.

6. *Mount of Olives, rock of the ascension*

There's a small rock (size of a year-old baby)
And in it, the deep print of what's undeniably
A man-shaped foot—the down-thrust of Jesus
As he jetted skyward, a man-carved joke
Or shameless fraud or natural accident?
Too late to know. This plain dome at least
Has shielded the print from its destination—
Maybe endless sky—since sometime before 392.

We're here alone. The Arab child,
Whose key let us in, is back outside
Playing hopscotch with raucous friends.

You say "Look. This could be my last appearance,"
Then shuck your shoe and set your huge
Right foot in the print.
And stay with me.

21. A HERON, A DEER—A SINGLE DAY

A dull tin noon and, struck down on us
From the crest of pines, a heron—the one
That's brought me each winter solstice
For twenty-six years now whatever code
I've earned for the past year, need for the next:
Vast as a stork in a child's old reader
And fierce in the head as a demon deputed
To pluck out human eyes in vengeance,
Bolt them down hot.
                                        Yet our two faces
Broaden—eased, assured once more
Of witness at least: our names and precise
Address still known to Guidance Central.

Midnight mist and roaring cold,
We roll toward home from Christmas-eve dinner;
And there in the glen, frozen at the verge,
A six-point buck, young in eye
And grace of joint but flat-eternal
In steady witness. We slow to spare him—
Or think to spare a soulless thing.

He spares us. Sustaining our glare
A long instant of still composure,
His eyes consume whatever we show.
Then in a solemn choice to leave,
He melts a huge body, graceful as girls,
Through two strands of vicious barbed-wire.

We pass unscathed, drive in silence
A last slow mile, then both laugh sudden
At the sight of home. *Seen,* well-seen
But spared to pass.

22. FIRST GREEN

All ancient hopes are not, by nature, lies.
The dream of green does not preclude new leaves.

The fact that here in drystick winter
We long for spring, new life on limbs,
Does not mean spring will not transpire.

That intricate all-but-smoke of green
On the smallest trees at the riverbank
(Their upmost hands) is only the billionth
Promise paid—resurrection,

Frank hint of endless rounds in steady light.

23. 15 MARCH 1987 (TO W.S.P.)

Today I've lived my father's life—
Fifty-four years, forty-two days.

Father—there beyond that wall—
I beg to pass you, beg your plea

For excess life: more earthly luck
Or a longer sentence in the old appalling

Gorgeous jail in which you craved
My vivid mother, made my bones.

24. 16 MARCH 1987 (TO W.S.P.)

Given. Today I exceed your life
By an extra day of gray warm rain;

And there just now through glass on the air,
My heron soars in to work the pond—

"Symbol of longevity" here this year
Long past his usual winter stay

Despite two snows and his mythic age:
Tall slate-blue spirit, never leave.

25. SPRING TAKES THE HOMEPLACE

A long wet winter since I saw the house
Pounded hard by August sun—
Choked in stands of waist-high grass,
The lumber scrap of renovation—
And even now, all I have is pictures:
A cousin's color-snaps last fall.
The grass is scythed, the scrap hauled off,
The view from the window where I saw light
That bleak first day is clear again—
Straight sight to the road I took to leave
More or less for good, barring childhood visits
To Ida, not the place (Aunt Ida, saint
Of my saint-strewn life).
It's stood through
Three snows, hard sleet, the quick reversal
Of a ten-year drought—empty still,
No tenant yet. At least I've heard
No word of fire; so it must stand
Or crouch (*crouch* or *lie*?)—snoozing snake
Laid on the long lot, digesting its century
Of food: our lives (Rodwells, Drakes,
Prices, Rowans, Huffmans, Swifts).

None of us there to meet the spring,
Throw the doors wide on green-gold light
And acknowledge the silent service of walls,
A good tin-roof, and heart-pine floors
Through hateful cold.
So from this distance—
Eighty miles—I grant its virtue,
Grant our thanks (living and dead).
And these eyes roam the yard in memory,
Hunting a bloom to deck the door.

Ida's roses were long since blighted
To thorny sticks, razed and burned;
The rows of annuals long since a wilderness;
Only the tall old fig survives—
Backed against Buck Thompson's shed

(Where he stored the coffins he sold, a sideline
With sweet potatoes and brightleaf tobacco).

Life creeps up dry spongy pith
Of limbs that still bear pounds of figs
For cardinals now or cocky jays,
The sticky milk of ancient sap—
Loyal, punctual, undeterred.
No leaves yet, no fruit till August.

But from here, in mind, I break a stick;
Wait for the sweet milk; smear my hand
With its proof of lasting, in a long straight line
(Opalescent, warm in the cool day);
Bear that to the front door, press the hand
To a brass knob turned by all my kin
Through a hundred years. The door breaks open
At last.
          Spring light! Now rush on past me.
Flood the rooms.

26. THE RESIDENT HERON

Twenty-eight years this pond was visited
Briefly near the winter solstice by a Great Blue
Heron tall as a boy and famished
As sand, a single bird distinguished by a growth
On the back-folding joint of one of its legs.

A month early this year, my eye caught a flurry
In the yard well beyond me, the lilac rush
Of something fairly enormous landing. When the image
Resolved itself, there stood the heron—
A heron, these legs were healthy and taller than before.

He stood in the gravel drive sideways to me
Long enough to let me learn his presence and frame
The questions he plainly set—is he mine
(My old bird healed and bigger now as he nears
His thirties) or am I his? If the latter,

What next? Then in the slowest motion, he triggered
The awful process of levitating
Up and off—the twenty yards to the pond's
Deep end where, each day since, he's gorged
His flat blank face in my presence:

Apparently a resident, even this noon since—there,
In a hard sleet-storm—he stands, braving
Whatever short or lengthy trial fate has
In mind for the local livestock: me

And the few million more live forms he watches daily
As king, angel, ultimate judge or famished bird.

27. LIGHTS OUT (TO E.R.)

A whole day of sleet and just at dusk
The power fails. We're left to face
A frigid night with only the warmth
Of a squat woodstove for thirteen rooms

And I with a fever and all the hours
Of no way to read, watch a movie or type
(Sob for Fate's inveterate fool);
So I watch the jagged blade of an oil lamp

And try to mime the altitudinous
Thought of a monk winging a mind
Blank as ultimate Buddha at simply a wall.
An eon turns, I pass the first stars,

They vanish behind me. And home at dawn,
Even my name is unseen smoke.

28. THE RACK

Weeks of threshing the family photos,
Gleaning faces to feed a memoir—
I start each day expecting sadness:
The thousand captive grinning eyes,
Long since blind in red-clay graves.
   I find no fear on any mouth
But frank displays of a taste for time
As unassuaged as an alley drunk's
For dollar wine.
                    To have watched each one,
From my own start, and now to set
Their secret down for a world to watch
And own and judge—*More life. Bring it on*:
A gift as big as any yet
From whatever unseen hand endows me
And stakes me too on the desert rack
That will parch me soon as dry as they—
A random ghost, all face, no voice
But maybe these lines.

29. JIM, WITH AIDS

Thirty years past, we were all but boys—
Full of ourselves as Christmas dinners
And ready to feed the world our bounty
Yet bound by a single ceaseless craving,
Beauty in all his licensed forms
And one illicit:
                                        Phosphorus flares
On the black horizon—music (a siren
Train of voices, vowing bliss),
The signal shine and pulse of verse
That also pledged safe harbor, rest
And the endless unpredictable faces,
Proffered and near, that we both worshiped
But only I reached toward and touched
And saw smile back.
                                                    Now struck still,
I only watch—no reach, no touch—
While you, desolate as Lot's salt
Wife, are eaten in agonizing crumbs
By a fate more famished even
Than we.

30. TOM, DYING OF AIDS

In seven years you took my picture
A thousand times—in New York mainly
Ringed by gawkers, muggers, geeks—
And you as high as any bystander:
Lobbing me jokes like booby-trapped balls,
Tying your limbs in sheepshank knots
To break my pose and make me yield
Or asking me questions God will blush
To ask at Judgment. I'd laugh and answer;
You'd click and brush my hair aside
Or turn to a geek, "Ain't this boy
Fine?"
        I always came out
Looking like me. Others complained
(Nobody likes the you you like), but
You agreed—*It's you. I just* found *you.*
   Today I hear you're nearly lost,
Under a hundred pounds, eyes out,
Hid from all you saw and served.
   But Tom, I find you—see you still
In parks, up alleys, wrenching your face,
Your wiry limbs, into clowns and monkeys:
Finding *me.*

31. FISHERS

Mid-September noon—warm on the porch,
Reading the rowdy life of Saint Paul
(Our oldest lover, hottest scourge),
A killer hurricane grinding north
Eight hundred miles south and I as calm
As the pond beyond me, poised for a visit
From Monet at least: that posed and lilied.
   And there a sudden heron lights,
Slow motion in the near-edge shallows
Thirty yards off.
                              Can he be the blue
Transformed crudescence that lit in the drive
Last winter, giant? No hint, no sound.
I freeze all the same to grant him ease.
   Blue, yes—the lilac brown of rabbit fur;
But something here at this end repels him.
He lifts again—a jokey wonder
Of struts and flaps that would ground a flea
Yet buoys him from me, slow as he came
And at least as fine.
   Is it me or some other lack he scorns?
If I knew, would I care? Could I move some way
To lure him back; could the world adjust
Its gilded, pocked and horrent hide
To earn his grandeur, grant him welcome?
   Skip it. Eat this limpid air,
An early merciful autumn food.
   First time in years, I barely ask
If my blue fisher trolls for me.
Today he seems a skittish bird—
Not more, none less, a freak of the light—
Creaky, cranky, good to see.
   I wing a brisk thanks to the hole he's left
In the pond's dumb patience and return to Paul.
   Paul, fierce dwarf! His brutal hand,

Relentless eye, fish the whole flat
Mare nostrum boiling with us,
Our scaly souls his tasty prey.
He'll stand and gaff us, love us briefly,
Then hand us up to thc hungry sky.

32. YOM KIPPUR 1983–1988 (TO D.S.V.)

Sundown a full five years ago,
We threaded streets in east Jerusalem,
Fumbling a way to the Wailing Wall
By hunch, no map.
                                        Then sudden blood
Thick at our feet, the dim alley
Paved with blood fresh enough
To gum our shoes and rank with the iron
Stench of a massacre, minutes old.
    You found a sign, *Street of the Butchers*—
Flayed, gutted lambs in reach of our hands
(Three hundred maybe, blue as bruises)
And not one visible human in the stalls.
    All killed by me, I suddenly knew
And jogged ahead to claim my crime.

33. JIM DEAD OF AIDS AN HOUR AGO, 25 SEPTEMBER 1988

Full moon on Earth, calm autumn night,
And word of your death in the telephone voice
Of a decent man you taught years back
Who saw you through.
                                        Full moon, you cold
In warm Key West. Old slave of the sea
(You'd walk through fields of broken glass
For a smell of surf, its battering light),
The blind avenger that cored you out
And swamped your mind dies now with you,
Drowned in the final towering surge.
   Full moon, flood tide, drew you at last
To your best height. Death and victory—
The killer killed.
                              Sail far, kind
Ancient luckless boy.

34. TWO (TO D.L.)

Twenty-nine years of the Great Blue guest,
A clutch of poems to mark his descents,
Even his recent phoenix-change—
Entirely renewed, though lone as ever
Near a me companioned, me fitted with help
From my own kind: a steady soul,
Intent beside me, mind on me.
  And now cold noon, writing at the window,
The pond mud-yellow from last week's snow,
I catch the usual skirmish of blue.
Two Great Blues rise from the near deep end,
Foiling the laws of aerodynamics
One more time and clutching at air—
A second pair on the place, fed and flying.

35. EASTER SUNDAY 1989

Drollest day of the calendar year—
A battered corpse alive again,
Upright walking, to the consternation
Of a covey of former fair-weather friends,
Who gave a new meaning to "left in the lurch"
Last Thursday night. Yet here he's back
And with nail holes to prove it in the midst of a cold
Fish supper they've somehow managed to cook,
For all their gob-stopping shame and grief.
  Me, it's coming on evening here.
I've had a hot lamb lunch with cheesecake
Somber as strontium, and rolled outdoors
To the pondside deck, ready as ever
For my annual call from the Galvanized Stiff
Who made this universe at least,
If not zillions more, yet brings me too
The flabbergasting uproarious news—
You may, at will, companion me
Till Hell frosts over and countable time
Is swapped for endless alternations
Of light with restful dusk and angel
Serenades in earnest of utter safety,
Sure tranquil dawn.
                                        A slow
Warm hour of earthly twilight, the pond
Now still as a marble slab—the fish
All sink to early sleep; small birds
Jitter as ever near night, afraid
This dark will be the one stamped deep
In their hot brains, the dark that lasts:
No dawn, no food.
                                    And I wait too,
Calm to the passing eye but edgy,
No visit still.
                              Then a streaking shadow
Blots my hands; I look straight up—
A hawk, fervent as any bullet,
Flings skyward through the failing day;
Takes the final western glare

And melts in my sight, melts for me.
  I let that be my manifestation
For one more year—my sign, proof,
Grounds for hope.
                What blistered child
Abandoned sleeping by his monster father
In desert scrub has more, has less?

36. TOM DEAD

More than a year of utter silence—
Stashed in a sister's merciful room,
You the mute black hole in its midst—
And now this word of a death that ate you,
Cell by cell to the livid bone;
Then sucked at the marrow till the mind, aghast,
Parched and shrank and shook in the skull:
Grit in a rattle, your final music,
Who for generous years in sight and hearing
Made a visible line of silent praise
From nothing but my own dying face
And the thousand other faces you played,
The thousand smiles you forced to light,
All dying with us but slower than you.

37. DOWN AND BACK

First hot spring day, humid as Delhi
And a muttering thunderhead on hand,
My two legs jitter like galvanized frogs—
Banging the baseboard, rocking the lamp.

I kill the phone, wheel to the sunporch
And play the eighteen-minute tape
Of my hypnotist's disembodied spiel—
Me in the clouds, then gyring down,

Then into the warm lake, through its murk
To the door in its deepest silt, then *down*
Till his sovereign voice commands my mind
To end its pointless self-torment

And oar back up to cooler light
With legs becalmed as bathtub boats
And the musky scuppernong globe in my mouth
Of sane return, a sober man.

38. THANKS

This fabulous loneliness dense as diamond, now my home.
This frozen thrilling air my lungs have learned to breathe.
These hands, serene as water birds, that know no need
To reach or take or love or kill.
                                        All burn a silent
Praise of thanks to what or who has worked such peace.

39. SCANNED

The annual scan of my spinal cord
Took a long four hours a week ago,
And now my surgeon breaks a silence
That had started growing teeth and claws.

"Clean, *clear*! I'm more than glad;
You've outlived your old prognosis again.
Course, I'm convinced there's tumor there;
Convinced we'll have to deal with it yet—"

Laughing, I stop him and prompt the truth,
"You were sure I was dead five years
Ago." Now to keep him foiled
And glad—not, to be sure, entirely

My job.

40. THE NET

Five years since and I sit here winnowing
The hill of mail I got those burnt months
In '84. Then I could hardly
Force my eyes to see the lines
They flung toward me—hot protestations,
Hopes, vows—much less catch them.
   Now though, safe through one more gauntlet,
I haul them down at last, brace and read
Each—safe as stories. One stranger writes
"I've got a whole convent of nuns praying for you
And they get *results*."
                                        So, plainly, they did
And all the zealous rescue squad
That, flinging lines in near-pitch dark,
Managed unknown to weave this buoyant
Iron net I ride today.

41. *NEW MUSIC* IN CLEVELAND

Nothing but words tapped out in a room
While the merciless eel ascended, blind
But upward bound—my racing brain.

Five years on, the words and I
Are live at the edge of a poisoned Great Lake
That still, from this high window, at noon

Roils and foams with an ancient fury
It will not yield. Nor I nor those
Mere words that burn on strangers' tongues.

42. J.H.

Big-eyed and trusty as a Labrador—
Six years ago, I'd have stoked each cell
Of my dynamo to incandescence
And fined my aim at the one hid atom
In your broad mind that needed me
And would warm in my pure heat and pour
Your central private essence—food
For which, those years ago, I'd gladly
Have given my hoard of goods:
Nostrums, gewgaws, rattles, flutes,
Sextants, talismans, torches, runes
And a deathless pledge.
                                        Seated now
I shine this honest useless smile
That you shine back, respondent moon.

43. MOB QUAD, OCTOBER 1955

Thirty-four years ago this week,
You rapped on a medieval door,
Heard my "Come in" and took four steps
That entered my life.
                                        No handshake, names
But within half a minute, I saw your secret—
Chill to the eye as the city round us,
You burned the constant self-fed light
I'd waited all my life to see;
And since I guessed I was your Balboa,
I rightly guessed you'd welcome and warm me.
   This far beyond, I watch you still
That autumn dusk; and in that light,
Still I bathe these empty hands.

44. AT HEAVEN'S GATE, MAY 1956

Tomorrow you pass your twenty-first birthday.
We'll drive with two carloads of friends
To Longleat House in the country near Bath
And sit on a hill called, understandably,
Heaven's Gate in frail sunlight
That nonetheless gilds each visible cell
Of your plentiful hair and makes you, not just
The birthday boy but the present goal
Of more eyes than mine—three horsefaced
English girls with double-cream skin,
A strapping stereotypical spinster
And six agreeably coltish Rhodes Scholars
Who frisk the sight and fact of you,
Coolly helpless as if they watched,
Say, Leonardo sketching curls
Of twining water in a turbid weir
While all gnaw chicken and drink cold cider,
Mindless that not one soul among us
Will ever know a finer day,

Though you and I built a finer night
Hours before, twining together—
Hot in a freezing room and bare
As gods exchanging ichor slowly
With rich side-dishes, celestial garnish
(No words, all thanks)—telling ourselves
In silent code that this thick dark,
This sage negotiated joy,
Would stay walled deep in our two minds;

And so it has, thirty-three years
(The span of Christ) till, here, I write
This plain recall, sharing at last
The secret huge exploit we dared
As you stood, frank, in the gate of manhood,
Meeting my gift with a full return
That's in me still: undiminished,
Food for life.

45. BOAR'S HILL, SPRING 1958

Trailed behind us the past two months,
That buried line of dark oases—
Bleak rented rooms in which we joined
To dowse for nurture and never failed:
Tresco, Compton, Oxford, Edinburgh,
St. Andrews, Cambridge—indoor wells
That quickly bred astounding foliage,
Shade and rest.
                        But here at last,
A sunbaked Sunday, we lie in foot-deep
Grass in a clearing not more than a hundred
Yards uphill from the stately homes
Of culture princes—Gilbert Murray,
Bridges, Masefield, Arthur Evans
(Who found, then half-invented, Knossos).
We mean to read till dusk at least,
Then dine at the Tudor Cottage in Iffley
With maybe a dusky after-hour
In your dim room, ivy-hid.
   But the clean sun pounds its own intent;
And sworn as we are to work apart,
The merciless weight of curing light
Engorges both our starving skins
Till soon, obeying helplessly
And plain to see, we meet full-length—
Calm face to face—and through the screens
Of cotton, wool, we conjugate
In flagrant disregard of nearing
Human voices, laughing high.
   My first and only implication
In an act as common as outdoor mammals
And aimed at no iron lasting construct—
Life together, deathless love
(We've laughed them both well out of sight).
Yet here it burns, these cold years late,

To light a numbing autumn day—
The quarter-hour we burned through clothes
And our rash vows of levity:
Young and ready, grinning broadly,
Blind as blood but undismayed.

46. A HERON, A DEER—AGAIN

The two together in one more day—
Morning, a young and trusting doe
Materialized by the drive out front,
Unspooked by cars or us at the window
And gone as strange and quick as she came;
Toward dusk, the sudden slate-blue flash
Of a heron, broadside, climbing air:
All knees and elbows, immensely strong
And streaming awe, though awkward as any
Clambering kid.
                                        Thirty-one years
Beside this pond, they and their
Progenitors have, at the least,
Registered me—a dazed smiler
Straining to read their bold recurrence,
The magnanimity with which they print
Their emblematic shapes on a world
That, year by year, compounds the warp
Of the trap it weaves to end them both
And all their kind.
                                        Refuge, rescue,
Where to hide them, where's sweet water,
Fish, clean grass, deep woods and lakes
That rest unshook in natural bounds?
   Nowhere but this silent cube
Behind my eyes where, day by year,
I store the weight of the heavy grace
Of, at the least, these slots on tranquil
Blinding light—a bird, an elegant
Quadruped, glimpses of their normal
Daily hunt for food or usable
Upright phantoms of God, thrust
My way on land to which I hold
A deed these few quick years.

47. SPIRIT FLESH, 1960

Horn Branch, its homely pond, accept the snow.
Weeds and scrub hunker their winter crouch
This last gray week before the darkest day.

Same branch, same pond and these weeds' hardy forebears—
Three decades back we lay in summer dusk
And counted fish: their skittish leaps for bugs,

Their agate eyes. Still nothing we saw was half
As fine as we—our coal-black hair, our eyes,
Your seamless skin, pure and taut as a bolt

Of creamy silk. Just at dark a snapping
Turtle surfaced, big as a tub;
You named this *Turtle Spirit Pond.*

He's down there still, realer by the year.
We're here, still hot to yoke on this white page.

48. ANTIPODES, 1969 AND ON

Late summer, then fall, then six more years,
You took this skin (that had been no use
To another human for a long dry spell)
And paved it, plated it—scalp to heel—
With your frank need and the will to serve
Till I could pass myself again
In random mirrors and not recoil;
Till—night on night—I drank the view
Of your gray eyes consuming me,
Healed by the salt of our joined laughter.

49. FREE FUEL, BYRD STREET, 1948

Five days shy of the solstice, ice
Binds the pond, glazes my ramp
To a slalom chute; so back I skid
On forty-one summers to you and me.
Hot dark, twin beds, a sweephand clock,
A penlight to read it and our two scorching
Separate forks—panting for touch,
Though touched by nothing but our sealed selves—
Are pounding down the course we've set,
Come first, fling farthest, till each arrives.
   Who won, remember? I know the time—
Forty-four seconds: we were both that green,
Both under sixteen and chocked with seed
As any silo west of Wichita.
   No word of you since the early sixties—
Your first divorce, bourbon-soaked.
Still here we stretch indoors again
And stoke the coldest day all fall.

50. FIRST LOVE, HAYES BARTON, 1948

Your room was a short two blocks from mine,
Though straight uphill and the close equivalent
Of two light years. I'd never knocked,
Never said so much as a word to you;
And still I'd lurk on my cot by night,
Weaving a burning Nessus shirt—
The ways to make you, first, my friend
And then the naked mate to my skin:
   (Leave your window open late).
I'd offer my hefty savings account
(Take this, shut both your eyes, lie still,
Take me—*this tidal surge of worship*
I ache to pour down your tan length.)
   Lave's the word for what I needed—
To lave you day and night with the honor
You'd more than won by your strong head,
Two eyes the shade of a desert zenith
High noon, midsummer, and a grin like dawn
On scalding night.
                                        Never—no hint
Of my dammed flood, though we laughed through sophomore
Latin class and senior P.E.
   Still—forty-one years—your Christmas card
Kindles the face you earned and gave:
Imperturbable tall Hermes,
The Guide of Souls.

51. ELEGY, BYRD STREET

Three days—two poems—ago, I wrote us down,
Pounding our racing bodies side by side
In August night and both triumphant. Three days

And here's the final word on you—your name,
A date—in our old school's newsletter: dead.
No explanation, fifty-two years old.

Of all my earnest mates then, first to go,
First to know how near our robust skin
Thrust toward the absolute ecstatic goal.

52. 1 JANUARY 1990

Clear New Year's day, a fresh decade,
Washed light and the sky a lidless ceiling;
But last night I woke at four

And, helpless, underwent the passing
Of a bitter grainy cloud, black loss—
The half-turned heads of all my *gone*:

The dead, offended, lunatic, fled
In anger, fear, self-entrapment,
Cold repulsion, paralyzed sloth.

A slow hour I worked to turn
One face my way, both eyes to mine.
Not one agreed; all took a last step

And vaporized. Up, this sterling day
Alone, I court the hurtling fickle sun—
Pale whore but free this noon and speechless.

53. SAFEKEEPING, 1963 AND ON

You again, back by night in an entertaining
Instructive dream—both of us
Young as in fact we were and locked
In one more run of our main event:
Using you, stretching your compact
Trunk and limbs, your dropdead face
And a soul as huge and helpless as Newark
On the Junglegyms of dare and danger
That always certified you fit
For every soul-depleting trial.
   In this case here last night, you hunted
Chest-deep in the sumps of Hart Swamp—
Scenting, sighting cottonmouth moccasins
And gentler than both our mothers' hands,
Thrusting a deadly head my way;
Then returning the unharmed dragon
To its chosen tree as if its safety
Were crucial to the wheel of time
As yours was not.
                              Near three decades
Of liquor, wives, stunned kids, grinning
Leeches, your frank though glazed and bottomless
Thirst for poison—all I have's
Your phone voice maybe once a year
(Entirely itself, prodigal cello)
And here the face I find in dreams:
Prime of faces all my life,
Undeterred in radiance—mere fact
Still safe in my sole mind,
Your last refuge.

54. GIANT

Only this humming radiant boundary—
The band of light that hovers at his body
And seems another product of his sleep—
Defines the length of a frame that dwarfs the Urals.
Only a steady sigh of breathing moves;
Its cool mist feeds the riot of deep moss
That coats the floor and unseen walls of a cave
Where, unrecorded time ago, he chose
This ledge to start his urgent sleep and dream.
   Or are the cave, ledge, moss, the mist, the light
And that titanic body likewise dreams
Borne on a web of disembodied mind
That dreams and constantly creates our world
At least—the spinning furnace core of the farthest
Quasar, blackest hole, the lethal bow
Of hungry keen Orion, tender limbs
Of the Pleiades, you and me to the root
And every jigging universal atom?
   Or is our own giant folded in the sleep of some
Archaic dreamer (larger, smaller, past
Our power to think); and he in turn?—

The tale
I told myself at six years old when Hitler
Killed the children in his reach and reached for more,
While in a country suburb, lone as Lindbergh,
I trawled the woods and piney air for rescue—
Building a safer world at every glance:
The hectic trust that life described some logic,
Moved at the will of one tall smiling face.
   I couldn't know I'd innocently found
A thought almost as ancient as my sleeper,
Conceived and reconceived by priests and children,
And always balking at a final blank—
What happens to his world when the giant wakes?

In my case, fifty-seven years of me
Have felt unbroken—seamless, good or bad,
Except the hours I lost to anesthesia

(Blackest of holes, no fear, no hope, no help)
And those rare nights when sleep herself becomes
A wordless thoughtless merciful black box.
   So I assume he dreams on undisturbed;
And since the boy who found him dreams in me—
The nest of Chinese boxes, each in each,
Where every model of my former selves
Dreams still—I move on now in wary courtesy
(Soft tread, no cries) in slim ferocious hope
No dreamer wakes.

55. MAYA

Found this note of Einstein's, late
In his life on an old friend's death—
This death
Signifies nothing. For us believing
Physicists, the distinction between past, present
And future is an illusion, even if a stubborn
One.

In adolescence I wrote him
More than once—would he sign a portrait
Drawing I sent?
No answer then;
Now this old-man outright claim,
More useful.

56. 13 FEBRUARY 1984–1990

This clean new wing of the house looks east;
So eyes, that match their wide selves
In photographs from '84,
Scan the pocket-pond I've scanned
These thirty-two years of human noon.
   Frequent sights of former me
Materialize by willows, coves—
Plain as the days I shucked them off,
Dry as snakeskins, faithful molds
Declining to fade—tall boy, lovesick
And proud of his wounds; eventual man,
Part-healed, still hunting.
                                        Is any actual
Atom left that spun in place,
Even six years past as I cranked these lines?—
Hardly in my salvaged frame, though
Maybe hid in the cores of rocks;
Thickest plate on the shell of the dozing
Turtle, my senior. Maybe far
Inside the heart of these numerous eager
Boys, my ghosts—assuming they lead
A hardy life beyond this mind
That sees them now, amazed in thanks,
While they wolf down their plentiful lot:
Young and way too dumb for fear.

THREE

JUNCTURE

In Book VIII of *Paradise Lost,* Adam and Eve entertain the Archangel Raphael in Paradise. At the end of a pleasant luncheon during which the angel tells too many secrets of Heaven and the Universe, Adam tells the angel of his own erotic infatuation with Eve. When Raphael warns of the dangers of abdicating reason, Adam turns table and asks Raphael if the angels enjoy sexual relations like those that delight him so dangerously? Raphael blushes and responds.

Whatever pure thou in the body enjoy'st
(And pure thou wert created) we enjoy
In eminence, and obstacle find none
Of membrane, joint, or limb, exclusive bars:
Easier than Air with Air, if Spirits embrace,
Total they mix, Union of Pure with Pure
Desiring; nor restrain'd conveyance need
As Flesh to mix with Flesh, or Soul with Soul.

Pure we were that late summer week
Ten years ago in the Land of Rain
So blessedly dry that, strong as we,
Light succeeded in finding our lives
Hid in the least of a ring of huts
That made a Mom and Mom motel—
Two husky owners (Mim and Dit),
Big laughers both with dutchboy bobs,
Yapper dogs, a first-rate kitchen,
Fake pond size of a wading pool
In which tired travelers fished their dinner,
Famished trout longing for the pan
(You dropped your hook; they struck like sharks)
And just the shaggy butt of Mount Hokum
Between our sleep and the ocean endlessly
Gloating beyond.
                Though we hadn't confessed it,
What we were after was finding the walls,
Nets, bars, traps, hooks
In both our minds that foiled the mute
Clandestine will, total mixture.

*

The second day you'd planned a trip
Up the Mad River in a mail-tourist launch—
Dawn as our flat hull spanked up the delta,
Struggling past unthinkable hemlocks,
Eagles thick as gnats on the boughs
And bald as Mount Shasta, pioneer wives
In aprons and grins avid for news.
　Lunch on a clutch of languid rocks;
You half-bare an arm's reach past me
On a private slab, amply rewarding
The sun with partial views of a form
Well-made as anything animate between
The southernmost cell of your pelt and the first
Live sequoia, all rings intact
With sabertooth clawmarks hid in the heart
(My thought, not yours who hardly knew
The point of a mirror). How did I nap?
You napped, I mimed exhaustion and followed.
　Cool afternoon, the rush downstream.

Safe back, drugged with calm, I flung
My slack bones prone on the broad bed
To sleep an hour of late gold air
Until you woke me with a rocking hand
On the nameless plane where vertebrae stop—
Your blue eyes the streaming core of the room,
All the rooms we'd warmed in six years:
Cornflower brands that signed a way,
Lights that hailed me on you from the start.
　I swam up ready at the silent call—
Silent because you'd never yet
Conceded the force that worked your eyes,
Hands and body: rank as roots
That shatter tombs through generations—
And found your determined face, astounded.
　You granted at last a hunger deep
As the parched moon's pull on the nutrient tide;
And you worked on slow but *worked* in time,
Disclosing me to the failing day,

Cherishing me with the grave obeisance
Of newborn creatures to their generous kin;
Then bearing down on me at angelic angles
More intricate, more deeply cut
On the air's dry plane than any meeting
In Euclid's dream of perfect juncture—
Mitred joints so true no chink
Of sun could pry.
                                At the tall apex,
Open-eyed, I prowled the reaches
Of your whole mind—each muffled plan,
The throttled shames, pockets of joy
And dauntless trust—till in one broad
Eventual glide, I was all you,
You me, we single.
                                An actual minute
In manmade glare so loud the walls
Refused to hold it, tossed it back
To baste our single glorious hide;
And then before the bond could part,
I rose on you and repaid the gift
With ample interest, a fortune earned—
Unshielded passage to all my life:
Each craven, brave or baffled atom
Offered frank for your inspection
In unconditional surrender
That you accepted with a speechless smile.

Forty minutes, give or take,
We strode that dense seraphic air—
No self, one mind.
                                Then slept and woke
In early evening, light enough
To guess your face and you guess mine—
Familiar grounds, separate as twins.
   I think we called our daily names;
I know we proudly thanked ourselves.
No other mention, then or since,
Of a grace to match man's acquisition
Of the use of fire or the principle
That trees make wood and wood feeds flame

Or Adam's retrospect of Eden
From the stony ground he'd dig for bread.

Ten years gone, four more meetings,
Earnest tries with wiser minds
And grand results in grander rooms
But not again—never, none,
With no one else, not that cellular
Transmigration when willing you
And willing I made of our selves
One sizable brief kind holocaust
To be, in one dim rented room,
A speechless broad tall compound creature:
Fragrant, fertile, unforeseen
And soon extinct—its only future,
The white museum of these black lines,
Whatever selves we bear from here
Through later fates in tranquil hands.

No complaint—endless praise,
Thanks the length of this conscious life:
An afternoon's pure desiring;
Entire union, unrestrained.

YOUR EYES

Eyes, kind eyes, young master there in sunlight—
If you would let me kiss them steadily,
Three hundred thousand kisses steadily
Would still not satisfy,
Not if the waiting harvest of your lips
Stood thick as bursting sheaves of summer grain.

after Catullus

LOST HOMES

1. *An Iron Bed in Granville County. A girl aged twelve.*

The night before, he slept in our room—
Mine and my next-oldest sister's room.
Sister was eighteen, aching for twenty
And deep in love. Her beau, about
As thrilling as dust, had phoned up sick
In the midst of supper; so she cried herself
Unconscious by dark. Once Sister slept,
You could entertain a one-ring circus
At the foot of her bed; and all she'd say
In the morning was "I sure did dream
About music all night."
                                        Me though, ever
Since Mam died four years ago—
I took a little string of feverish naps
With a lot of lying there wide awake
In the hot or cold dark, forcing my mind
Not to haul out the mean old pictures
I'd already stored too many of:
                                                    Mam
Trying to bid farewell to five
Children and a broke-up husband
And still crack jokes as her life seeps through
The hot bedclothes and down and gone. Then
The heart attack Dad underwent last year,
His left hand always colder than his right
When he holds your face and searches your eyes.
He'll always say "Girl, who do you love?"
Then he cups your face and tilts it towards him
To hunt your eyes, whatever you say.
Whoever I mention, he understands
It's always him. Even as late
As this last afternoon, he asks again.
   Thank Jesus, I come out and say "Oh you!"

His eyes fill up and, before I can
Say something dumb and untrue like "April
Fool!", he somehow vanishes from the room—
Just leaves, no memory of his back in the door
Or any sound.
                    I'm young enough still
To know the world is more than half magic;
So I stand and think "He's changing *now,"*
Though I don't think how or into what.

So night—deep night, past three o'clock—
I was bolt awake in the cat-fur dark,
Staving off that grade of awful picture
By naming the principal rivers of Asia,
In order by length with tributaries,
When mine and Sister's door spoke once.
It had these hinges older than Hell; so
If you opened it fast, it said
"Goddamn your soul!" Slow as now,
It just said "*Gawwd*" like old country
Preachers addressing His Honor.
                                        Nobody
In our town ever locked doors; the only
Crime was suicide. I thought
It was Aunt Dot that came after Mam died
And all but killed us, on a daily basis,
With excess solicitude—you couldn't belch
Without Dot vowing you had TB
And sewing your shroud. She was also prone
To stark nightmares and joined me once
Or twice a month, having undergone
Some plunge through space or—swear to God—
Being wed in public to a strapping buck,
"Black as boiled tar," that all the family
Kept assuring her was white.
                                        So I rolled to the wall
And played hard possum, halfway snoring
While Dot slid in beside me and froze.
Then for once I managed to fool myself—
In three more snores, I was truly asleep
And launched on dreams of my own, mainly good.

In honesty I won't specify, though I can vow
Water would have flowed through it somewhere, warm.

In all those years between Mam's death
And my leaving home, I spent a big share
Of every night in boats alone
On thick tan rivers or, faster, bound
With a steamer of friends towards what we hoped
Was *The City Called Fair*—that curious name
For my destination always came to me
When I sailed with friends but never alone.

Whoever was with me that last night,
On the same iron bed Mam bore me in,
I ought to have known—that deep asleep—
It couldn't be Dot. Unused as she was,
Dot slept like a fired cookstove in August.
You had to keep turning, to brown yourself even.
But still in what I dreamed that last
Night, I moved through a chalky winter sky
With afflicted trees; and in my wandering
Mind I shivered hard.
A real
Hand reached in like rescue—cool
But warmer than all my dreams—so
I knew it was bound to be somebody else,
Not Dot or my sister. First I wondered
If I was scared—no. I waited for word—
Not even a breath.
Next I wondered
Where it touched me—it rode so light—
And then I guessed it was on my hip,
Somewhere high on the bone, riding easy.
I was on my left side, turned away;
And since the hand never flinched or moved,
I may have wandered off again.

Anyhow next thing I was somewhere else
That took me awhile to recognize—
I had maybe dreamed myself back in real life:
Me as a young girl, lean as a finger.

I lay the same in this same bed
In the same deep dark; but my body was younger
And leaner still—eight or nine years old,
Turned this same way and with this other body
Flat beside me:
                                        Dad, to be sure,
The same as now but that much younger
And his left hand laid on my hipbone.
My mind hung on in that child's world,
Hoping to know if this was a picture—
An old snapshot—or life, life moving.
I thought *If it's life, one of us will move*;
The hand though was locked like me in dark
In that old place in my old life
Or dream: I still wonder.
                                                        But this last night
When I was finally awake and present—
Well before light—I'll have to say
I understood my partner was Dad:
Dad live, with all his blood pumped through him,
Was next to me in bed in the night.
   Someway I thought the usable truth,
He's just this lonesome; and then I tried
As hard as I could to talk from my mind—
No words, no breath—and say he was welcome;
To say *Stay here as long as you need,*
Take all you need, I need not to fail you.

Like I said, I was twelve. I knew enough.
To be sure, I couldn't know what'd happen
If that grown a man—and my own father—
Had read my mind and set his hand,
Or whatever part of his strong body,
To work his will and take his need.
   I might be one of those TV women,
Every day of the week now, that stands up moaning
In public sight and blames her people
For her own failure to meet bald life
And stay upright on her scarred two legs—
It can be done: I hope to tell you.
   I might have scalded kids of my own

With my grown famishment and passed my hurt
On down the centuries like war and greed.
I might be Mother Teresa, or better,
Be taking my desperate stand in God's
Teeth to blind my eyes to the four-way
Wreck He lets the human creature make
At home and abroad.
Home was where
I felt I was that final night, with
My dear dad having chose to be
That close to me, his still-unravished
Wakeful bride, the night before he'd
Take his death. It was so near perfect,
So sweet to know, that again I sailed off
Into calm sleep. And when dawn woke me,
He was recently gone—his place on the sheet
Still hot behind him, the press of his head
In the pillow still damp.
Home—I know
I spoke it out, the actual word
In that thin light.
It woke up Sister
And she said "*Gone?* Gone where on Earth?"
I let her believe it and said "Search me."

Early that evening they brought Dad home
From the floor of the warehouse where he fell
From the highest loft—pitch-down on his face—
And not one spot of blood, one bruise or
A word. He looked fine as polished wood;
And everybody said his heart had failed,
The second ambush he'd waited for.
Hard as it sounds, I hope it was ambush.
Like a cornered thing, I watched every face
For a glint of news it was something worse—
Nobody but me even seemed to guess
If he chose to dive.
I'm more than half-sure—
Most days, even now—that no man that young,
That packed with glee and the hope of more,
Would endow me rich as he did in the dark

With that much tender need and trust
And then plunge out of my sight, my life,
The rest of *his* life and the lovely world's.

Even now towards the end of my time,
I can say I've loved life more than half
And pray for more. I've moved through seven
Houses since, with two kind husbands,
A girl and two boys (each boy thatched
With Dad's coarse hair the color of grain).
But in my mind or in the world,
I've still never called but one place home,
One night, one bed.
                                        I own it tonight
And—widowed again—I'll rest in it deep
If my own heart, that's stood so much,
Will stand me telling you what I've told.

2. *A Single Bed. A Back Street in Venice. Two young men.*

Fifteen or twenty more dollars a night,
They could enact this solemn start
On the Grand Canal, if just in a garret
With a dim slot-window.
                                        Still it's Venice—
A clean room with a locked door,
Two tall windows on a dwarf piazza;
And while they hear no actual water,
No lone cry from a spare gondolier,
The family home in which they've found
This private air is more than half-
Adrift on morning (the morning borne
On a tan Adriatic) and yielding, atom
By limestone atom, to the sleepless gnaw
Of an indolent sea yards away.
   The past two nights they shared the room
With a pair of jokey college friends
Who left for Rome in pre-dawn dark.
Now as a light like primal shine
Endows the room—bruised black chairs,
Muddy tile—with a blinding heat
That soon begins to sound in silence,
A Gabrieli bronze fanfare
Climbs both their minds: muffled, slow
As if this ancient cubicle
Has waited eons for their one visit
And will not let this single chance
Expire untasted, unproclaimed.
   Three yards apart, both hear it plain.
Separate, they hope it strengthens round them;
Hope the wizened crone whose pallet
Creaks beyond their massive door
Will snore on through it, unamazed.
Both wonder *Chance for what and how?*
And neither stirs, though the glory
Builds to a reckless pitch and threatens
To stagger, crumble fast.
                                        Then the older
(Just turned twenty-three; a former coward,

Chilled and starving) throws off his sheet
And moves to the younger (a month away
From twenty-one), sits on the narrow
Edge of his cot and, finding clear eyes,
Names the day—"Good Friday. Morning."
   The younger nods, oblivious
That what he brings to the awful day—
This opulent light, this city noble
As any built—is a head, a face
Of preposterous majesty: fit to be here,
Fit to bear frank human worship,
Worthy goal. The younger smiles,
Slides left to make a narrow harbor,
Says "Then rest."
                                        The older thinks
Good Friday rest, accepts the welcome,
Joins this body splendid as the dark
Cadenza flooding down the slatted
Sun that finds both bodies warmer
Now and half as strong
As its own star-born killing shine.

Thirty-three light years fling on—
Older, younger: each can still
Recall the weight of every beam
From that high window, taste the welcome
Salt of healing shine from God
On His death day in that one cheap
Dissolving room, the secret home
They never leave.

3. *A Cleared Ring in the Blue Ridge Mountains. A boy aged twelve, now a middle-aged man.*

This ring was here, way before I found it
When I was twelve. I'd packed me a dry lunch
And left at sunup to climb Table Top, not a hero's
Job. She's gentle-sloped and flat when you get
There but thick all over with cedars and briars—
So I thought, so Hedly told me each time
I claimed one day I'd try her (he's my dad
But, this far gone, I'll say the pure truth:
A vicious bastard stalled in my path).
  I took my damned time in the morning chill and kept
My sweater on well past nine when I had to scrabble
The last fifty yards, perpendicular in full
June sun. Wet as I was and both hands cut,
The minute I brought my last foot up and wavered
On top, I tasted a quick wash of sweetness
That I guessed was partly blood in my throat
But mostly the final recognition by a living
Thing that he's found his place, where he ought to be born
If the chance returns.
                                    I felt it that strong, even standing
Where it looked like Hedly was right again—mean scrub
And briars. I said to myself "Bring the hand-sickle
Next time and clear you a bed." I thought
I'd spend some nights on top and learn
A few things.
                        My body was still hairless as iron;
But shortly below my flat breastbone, I felt
A station warming up—some new broadcaster
That was hell-bent on drowning the air with his news.
From the earliest time my mind recalls,
I'd listened hard, more or less every minute, for some
Slight message I'd last out the meanness
Of parents and kids—I mean real blood, drawn
From my body. I'd also known for two hard years
I needed language lessons *fast*. I knew,
When the thing that rules our bodies struck in mine
And stocked me full of a man's ideas and the skin
To use them, I'd need to be ready to cooperate.

A thing that strong wouldn't speak the tongues I learned
From Hedly and my scared mother (she spoke through him
Most days anyhow, even when I was hooked
To her, sucking—he made her pass her words through him,
Except when he left; and by then she'd forgot
Her own mind and voice).
So while I tore through underbrush,
I said out loud I'd get to the midst of Table Top
And lay myself out an actual room
With green walls, a floor, all but a roof. Then
I'd be in serious business to start my hunt
For what I'd need in years to come, if my
Child's body really did reach out and be a man.
It very near killed me, finding the ring, dead
In the midst of that quarter-mile space—a circle clean
As a washed dinner-plate and damned near as round, just gnawed
At the edge with low dogwoods, half-trying to live.
I said right off *It's somebody else's. Haul-ass*
Out.
But wanting froze my feet in place,
And I frisked it for signs of who or what. No mark
Of a footstep, no fire ashes, just bare sandy dirt
In an ○ sixteen feet across at the center.
I'd heard of a place called Devil's Tramping Ground
Where nothing live could last, south of Raleigh.
But also right away, I knew the Devil had never
Set hoof on this Green Table. On her back here
I was safe from him, his henchmen and the humans he'd won.
Any harm would come from the same direction I'd met
It before—man or beast (I've mentioned Hedly
But not the yellow maddog I cornered too close).
I was no churchgoer, then or now; but I knew
Full well I hadn't *made* the world. So I bowed in the midst,
Then and there, and thanked Whoever cleared
This home and kept it waiting and brought me here
In the throes of my need. And Who- or Whatever signed
You're welcome by sailing a black cloud past the sun
And throwing me into deep night ten seconds. I chose
To read it as *Welcome* at least.
The rest of that day,
I scouted the whole of Table Top, telling

Myself any minute I'd stumble on robbers counting
Or a boneyard of orphans or—the wildest thing—*safety*:
No sign of humankind, though a world of bones
That had to be beasts, that small and fierce.
By late afternoon I knew if I meant to get down
By dark, I'd better go. Still I took myself
Back to the ring, and one more time I thanked
The sky—I could see it, clear as I'd ever seen:
The bluest perfect hoop above me, *listening*.

Years to come, till I left for life, I'd make
My secret way to the ring, all times and weathers—
Not a human soul knew, unless you count mine (Hedly
And Mother thought I was "hiking"). I'd spend
As long as two nights running, stretched out asleep
In the absolute midst, more times than most boys
Catch a ball. I was twelve and finally seventeen;
It lasted, stronger by the visit, that long.
And it taught me the following, secret to now.
If I could keep myself clear of dreams
Till the true midpoint of night and dark, I'd glimpse,
At least one time a year, these huge events—
Confirmable deeds—in the sky above me, dim-lit
Battles of Love and Hate where the brave truth wins,
Though it takes most grievous pain and loss.
If I
Could last till the instant of day, I stood the chance
Of seeing—once—the population of the air
We breathe, not motes and germs but the hidden
Traffic of good and evil, the angel freight
Of ruin and grace: splendid to watch.
And once
My body fledged out full, if I would show
My skin entirely, stand upright in the midst
At noon on the longest day and let the sun
Alone fire me to strow my seed in a high
Arc out to join the dry Earth, I'd guarantee
The future life of humankind and all
Its brethren, live or dead; the streams that—through
My will—would swarm with food for every mouth,
With endless water for our dry throats and the baking

Land, deep as roots drink.
                                        Swear to God,
I know I pushed that far toward entire knowledge,
The perfect service of man and things, entire
Worth to learn the names that unlatch time
Herself and lead to bliss for all good lives,
All harmless things that do brave duty. I was that
Near wild, that near to killing my whole family,
Teachers, schoolmates and that near *right.*
                                                        I'm back
There now as I tell you this—forty-odd years since,
Having come this once to see my mother buried
At last, covered neater than even she hoped
Down back of the house she kept so clean no human
Could grow.
            The ring is swept and bald as ever. I all
But see the print of my young foot. I kneel to hunt
For any sign my seed has bred the least reward—
Nothing, warm sand that honors my touch.
                                                        I've seen,
Of course, how blood-red flowers crowd to the barren
Verge of the ring and flaunt a mystery they retain.
They're new, here anyhow—new to me—and only
When I turn to leave do I risk the thought they've
Waited long to thank my childhood and lure
Me home.

SIX MEMORANDA

1. IMPRECATION

That there in a town like the stuporous skull
Of a matricide—coprophagous grubs—
We denied ourselves three days, two nights,
The solace of common skin on skin,
Attainable ease,
And are punished here in words.

2. BED

Display this photo of an unmade bed
In a faceless thirty-five-dollar motel
To three random strangers. Solicit guesses
At the havoc wreaked on helpless cloth—
Lawnmower salesman thrashed by nightmare,
Silver-wedding couple faced east and west
After one perilous commemorative try,
Father and child paused hopeless here
In flight from what had seemed endless home.

Ask me—*Cooling surface of the bottomless tank*
In which you and I first oared down to anchor
In all that was permeable, mutual skin.

3. YOUR LIES

Your lies
To spare me
Spare only the room
In which you crouch—
Desolate child
At a mother's corpse,
Guarding her cold right
To your sole love.

4. YOUR DEBT

You harp on the enormous debt you owe me—
Repayment could be made on easy terms;
But though you've sapped my hours, sapped whole years,
And though your slightest whim has been command,
Still I must walk before you like a shield:
Absorb, turn, take the thrusts that aim at you;
Be sanctuary for you from yourself,
Stand as faithful bondsman for your crimes,
Shoulder burdens you refuse to bear,
Weep tears you ought to weep, kiss your dry eyes.

after Stefan George

5. MONDAY, JUNE THE SIXTH

Huddled above you Monday, June the sixth,
When I had given what I had to give,
I said the truth—"I love you"—in your ear;
Then felt a shudder grate down from your eyes
And offered quickly "If that makes you worse,
Forgive me please."
                                        You turned your face aside.
I said "Where are you?"
                                                  —"Still right here" you said.
—"*How* are you?"
                                        —"Been this happy once before."
So I slid down, extended your left arm
And kissed the two scars parallel as rails
Where you had slashed your veins eight weeks before.

6. FAREWELL WITH PHOTOGRAPHS

Time is mainly pictures,
After a while is only pictures.

Five years, for instance—all but two thousand days—
Will resolve to a few dozen pictures in time:
Of which, if ten give long-range pleasure to their veterans,
Thanks are due.

Thanks then for time—
Deep-cut pictures,
Mainly delight.

WINTER 2

The images of fall are sought in vain—
Have fallen, rot, are locked in winter cold.
The field is blank; the tree that once stood bold
Is cowed by wind but soothed at night by rain.

As I am soothed who rest now at the close,
Hearing the year's last question to the sky,
Waiting the answer to that rising Why?,
Trusting an answer when spring's coming shows.

after Hölderlin

LAST VISIT

I found the old nurse you envied, Mother.
She naps, for good, in weed and scrub;
And the least I owe is a few last flowers.
   The dead chew bitter cuds of pain;
And when November scours the woods,
They're stunned again by our neglect,
Safe as we are, quilted in down
While icy nightmares plow their sleep—
No partner, no low pillowtalk.

Dark and late by the whistling fire,
What if I see her rocking slow?
What if, this blue December night,
I stumble on her curled by the hearth,
Back from her unending bed
To guard with rheumy steady eyes
The child I was, this broken man?
   What do I tell her selfless face
When cold tears pour from empty lids?

after Baudelaire

AN AFTERLIFE, 1953–1988

Thirty-five years, a gory rake—
My parents scrubbed in laughing prime,
The Kennedys, King, sixty thousand
Baffled sons in Vietnam,
The countless thousand sons they offed,
Mobs of flower-handed girls
Keening for rescue, blazing kids,
A normal stock of routine pillage,
Lunacy, rapture, genocide, famine;
And then my legs unstrung, both frozen,
Me flung down to sit through what
May be of time, need, gift.
  But here, a clear warm day, I come
On a hare-brained backward lunge, trucked up
In a black wheelchair by chuckling friends
To scout my youth and hunt the cabin
Where I passed a slow ten summer weeks
With boys smooth as baby birds—
Mild, still naked-hearted toward
A world they'd barely dreamed was mad.

We've got a key from the owner's son;
And once we pass a final gate
Where hemlocks start, I know each rock,
Each fern primeval.
                                No tears yet
But a blunt amazement humps up hot
In my dry mouth. When we break in
On the heart of the place, it's beating still,
Though derelict for more than a decade.
  The eyeless rake only groomed this hill
Where I worked my twenty-first summer—guide
And shield of a dozen tads, ten to twelve,
In a likable bonded warehouse and playground
For bored sprouts in the dogday swelter:

Summer camp.
Sequoyah after
The red inventor of Cherokee writing,
Laid up half a mountainside
In the floating Smokies by a fierce-eyed saint
And ramrod dreamer—Walton "Chief" Johnson
Never saw a boy whose timbers he
Couldn't shiver and brace for stiff headwinds:
Manhood! Seize it! God's high hope!
Your very name is on His *lips!*

Chief's daunted too, buried uphill
In magnanimous block-high hemlocks
Straight as the hope he nursed for man.
The swarms of boys are random-sown
Through a turgid world that may or may not
Be one amp of voltage brighter
For his husky ardor, sleepless labor,
The force of this nursery he gouged by will
From granite and the hearts of trees.
I've been away since that last morning,
August 1953, when I
Left to lurk for two more years
At home and college; then the headlong
Spiky trail of my getaway, the mottled
Roll of Chased and Caught—trawling
Love in phosphorescent cities,
Unthinkable limbs and music dense
As baled swansdown or sunbaked mire—
Through that much time: no bitter month.

Same eye today, same skull—I hunt
Chief's house, the office, sick bay, lodge,
Library, crafts house, breezy low dining hall,
Oval ballfield, a waving swell
Of foot-deep turf uphill to the cabins
Propped on stilts.
I try to see
Two hundred yards toward where I guess
My cabin stood. Young blue cedars

Fog the view, but I point that way.
And my tall friend says "Here you go."
Two more join and, while I cheerfully
Yell "No need," they lug me up.
The chair rolls game on ground rough as gator
Hide.

It's there. Steps rotted, roof pocked,
Charming as a hatchet-built filagree box
But efficient as watchworks, host to nothing
Bigger than mice, squirrels, the brindle
Panther.
A friend says "Ready?"
I think
He means "To roll downhill." And set
On stemming a risky flood, I say "You
Bet."
Three bearers lift me, levitate
Three pulpy steps, park me safe
Inside.
Thick air, cool as evening,
Brown as dusk—there, *here*
I finally am—thirty-five ticking
Years down a ring road.
The eight
Bunks swim up first from murk—
Four two-tiered six-foot canvas slings
That once stretched taut to sleep light bodies.
All but one are ready to serve
This moment—vacant, clean and dry
(One's torn and fallen, the one that bore
My sole bedwetter, a chunky towhead).
Mine, the right-top sling by the door,
Suddenly stops my hungry eyes—
The boy I was those seventy nights,
Crusty with love as a cross with blood.
Hurried taps of the pressure valve
Would spare my mind, my mustang body,
Its devastation one more day;
Then through six hundred dreaming hours—

Tads sighing round me—I'd build designs
For my doomed try at knotting myself
In Gordian toils with a lanky blond,
Noble as Neptune, healthy as lye
And bent on yielding me nothing but shame
When what I craved was joint safety.

(*Safety!* The eros-octane in me,
Spilled and lit, would have jacked the crest
Of this hefty outcrop a quarter-mile higher
In chattering dark and crazed the skins
Of all live creatures in a five-mile arc
Like air-thin china in a runaway kiln.)

One friend, a camper years after me,
Says "Where's the plaque with your boys' names?"
 I say "Plaques came well after my time"
And look to a tidy line of boards
Nailed at the eaves. Dim as we are
With me hunched low, I see no words
And turn again to study my bunk—
The night I rolled in after twelve,
Back from a long day-off in Asheville,
And vaulted into my covers to feel
The chill depths lined with chillier rocks.
Both feet clenched, suspecting worse—
A snapping turtle or frosty snake
Mad for heat and a chance at fury,
Fond welcome home from the comatose boys.

A friend says "*Ah!* The Great Memory falters!"
He's stretching a match to the webby heights—
A brown plaque, maybe nine by five
And older than most, apparently blank.
But then he reads, a blind child groping:
"1953—Reynolds Price, Counselor—
Paul Auston, Jim Avary,
Ed Grimsley, Buddy McKenzie,
Tommy More, Raiford Baxley,
Terry Brookshire, George Harrell,

Jonathan Lindsay, Lester Shepherd.
Ten-week campers: Bill Barrington
And Randy Floyd."

Stunned as a beef at the abattoir door,
I hear the dead names hurtle through me—
Searing, healing, possibly both.
   As six friends gang at the wonder site,
I sink in merciful isolation
And watch a line of figures scramble
From an unsuspected open grave—
A dozen boys, twelve heads for the names,
Big teeth, chopped hair, a team of voices:
None cracked, each laughing, not a tear
In the loaded days.
                              And none from me,
All-Purpose Font, those days or now.
Halfway uphill, jigged in pain,
I'd wondered coldly why I shanghaied
A weekend's rest for a retrograde,
Dead-sure to appall—*Broke-Down Me*
Hunts Me At The Full: hard boy, primed
For a life that looked in this pure air
Plainly unending, a noonday glide,
But ran a quick hot thirty-one years
Toward an unmapped iron murderous wall
That ended me.

                              Here though, reborn—
Amply friended, spoiled as a pasha,
Unmanned in a fecund afterlife—
I watch the boys' eyes sink again;
And I hear these lean words, mute though clear,
The pitch of Hopkins' "Felix Randal":
How far from then forethought of, all
Thy more boisterous years.
                                        Boisterous, good
To see, starved as a stoat and wild
To couple—for *chance*, bliss, mayhem—
Impeccably kind and cruel as the child

I'd only just been: now this snowcapped
Hulk on wheels.

How far from then
Forethought of. But grand.

Before a friend can turn from the wall
And smile down toward me, I watch the coals
Of my sequestered phoenix pyre
Flare inside me, light for every
Soul in darkness.

Grander still—
Young, I stood here, cocked but blank.
Old, I sit in a hole my green
Self cut in this clean air, seeing now
In my new head a sight my green mind
Never dreamed—the eyes, lips, talons,
Rampant songs and muffled names
Of incontestable angels hid
Past this roof, past the blue abyss—
From all but me, the sole relay
For man on Earth and earthly beasts
Of seraph hymns in adoration,
Praise, undying blame and glee.
I breast their scalding tides of anguish,
Drink their essence—pain and promise,
Grace and torment—

Know the back
Of God's right hand (my teeth still taste
His acrid blood), know Death will somedays
Stall at a door if strong eyes bay him;
Know he marks strict time in silence,
Final friend.

One live friend moves,
"Sure, let's take it." His broad hand reaches
For the coded plaque still aimed at time,
A plucky voyager.

My own hand lifts,
Unspeakably strong, to stop him there.

"It lives here. Leave it." I trust they see
The choice is mine, a power earned
In walking toward the boiling core
On shards of broken mirrors barefoot;
Then returning, charred but me.
Let this pine board endure its earned
Fate in place here—bearing its news
To silence, nestlings, the stone-deaf adder.

My friend's hand drops, though no friend kneels
And no head nods to the solar flare
That fuses light herself with time
Behind my brow, this bony ridge
That bears the fire—outright knowledge
Of how to stay and how to leave,
What to hold and when to loose:
The only secret, *utter loss*;
Glad surrender of every hope but the life
That, breath by slow sweet breath, confounds
An end.

I blink a long instant,
Rig my grinning mask to join them—
Affable gimp.

Two more minutes,
They bear me out and down again,
Heavy but likewise potent as pig iron.
Flung toward dark, a homing bird.

IV

THE UNACCOUNTABLE WORTH OF THE WORLD

(1997)

ONE

AN ACTUAL TEMPLE

FOR DOUGLAS PASCHALL
1944–1994

That week we spent in the Nashville Parthenon
Motel—summer of 1982—
The downstairs bar was quilted in would-be
Country stars, teams of hulks
At a muscle-man convention, and you and me
Exhausted after twelve-hour days
Of nudging fervent elderly tyros
Through the Cumberland Valley Writers Conference.
   Their mountingly desperate tries at plain speech
Had us both deep into Scotch by midnight,
A sensible if costly resort
And no solution to the endless puzzle
Of how to spend our slim reserve
Of journeyman skills at love and service,
Our orphan minds.
                                   What we never tried
Was crossing the road—I could still walk;
You hadn't turned forty—to Centennial Park
And the full-scale cast-concrete Parthenon
On its green apron of American lawn
Flat as Kansas and as unlike the home
Of the blinding original, hung above Athens
In bone-dry air, as modern Athens
Is like new Nashville: both mugged in smoke
From prowling cars of men more bent
On hunting meat than any Land Rover
On the blistering veldt.
                                        She waited though,
In the looming folly of the world's one full-scale
Replica of the sanest human try
At honoring the force of chaste wisdom
And anchoring down, for the upper flank
Of a dead Confederacy, the grave Athena's
Durable offer to heal the single
Cause of pain and hatred this side

Cold Olympus.
                    Normal men that we were,
Parched, famished for the routine fare
Of our whole starving race and kind,
We might at least have crossed the road
And asked a god for the proffered cure;
But we reneged and never saw her,
Not that week.
                    An all but infinite
Decade on, with me paraplegic
And you now under mortal assault
From the same brand of butcher, can we make the trip?
No strain, no need for you to roll
My chair so much as a yard across
The simmering asphalt. Yearning lifetimes
Under our belts, we've earned our wings
In the mental flight we dreamt of in boyhood.
   So one joint lunge at levitation,
Perfect freedom (still by night)
And we're painlessly there. An instant's clamor,
Our weightless real immortal bodies
Wait on the grass, faces raised
To the dark portico, the colonnade that—
Lime or marble, then or since,
Greece or middle Tennessee—
Shades the bronze doors, more than double our height,
Which hide the vanished presence of the gray-eyed
God herself, chryselephantine,
Armed with her helmet, shield and snake,
Expecting us.
                    We drift through choking
Molecules of bronze into trapped holy air
And pause in the space of her long absence,
Smart enough with all our wrongs
To ask at least, in unison now,
For her benediction on our balance of time—
Days or ages—the overflow
Of power she's earned in the unstained act,
Inimitable, of guarding her core
From longing for the flesh of mortals,
The hair of gods or the touch of need:

The banked outrageous fire of virgin
Solitude.
Does her head incline,
Her gaze stoop toward us?
I'm blind in the night
And turn to you. You're facing me, likewise
Blinded and balked.
Grace arrives,
Stunning as ever in its habit of landing
Moments before or after it's despaired of.
A fast decaying glare surrounds
The trail it leaves and lights Athena
Parthenos, frozen still
In self-sufficiency, both hands clenched.
We understand we've laid the blessing
On ourselves in her chill presence,
Won our permanent reprieve
With nothing but two thrusting minds
And four hands barnacled with blundering
Through packed years of take and give.
Before we grin and preen on the gain,
The god speaks on the cringing air,
Her voice a keening silver path
Conceding our win, the risk we dared,
The prize we bear on shoulders unexpectedly
Broad for burdens—*Leave here now*
In mere brute courage, noted by
My spotless heart for lives the gods
Themselves adore: lives threaded with
The smoking blood that burns unstanched
Through gathering night (for all your fears)
And will not cool.

NEW ROOM

This house, a hurtling thirty-three years old,
Bears crowded freight—the woman who built it
Was killed soon after in a head-on wreck
The day she got her first driver's license;
Her husband and daughters left it cold
The day of her funeral and sold it to me;
My mother spent one night here, freezing
When the furnace failed, then died four months
After I took possession in characteristic
Lone-wolf guise.
                    Yet decades turned
On the spit of romance, even lasting devotion;
A plague of robberies and a housebreak with gunfire,
The years of the eel encysted in me;
Two good legs lost, howling terror,
Blank pain; this long survival,
Still in these rooms and the pond beside me
Ringed with mostly silent life
That's often edged toward the rim of speech
And mouthed what may be my whole name.
   Now to mark our *Christusjahr*
Together, both alive and waterproof,
I've built this big gymnasium room
In the doubtful hope of working off
These yellow pounds of a sedentary decade,
Leeched to my gut like starved young love.
   Mocked, left and right past walls and tables
Densely thronged as a minor Levantine
Capital's forum, by the stone torsos
Of headless presumably black-haired victors
In assorted ancient nude events—
Well-oiled wrestling and mirror-gazing
Apparently (by their blind self-pleased eyes
And flaunting invisible smiles and nods)—
I roll a first turn to bear me over
The new threshhold: a geezer, pudding-

Waisted and dreaming his long-gone limbs
Lean as walnut and furred like the fresh
Spring antlers of that young buck who walks
My woods, a god himself all but surely
Unfed at winter's edge.

THE DREAM OF THE COURT

I arrive—spiffed, winded—at the Supreme Court
In snow-plugged Washington only to hear
From a guard in the lobby that I'm late, please hurry.
   When I ask "Where to?" he says "Your *reception.*
The Japanese are honoring you
As their first liaison with the Court
At a formal elevation in the far west wing."
He waves me off as if I know
The ground plan minutely.
                                             I wander long minutes
Down a rail-straight corridor, carpeted gray
On floor, walls, ceiling; and only when
I catch the treble chat of voices
Does the slowly appalling truth break on me—
"I'm a *lawyer!*"
                              Before I can howl and bolt,
I'm there in the humming midst of my party,
Though my hosts have dwindled to a distant three—
Two men and a woman, oddly tall
For Japanese but wrapped like larvae
In court dress of staggering red and gold
With fish-white faces.
                                   None of them seems
To know a word of English; but they bow, draw near
And extend inestimable lacquer plates
Displaying the last of the finger food—
Tiny elaborate carvings of smoked shark
And what may be mushrooms or pressed seaweed:
Dried knots of apparently organic matter.
   I bow and swallow a knot or two,
Cold and bitter; but I think *Never mind,*
It's the Supreme *Court*; and I actually say
Aloud to my hosts "My parents will take
Great honor in this." At last they smile
As I think *Is there no one alive but my parents*
To share this ritual elevation?

*

Awake, I'm actually laughing alone
In the dark of my hot sheets, brimming straight
From the cuckoo dream with my mother's laugh,
My father's more nearly reluctant chuckle
At the awful news, though they've been outlived
Three and four decades by their outlaw son.

FIRST CHRISTMAS

Two early Christmases in my mind—
The first dim as a post-op drug haze
(Our jittery terrier eats a pill
Father drops at bedtime and greets us
Dead beneath the tree when we rise
For Santa; I'm three years old), the second
Gleaming a little higher like a lantern
Smoking in a room under fog (my main
Gift a Dopey doll from Disney's
Snow White, 1937; so I'm four
And take Santa's sooty broad thumbprint
On the white plate where we'd left him a biscuit
For testimony at least as real
As a face-to-face sighting at my bedside).
   Another year before I'm given
The plaster set of the Holy Family
With assorted guests and attentive beasts,
All their eyes betraying the legend
Stamped on their bottoms—*Made in Japan*—
So till then, and the learning that starts with the sight
Of their two blissed-out faces yearning
Toward the mangered boy, I have no model
For boundless love but my luckless stone-broke
Tall young parents:
                    an adequate stop-gap
Spectacle still burning here fifty-seven
Years on, though selfless as water,
Their steady eyes.

LEGS

I always enjoyed you—straight as plummets
Once you'd corrected, on your own,
The near-hoop curve you described at my birth
And aligned yourselves with the classic template
For well-turned strong young male legs
In mid-America before the Second War.
   Then once we'd mopped up Hitler and Tojo
And launched me into the stinging suck
Of puberty, on cue you sprouted
A dense black pelt of tensile hair
On which I prided my desolate young
Self: one of my rare occasions
For pride through that five years of mopery,
Isolation and lust more potent
Than the average Siberian nuclear melt-down.
I even recall the favorite compliment
Of my college freshman year—a towering jock
In the musky dorm shower looked my way
And said "Good legs, Reyn. You a distance man?"
   Turned out I was, you two and I—
No actual races but fruitful walking
Down most of the sunbaked pavements of the West
With forays into the dimmer alleys
And rooms so dark I still can't swear
They were rooms at all (with walls and roofs)
And not mere circles hastily scored
On the heated Earth for the hurried rites
Of a slatted afternoon on a cot
Or an entire night of conjugation
On the packed dirt floor.
                                        In all of which,
You served me impeccably, twining yourselves
Into knots round the writhing magnets
Of eyes and bodies I'm powerless still
To believe we plumbed *(promise we did)*.
   Then I failed you, my spine cored out

By the blundering eel; and now you wait
On permanent duty—loyal Gurkhas
Minding your post through hail and wind
Though no order's come for a cold decade
From the HQ cornered high in my skull
Straining to reach you by wire, smoke, flags
But mute as a millstone to anything south
Of my upper chest.
Still you wait on,
Number than pilings, knee locks gone,
And prone—for your own unfathomable reasons—
To go rail-stiff, thrust straight out before me
And jitter wildly enough to fling me
Out of the wheelchair: a helpless lab
Frog wired to live voltage. We've kicked over tables,
Punted several squatting friends
The length of a room or square in the nuts,
And interrupted solemn movies and concerts
With our hapless interpolated tap routine.
No complaint. Tap on. The unhooked haywire
Bouts of drill keep your muscles bulky,
Keep lethal blood clots moving and seldom
Permit me to slump or languish for more
Than a minute, dazed or bored.
Regards,
Old logs; if we hang on long enough—*too mean*
To die—they may yet learn to reconnect
Us.
Meanwhile, dance.

THE DREAM OF ME WALKING

In just the last month, three friends have said
"You walked upright in my dream last night."
Since in my own dreams I've never sat down,
I wonder whether they're being told something
I need to know.
                                        The chance of self-
Propelled locomotion is immensely unlikely,
But maybe the joined intensity
Of the three friends' dreaming will help me walk
Occasionally through my own sleep
Since—four or five years now—I've mainly flown:
My arms in broad slow condor sweeps
That never lift me high off ground
But never fail.

MID TERM

Near forty years of entering rooms
Where something between a handful and fifty
Faces meet my arrival and give me
Somewhere between one minute and five
To rivet them to me in house arrest
Before they drift on out the window
For whatever better they've got outside—
A finer body than mine to grapple,
The day's first nap or a secret beyond
The reach of my boldest guess or longing—
Leaving me only their cooling hulks
To chatter at for under an hour.
   Maybe I've talked at two thousand of them;
Maybe of that crowd, an honest two hundred
Have flashed a grateful *Oh* or even
A discernible *Cheers* with lit wide eyes;
Maybe another forty or fifty have waked
In the night years down the line and felt
A dug-up lost line of verse in the shape
My voice pressed on it once—*Therefore let the moon*
Shine on thee in thy solitary walk—
Or a speech I gave them in the angel tongue
Of a human exalted: Keats' final words
As his lungs collapsed in the Roman cubicle,
To loyal Severn who'd watched him for days:
Hold me up and do not be afraid
But thank great God it has come at last.
Signs I've smuggled them, charms against fate
And the loveless dark, the chill adjacent
Partner with dawn still three hours off.
   Here's proof of one, only thirty years late,
From a girl of the sixties (now a fiftyish mother),
A letter out of the blue from Idaho
With this one sentence: "*I would like you to know*

I cannot anticipate Hopkins or Shakespeare,
Even a sonnet, without a sense
Of absolute risk—what can happen to me,
The world, or the day—and I cherish the gift."

Sufficient reward unquestionably.

ALL WILL BE WHOLE

All will be whole and powerful again—
The land be level and the water folded,
Trees gigantic and the walls built low;
And in the valleys, various but hardy,
A race of loyal herders and tall plowmen.

No churches to encircle God
And pen him up—a common fugitive—
Then mourn him for a wounded plow-broke nag.
All houses open-doored and welcoming,
The potent air of boundless sacrifice
In all transactions between you and me.

No aching for the future, gazing onward,
But calm resolve to honor even death
So we learn earthliness and serve its needs
And never feel its ample hands grow strange.

after Rilke

ENTRY

Have you felt, in an evening, this slight force
Along your spine—a slow wind maybe
Or the grazing path of a curious thought
Pressing its way from skull to ground:
The need of thrusting forward and *out*
Toward some fresh body that's hooked your eye?
    More likely the wind you feel is me,
Your thrust a faithful echo of mine—
My own firm launch, delayed by dread
And padded by the monster patience that's come
Down on me since motion quit
And the chance of bald entry to any body,
However craved, was flat denied.
    What came was a surer unstoppable entrance—
Thoroughly mental but nonetheless perfect:
The silent invasion and permeation
Of every cell of your body, lean
As a lightwood statue of God's main child
Or the amplest gift to eye and taste
Since the birth of sycamore trees
Or rapids.
                You, entire, are far
More surely my old-style mark
Than anyone else in a packed decade
Of cool sideline benign quiet witness—
Your fused compound of frank command
And private doubt, Delphic eyes
And the skull of a swordsman at Marathon.
    So—easy here, this cresting arrival
Is harmless as saffron tapped from a lily,
Useful as rain on the heels of a boggling
Sunset ending a stunned August day.
And, look, I occupy you all—
Offering every gift I've earned
Or bought or seized in a taking life
(And what I know after so much study

Is a mere trick of momentary endurance,
The knack for lasting that's brought me here)
In return for the uncontested right
To colonize your mind, here on:
Mind and all the inner dark
Of your stronghold, a heat and a form
Of endless food to bear me on
Through my own fate and the fate of your children
Who flow from me now deep into your pith
And sure to thrive.

TO MUSIC

Kin and the boatloads of human beauty
Confided to my hands for knowing—
Nothing else in life or a billion dreams
Has equaled you for flawless care.

The oldest flute, a hollow wing bone,
Turned up at the base of a village midden
Twelve-thousand years old on the rim of Jericho.
The finder allegedly piped "Yankee Doodle,"
Its premier song in modern air;
And children claim the nearby Jordan
Slacked in her decrepit roll
To hear the revival of light's one sister.

Birds and wolves, famously; amorous frogs,
Sawing insects, clicking dolphins,
Rhapsodic whales and gasping divas
Agree to your glory. Often the sun himself
Sings out in thanks for God's other child.

TWO

DAYS AND NIGHTS 3

A JOURNAL

This third group from a notebook of occasional poems was begun in January 1992 and concluded in the spring of 1996. Again the poems exist to record, quickly and informally, the impressions of a short stretch of time—the observations which are likely to disperse if not promptly and precisely noted. As such, they have continued to be fixed in words and abandoned in a matter of minutes or no more than a few days after their arrival. Many of my human subjects hardly volunteered to appear by name, so precise identifications are given only when useful for the reader's or the subject's understanding. Likewise, dates are given only when relevant. The reader should not assume that all poems addressed to "you" are addressed to a single person; no "you" however is fictional.

Since a number of the poems concern themselves with a particular ending precipitated by the AIDS virus, I have specified in every case their dates and their subject—one man, Lightning Brown, a friend of two decades, whose eagerness to last (and to function entirely so long as he lasted) was awesomely heroic. As a man whose trust in the power of poetry exceeded any I've known, he wrote striking poems till only a few days before his death.

Reflecting on the one hundred fifty-five poems that have accumulated in the three parts of *Days and Nights*, I can hope that the reader will not feel unduly leaned on by intermittent glimpses of the paraplegia that became a condition of my life in the summer of 1984. In ensuing years my immobility has provided occasions whose increasing naturalness prompts observations that I hope are of more than personal interest.

DAYS AND NIGHTS

1. FOR K.W. ON HER BIRTHDAY

A male Canadian timberwolf who knows himself defeated will offer his jugular vein in submission to the snapping jaws of the victor, but the victor cannot or does not bite. Something in his nature prevents him.

after Konrad Lorenz

There's one cleared ring unknown to you or me
Where, three weeks into winter every year,
A pair of lean but fed tip-silvered wolves
Meet to enact a plain memorial rite—
The tragic end of life they must avert.

One crouches, dares the other's tall assault
(The death of each is in the other's power);
But then, to turn the year's approaching doom,
The taller creature balks, kneels, falls to Earth
And bares the tense hair at his pulsing throat,

Requiring mercy of his strong companion—
A thorough mercy granted instantly.
This primal mutual yielding near the core
Of our world's shut ferocious driving heart
Marks annually the day you came to light,
Whether to honor you for your broad mercy
Or merely as a parallel good gift.

2. F.H. AGAIN

Fourteen years and still, you here
On the Palm Sunday porch in the green and white
Revivals of beech and rank azalea—
Both of us grayer and me stalled—
You bring your old benign disturbance
To the lengthening day.
I haven't reached
For more than common courtesy
From one live human in two thousand days;
But when you stand to leave at dusk
I think *With half a nod from you,*
I'd actually rise and walk the face
Of this brown pond, studded with turtles,
To dock my life in the shadow bay
That waits in the pit of your strong neck
Where it subsides toward the ready target
Of your chest.

3. DURHAM, 4 JUNE 1984–FORT WORTH, 4 JUNE 1993

Today, nine years ago, I dug my way
Through ten stunned hours of mindless oblivion
While a huddle of miners hacked their own blind path
Along my spine, hungry to excavate
The vein of slick gray cells that longed to eat me.

They partly failed; I clawed partway to light—
This pounding desert light in late spring Texas:
Sufficient shine at least to see this page,
These low black marks that sign my endurance,
Roaring thanks.

4. HOME FROM THE CLIBURN PIANO COMPETITION, FORT WORTH

A week of talk from Steinways, crisp Kawais—
Three-fourths of all the talk some brand of chatter:
A faceless sewing machine for luckless Bach;
Rachmaninoff's moist tumescent neurasthenia
Dispatched with swift karate chops or torpor.
Then a kindly hometown boy from tan Navona,
East of Florence, burned his soulful trail
Through "Rachy Two" with hands like a perfect night
From moaning Callas—the bottomless power to mourn,
Heal, barely smile on dying lips that win
The chunky boy a round gold prize.

5. TWENTY-ONE YEARS

That long ago we drove ourselves
To the thermal pool and floated hours
In its uterine calm, naked as newts;
Then hauled our sapped bliss back uphill
To the cheap hotel; and on a bed
That had plainly borne the labors of love
For at least three generations of roamers,
We faced the choice of using the rest
Of our new lulled ease in joining our selves
In a trial knot of mutual skin—
Our excellent hides that were each then fine
As rawhide gets.
                    The trial worked,
Then worked (with frequent repeats and variants—
New-found knots as brilliant as any
Known to an Eagle Scout) for the years
Till I was effectively sheered off smooth
Below the waist.
                    Nine years of bearing that
With no loud grumble; and here again
You volunteer what we have left—
Your same hide, seasoned a little but still
As fine as a well-made glove containing
A trusty hand dispensing grace.
   I take it, new as a playground boy
Confronted with the actual dream
Of proffered skin, and offer it
What I have now, the parts that work.
They prove sufficient; you bloom on schedule,
Old Faithful mate.
                    Weeks later, basking,
I feel stripped clean still; in service again,
A scow called back from years in mothballs—
Eager to tow, dredge, breast high seas
If that brief duty bears you on
As it does me.

6. RECUMBENT, SLEEPING

You've hauled me up and down the rocky island
Through blinding sun and swelter. Indoors again
In my room's dusky cool, you topple back
On my wide bed and nod off instantly—
Two decades older than the you I loved
In that long summer of our first communion
And only better for the time consumed:
Calmer, sure of all your rangy hungers
But undiminished (eyes, hair and limbs).
   I know your present skin and mind
Will take whatever I offer in tribute—
My hands, lips, music, all my tantric stunts,
Verse improvisations grand as Homer.
In thanks, I merely sit and tend your sleep.

7. INDOORS

You stirring the lazy air of these still rooms
Are welcome as any caller since Christ
And not without at least his minor virtues—
A heart the size of Earth east of the Gobi
And eyes that blot light, young black holes
Imploded seconds past and starved for atoms.
   No one in this century-long decade
Has brought a more opulent sexier grace—
The whiff of Appalachian red clodhopper,
The overriding bronze eyebrows and eyes
Of Delphi's dazed victorious charioteer
And his bare feet: that tempting instep arched
To spring *toward* or *away.* Kindly choose.

8. LUCK

This big piece of luck—
That all my life, from age six anyhow,
The human pelt smoothed over a rack
Of elegant bones, studded with dark eyes,
Topped with black horsehair
And lit just under the rind
By the jet of curiosity, joy
Or random eagerness
Stokes me for the crossing
Of at least a minor temperate sea:
The Adriatic, say, or Marmora
And the Hellespont—not to speak
Of Horn Branch at the foot of this hill
We cling to gladly.

9. A CHIPMUNK GONE AT CHRISTMAS, FOR K.W. ON HER BIRTHDAY

While we built our Christmas tower around us,
Filled and glad to be ourselves
Again together and ready to hope

The tower lasted all our lives,
Silent and curled in a box at our base,
His small life fought like a clock

To last, a shut fixed timepiece pounding
The moments to stave back death.
And when he failed, full and glad

As we still were in our own kind,
We paused to stroke his cool torn hair
And, silent now, commend his brave

Lost fending-off of that long siege
Awaiting every tower and life.

10. LION DREAM

Four in the morning, the full moon breaks
Into my room and with it—in its
Humming wake—your full lion head,
Lion tawn and limbs eight yards beyond
Me stalled in sleep.
                                        I nod to send
You all the night-birds roosted safe
Around my bed—gray wings to lift you,
Bear you on still safe before me
Toward that still circle of a room
I know is waiting somewhere here
But cannot find, that final shelter
Which (like you, staunch sleepless friend)
I've longed to live in all my life:
The tower of utter needlessness
With its enormous lens on time,
No hope but sight, clear clean-lined view
Of all that lies before our eyes
And waiting past our present reach.
    Wait there. I follow.

11. FOR HUBERT DILWORTH DEAD IN HIS SLEEP

Open-hearted as a snow-fed spring stream
Barrelling down a canyon narrows
On its wide purpose toward the sea,
You had less meanness
Than the average day-old colt on its weak pins,
Less than the average grown man needs.
   Salzburg chocolates, Bond Street soap, Irish linen
Handkerchiefs by the pound from Shannon,
Fistfuls of silk ties, music
In every medium known, late phone calls
From Grand Hotels in America, Europe,
The back of the moon, and your concerned voice
"Friend, did I wake you?"
   Gifts, all gifts, all poured out on us
Through lucky years of you, dear friend—
Dear head, dear dark eyes: gone
And missed like a fine tree lost from the hill,
Like closest kin, near older brother.
Rest, rest now.

12. BACK AT MERTON COLLEGE

A warmer clearer day than any
We navigated in our years here,
Nearly four decades past—a city and buildings
Still under two palls: the recent war
(That quietly slid the bristling Empire
From the earnest grip of British hands)
And six to seven centuries of residue
From wood and coal and fifty years of petrol
Burned to ease the chill off yard-thick
Stone walls—uselessly: the chill prevailed
In every bitter stall but our own.
   Our silent burning, secret to all
But us by night, has—look—live coals
Still under this meaningless
Thick gray ash; and the golden fleece
You bore through mist on your strong head
Shines still today in sun both fiercer
And kinder than any we saw or felt
In our green prime.

13. AFTER THE ANNUAL MRI SCAN, CLEAR

What if I hadn't been in place—upright,
Gilded with love and gifts at fifty-one—
To take the blast that Your constricted heart
Required You hurl outside Yourself: blank dark?
What if I hadn't stood blocking its path?
   Whole tribes of Bushmen, herds of mountain goats,
A board of directors in the Chrysler Building
Poised to lay-off thirty thousand workers,
Or all the children of a highland village
Steep in the foggy north of Vietnam
Might have gone down in agony.
                                                  You elected
Me.

14. LIGHTNING BROWN DISCOVERS HE SHARES A BIRTHDAY WITH EMILY DICKINSON, 10 DECEMBER 1994

We've spent the whole month lobbing Emily poems
At one another—*After great pain* and *morning's nest;*
The distant strains of triumph, agonized—
And here the mail delivers this calendar,
Day on day of a thousand poets' birthdays.
   You turn to yours and shout "God, it's *her*!"—
A grace we'd never known you shared
With that remote uranium core from Amherst.
Then for a silent instant, your eyes flare.
   So now we understand you move secure,
In far more light than heretofore we'd seen—
The light the two of you lob back and forth
Across bleak years: the bald-faced truth,
Pain seized and worn threadbare, triumphant laughter.

15. AFTER AN AIDS BENEFIT, L.B., 17 DECEMBER 1994

Past midnight, here with bourbon in the chair
Where I sat out the last of my strength to walk,
You let me watch you wait out your own yielding—
The streaming eyeless mouths of our time's plague
That wolf you down in minuscule warm chunks,
Sculpting your face to concave lunar planes:
Still powerless to touch your hazel eyes,
The crouching eyes of some bent Chinese sage
Who, any instant now, will start to pale
And leave me facing only where you burned,
The mild welcome mist of your ongoing.

16. NEAR THE DEATH OF THE SUN, L.B., 21 DECEMBER 1994

Knot by knot, it leaves through our hands—
Frail yarn of light through the wayward fingers
Of our four hands that have staved off death
Past various absolute-last reprieves
To link, near empty, at the end of this year.
   Linked, the surge of voltage threading
Both our frames—one circuit—promises
Every good office and burden of fire:
In-dwelling warmth, dry crackle and respite
Of helpless hilarity, juddering blasts
Of shine and vision, the cooler shades
Where (eased and stoked) we slowly comprehend
And greet a mutual ravenous sane
Just possible will to last.

17. ON THE ROAD NORTH, L.B., 23 DECEMBER 1994

All day, since your rusty voice called with goodbye,
I've followed your climb up the map toward D.C.
And seen you plowing your L.A. childhood
Through my own past—the ebony counties
Of northside N.C. and southside Virginia:
The deep red gully of hundreds of units
Of scared-cold boys through the Civil War,
The only surviving American landscape
Terrorized by a slave rebellion,
The final days of the Revolution
And plump Cornwallis's blushing surrender
All cooled by day and chilled at night
By a few million trees in direct descent
From the native woods of thousands of Indians
Long since starved out or shot by my kin
To make lit space for the lovely fields
Of deadly tobacco grown by Africans
Hauled through a continent, a bottomless ocean,
To (unforeseen) endow white souls
Past any dream—the endless plummet
Of their balked longing and silent curse
That stirred the slow warm rings of balm
Which even now both scald and cure.
　You though—sapped by an inner dumb
Unstoppable mouth—have surely only
Gazed straight on in increments
Of a hundred yards, parceling out
An aged boy's few grams of strength
To cross your goal: four intercalatory
Days in safe oblivion at the heart
Of a country no less magnanimous or free
Of a scorched-earth history than gentle you,
No less consumed, no less susceptible
To grace.

18. THE DYING BELT, DOUGLAS PASCHALL GONE

Just as I head into the Dying Belt,
As my father called it—when friends and enemies
Roughly my age begin to wink out
Naturally—I find myself
Assaulted still by the wrenching off
Of far younger friends with stingier portions
At this long feed than I (and I feeding yet).
   Now you, Douglas, ground to death
In the monster claw of the crab in your vitals;
And the poem I wrote you a year ago
Still unpublished—well, you read it
And hailed me back through the wide air between us
(Tennessee, Carolina) with a Roman poise,
A courtly gravity becoming our best days
A dozen years back when we trusted each other
Through a dangerous night and walked out saved
In hot August dawn.
                              Vale, fratre.
Atque ave.

19. ANNIVERSARY, 9 JANUARY 1995

Because you mentioned the house this afternoon—
The house embroiled in its late bronze light—
I suddenly guessed I was near a milestone.

When we went to the kitchen cabinet and looked,
There was the posted card inscribed
By Inger and Pietro, thirty years to the day,

To welcome me here with salt, rice, wine.
The rice and wine have come to me, steady,
Three crammed decades. Only the salt

Has poured past limit: tanning my hide.

20. BESIEGED BUT STRONGER, L.B., 22 MARCH 1995

This second fulminant full day of spring,
We sit on the deck under leaves so young
We can all but read the old sky through them—

The dregs of a winter we ushered in
With appropriate quiet three months ago,
The balked dark solstice we'd only begun

To think a way past. Yet here and laughing
We sit in the young sun as you read poems
You pressed from the black time (words as hard

And likely to last as—what?—the voracious
Jet kingfisher that mines the pond
For life, the hid turtle's iron jaws);

And the air that courts us slavishly, shameless,
Feels for the instant like endless luck.

21. MERE FACT

This quiet life secretes these quiet poems—
Friends sicken, die, pets vanish, love rekindles,
Dreams witness mutely to impending doom—
And in the silent waits, I roll past time
So uneventful I could balance eggs
Safe on both my thighs through average days.
Weekends, before and after lavish naps,
I half permit myself to search the wall
Of loaded photos from my distant past
And replay thunder, lightning, sleepless nights
When my limbs braided with stupendous others—
Torsos, calves, necks, napes, assorted thickets—
And watched the muffled dawn declare itself
Eight or nine times in a single dark:
That frequently the miracle recurred.
So *quiet*—right. Earned quiet. Sounding silence.

22. THE WHEELED EROS

This black-browed Huguenot, young and gimped,
Comes on his scarred wheels to see me,
First time in four years, to say what I know
Maybe better than he (knowing the state
Of my own body eleven years now)—
He's lopped off for every practical purpose
Below the armpits; and the purpose that's got him
All but crazed is "Penetration—
I never got to penetrate a woman
In any loving way and never will."
He laughs and pops a vertiginous wheelie
But the howling crevasse that splits his eyes
Holds firm as a cleft in permafrost.
   How can I tell him what he wants to hear?—
That my four decades of thrust and take,
Taste and keep are lost and well-lost,
A minor amenity calmly declined
For the cool rewards of self-sealed stasis,
Gray-thatched content—when I long to stand
One moment and say "Oh never: see every
Cell that burns through my dry rind,
The shine and trace of wordless pleasure
From chock-full years—not memories but atoms
Of bodies and minds as fine as horse flank;
Hair like the distant strong undoubted
Weft of night, strung taut for me."

23. TWO FRIENDS, PARTING

Immensely sad
But think of the run of years
You had—the songs and pictures,
The salvage mission on two lives
Discarded, balked and furious;
The ten thousand decencies, the bumper meals;
The ring of light you shed around you
In town and country and famished mesa,
The belly laughter that bore your friends
(Me grateful among them) through parallel days
And nights as safe as the dogs, cats, turtles,
Chipmunks, lambs, and amorous graycheeked
Parrots that ate cold breakfast from our lips.
Sad—and worse. But only here
For this bare short space
As the one path ends, divides, proceeds—
Two seasoned farers-on hereafter,
Each amply gifted by a former mate
Who's separate now, beyond that slotted
Line of trees.

24. BACK, D.V.

Five years gone, now you're back
For a week's caretaking in the rainy spring;
And for the first time, we take our run
At keeping house (however lazy)
As a mutually functioning set of backs
In a space no longer terrorized
By the daily bite of paralysis,
The night's hot tunnel toward big-eyed death.
   So we move with a courtly deference
That might have done justice to a weekend with Jefferson
At Monticello or the Madisons
On their opposite hill. My compliments, sir,
And unpayable thanks—your obedient servant.

25. SAFE HOME

Any way on Earth to wring another poem
From the sight just now of two young buck
Deer stopped a hundred yards apart
At the edge of our headlights, coming home
From a week in trembling San Francisco?
  Parade ground pose—still as sentinels,
Fearless as the memory they broadcast toward me,
Coded voice: *Your absence was noted.*
Now you return. We halt this instant
To mark the event—recurrent but (recall)
Not guaranteed.
                And not sufficient
News in any known *vox humana*
To furnish a poem, though maybe in *Cervida*—
Otherwise, why such rites
For an aging householder in a county chocked
With near-pet deer, a threat to home gardens:
Common pests, graceful as comets
Stalled in their cold fading rounds?

26. ON THE ROAD

For six weeks drawn-out across the republic,
Reading scraps of my new AIDS novel
To ingratiatingly large clumps of people
Who've bought the book and will ask me to sign it,
I've met—face-on—more men than I'd hoped
In near sight of death (all thin as paper,
Some purple-splotched in the grip of sarcoma,
All shaking my hand, having spent their cash
On a stranger's prose); also the parents,
Mates and partners of men who've died
In the bottomless gut of a starved killer
Brilliant as any Nazi doctor
And a good deal madder.
To the worst-off man,
I could only say "Have you got friends
Around you now?"
His purple face
Wrenched into a grin—"Oh friends,
Lord God, I'm *floating* on friends!"—and his hand
Waved back at the empty room: he
And I.

27. STEPHEN SPENDER DEAD, 20 JULY 1995

Eighty-six years of eager life,
A palpable notch on the shank
Of European poetry, a long marriage
Resolved in devotion, two estimable children,
Hundreds of friends, a peaceful end—
And still I take your sudden death
Like the tearing out of a working arm,
Though with no further pain than the calm sense
That time has changed unalterably
And I have finally undergone
The forced assumption of that old downturned
Powerless mask that watched the blinding
Of Oedipus, Hector's corpse
Left cold for crows.

28. NAPALM, L.B., 9 SEPTEMBER 1995

The past six weeks you've lost twenty more pounds,
A tooth, big patches of hair; and now
The creature's ruptured the last few cells
That might have slowed it; so it's burning out
The final inches of your gut and, incidentally,
Has breeched your eyes: "They've begun to fire off
Tiny points of red and yellow light
That streak through my vision like UFOs.
Hey, maybe they're actually UFOs—
Nobody ever said they had to be huge
And parked outside or on the roof, right?"
   I'm glad to agree; then we both cave in
To genuine laughs that our two telephones
Render as cackling, when what I think
I hear behind your helpless voice
Is the so-far steady roar of a fire,
The so-far unstanchable conflagration
That has been you and is.

29. WITH A.T.M., BALTIMORE

Thirty-seven years ago this month,
You entered the first class I ever taught—
The gray-eyed Athena straight as a poplar,
Tall, dark haired and far more gifted
Than a tasteful billionaire's Christmas tree:
A tree that can speak a language of utterly
Adequate power to watch the world
And hold it out for close inspection,
Even rescue missions by hands no stronger
Than yours or mine through the centuries left
Of human life.
Seeing you still
Four decades on, undimmed by time
Or the hurts you've borne, I more than half
Believe again that time's not merely
Quick but just, not simply famished
But bountiful for actual instants
Long as your whole life till now.

30. WITH T.M., BALTIMORE

Both of us born the same hard year,
You five thousand miles to the east of me—
It's like a month with the bravest boy
I knew in my childhood to spend two days
Beside you here and gauge the force
With which you brace your legs on a cane,
Fix your beetling adamant eyes
And bay the lion in your veins
Like blond Canute by the chill North Sea:
This far; no more.
From the silent pause
Beyond that dare, the sudden boil
Of your deep joy proves your chance
At baying the white clandestine stalker
Is better far than any king's
By any known sea.

31. TENTH MRI

Nine years since the last expedition on my spine;
And the annual scan proves clear as bought water—
The surgeon's call, announcing the fact,
Has the boyish glee of an unabashed victor,
Which indeed he is, as I am his prize:
One of the hundreds lined behind
His pale white hands.

32. IN THE FALL, L.B., 28 OCTOBER 1995

You haven't been here in maybe four months;
But now in this literally azure day,
Your hero sister drives you over;
And we sit on the porch, leaves piling round us,
To do little more than face each other—
Little left to say.
                    I mostly face you
(You study the floor); and I memorize
The eyes, skull, skin the monster's left you—
Face of a Spanish monk, ecstatic
In a crazed barely candlelit El Greco:
An upward flaming emblem signifying
Pure Spirit as it launches skyward
Or all that death has failed to seize
As it mows across your live remains
By the hour, the breath.
                              When we stretch flat
On my wide bed for parallel naps,
Separate as felled trees merely adjacent,
I take the bundle of bone—your hand—
And say "Two tired old gimps."
                                   Your eyes
Turn slowly right to find me; you say
"Why is this just so consoling?"
  Near as I've been to the high black gates,
God knows I can't tell you; so for once I'm honest
Enough to fail.

33. NEAR THANKSGIVING, L.B., 15 NOVEMBER 1995

Home from a flat-out jaunt to New York,
I call you—guilty of a whole week's silence.
By now your voice is strips of paper,
Ancient rice paper poised to ignite.
  When I say I'm bushed from the city slug-out
But will try to see you by Sunday at least,
You say "Please, Saturday. No later please."
Then you say "They're taking me in again tomorrow—
For blood, I'm guessing. They think I'm anemic."
  Anemic? Even two weeks ago
Light lingered through the window, then on through you—
The porcelain sparsely bearded poet
You've aimed to be all your short life
And have now become.
                                   I doubt I can stand
To watch it again; but sure, I'll be there.

34. TOWARD AN ENDING, L.B., 17 NOVEMBER 1995

You're back in what you call "the clink"
For a pint of fresh blood (down the phone
Your voice is sane as a smart child's)
And we—three friends of yours—sit over tacos,
Rolling your plans to end it soon
On quiet tongues.
                                    A whole year ago,
Still writing three or four poems a day
And filling a schedule fit to swamp a drayhorse,
You told me "I won't hang on to go crazy;
I've got what it takes."
                                    In my own years
Of funneling drain, the one conceivable
Exit I ignored was suicide;
So what, please, is that—what does that take?
And did the friends of Roman Seneca
Sit in a tavern just south of the Palatine
And ask if he'd have the savvy guts
To lounge in a warm tub and slit both wrists
Before Nero could reach his throat?
Did they manage occasional grins while they talked,
Skittishly flicking dry forefingers
Through a healthy candleflame in their midst
As we do here?

35. THE DREAD, L.B., 21 NOVEMBER 1995

I'm starting to dread your ravenous life—
The plumb-line weight of daily guilt
When I haven't seen or phoned you anyhow,
Despite the posthumous distance of your voice
Whenever I wake you (most moments of the clock)
Or your stratospheric apparent indifference
To my prancing desperately meaningless questions
Of *How're you feeling? What do they think?*
Is there anything on the Earth at all
You'd like me to do?
                                        No sign this week
Of your stated purpose to clear on out
Before the hard straits. What could be harder
Than these slow minutes, the swarming—or frail
Threading hum—of whatever your mind,
That huge unwinking merciful eye,
Is poised above or foundering in
By the smallest measurable unit of time
As I stay home, longing for credible alibis
Never to see your skull again?

36. BIRTHDAY PARTY, L.B., 29 NOVEMBER 1995

Today comes the invitation to your birthday—
December 10th, a small party at the hospice
Given by the "Lightning Brown Support Team":
Can I be there?
                                        Can I be on the moon by morning?
Can you, or I, or the Earth for that matter
Be alive at dawn after this coming night
Which threatens frost to the frogs in the pond,
All vocally ardent after a warm day,
And everyone else's fixed intent
To run out a course that rounds a circle?
   Your telephone voice is less than the cry
A locust leaves in its abandoned
Self in the yard. No way to ask
If you wait in your dry husk only to clock
A last birthday, then fade altogether.

37. FORTY-EIGHTH BIRTHDAY, L.B., 30 NOVEMBER 1995

So ten days early I write you this ultimate birthday poem,
At least half-hoping you'll be elsewhere by the actual date,
One day after Milton's 387th and the day of Dickinson's 109th.
   Here, take this guess at a tailor-made Heaven
With every feature you'd likely request, if you had serious
Hope of Heaven (I have it for you; let's claim that's enough)—
A clean dark stream with wooded shores, sufficient banks
For a few nude swimmers who occasionally rise and, joined at the palm,
All but conceal themselves in thicket to couple safely
With cries on the order of panther wails and buffalo moans
While a tape-looped selection of Shostakovich's rare calm moments
Sifts through branches gripped by hawks and stern-eyed owls
Who may well envy the pitch of pleasure your face agrees
At last to show, unparalleled and a vast liberation
For you to acknowledge.
                                        Afterward, you withdraw to your house
And write one further shaggy poem of pawky eloquence;
Then head for City Hall and a long night's wrangle in the interest
Of some immensely unlikable citizen's last-ditch rights
Before you lay your dark hidalgo's eloquent skull
To final sleep—*final* only in the sense of the last
Willed act of an infinite day in an endless life.
   Hard as it's always been for you to take the slightest
Gift from the world, take this, lean friend, strict payer of every
Debt you've owed.

38. THE DAY ITSELF, L.B., 10 DECEMBER 1995

So it came, you with it, your voice firm again.
On the phone when I call to say "Happy Birthday,"
You forestall me and say "Happy Birthday"
Though I've got two months to wait till mine—

Which means that the mystery of today's renewed:
Were you marking time till the milestone passed,
And are you freed now to set your face
Toward the presently somnolent sleepless hyena

Pausing at the bright scalloped edge
Of your mother's afghan guarding your feet,
Seeing you only?

39. TURTLE DANCE, SAN JUAN PUEBLO, 26 DECEMBER 1995

My third time here at the rim of their motion—
A unison line of men, all ages
From four to well past stiff-kneed eighty,
And each in a white kilt, rooky hair
Crowned sidewise with evergreen, a belt of bells
And the vacant shell of a turtle lashed
With thong to the left knee.
                                                Dead-earnest signs
Say "No Photographs," and the big-bellied clown
Who partly leads, partly derides
Each step of an elegant slightly ridiculous
Transcendent turn seizes the Kodak
From a heedless Anglo woman, opens it,
Strips out the film in freezing dry daylight,
Then bows low and—grinning—hands her the black box
Gutted empty.
                            They've likewise never
Explained their point in this daylong trot
Of more than a hundred males, some lean
As midnight runaway horses, some larded
Like sows.
                    But scanning the rattling line
For an hour, I knowingly choose one face—
Eagle-keen—and plumb its goal: *Light,*
The pale sun, foundering, hauled slowly back
Above the nearest bowl of hills
For one more year or week or instant,
A frail warmth to kindle whichever
Eyes—boy's, girl's, a hare's,
The snake's—were guttering fast
Till these cold feet shook local clay.

40. A LONG STORM PASSING

That distant stripped tree, pinned by a flock of ravens
To the hard ground all last week, the western magpie
Steadily starved at the window (street-hood stylish
In his black and white duds); indoors, we two at table
Murmur our way through coffee and raisin bread,
Both declining to mention the mauled chipmunk
From three years ago, the life we waited near
For one sure breath or a flick from one jet eye
And neither came.
                                        Now silently you face
The white east window, light takes the pale broad planes
Of your full head; your dry lips count the ravens—
Shifting and big as old artillery shells—
Then say "Eight or nine. "
                                                    "Nine," I say,
"By my count, nine."
                                          At a shot the huge birds rise
A yard in the sky and settle back, at least
Confirming home in thin air cold enough
To kill us two.
                                 I know you've lived through more
Than they, for all their gangster jeers at daylight.
I know you very well may outlast them.

41. SNOW, L.B., 6 JANUARY 1996

Three years, maybe four, since this whole hill
Was sunk in snow and—pewter dusk—
Is likely to sink on deeper through night;
And I'm wondering hard if you're alive:
No word of you since Christmas day
And I too locked in now with dread
To drop by the AIDS House unannounced
Or phone and leave a message saying
I'll be there at noon tomorrow
Or sundown any day you name—if
You've still got a phone, a voice,
A mind to recognize my greeting,
Or (better still) the lucid moxie
To call my bluff and say "You vanished
Three weeks ago. Why turn up this late
Sniffing round a boneyard? Nothing here
But loose cells from a long-gone brain
That blames your ass for treachery."
Snow's all I see from this clean desk;
And what I hear's the *meep* of birds
In gangs at the feeder, desperate.

42. A CLASSICAL FRIEND

The better part of a year you've stood
In the clear foreground of what I see
When daylight wakes me or dreams mock life
And run me the film of my actual luck—
To have known you toward the risky end
Of your far-flung youth (dry Africa,
The hills of Montana, the odd real shaman)
As you rise to your full height
And face the Earth from a brief advantage
I also knew four decades past
When I was dark haired and deep eyed as you
But less the effortless natural lord
Of whatever space I paused to fill.

43. THE ISSUE, L.B., 2 FEBRUARY 1996

This gray leviathan stalled overhead
Is breaking up into frozen rain,
Trees crash; the lights and heat phut out
And here you are on the spared white phone.
The nurse half whispers "The tumors are back,
All in his brain; he's somewhat demented,"
Then puts you on.
                         And all you say
As I fumble for questions to break through to you
Is "*What's the issue?*" Every attempt
At contact, assurance, even the tries
At naming myself so you'll know it's me,
That you've known me two decades, is met with only
"*What's the issue?*" in your normal voice.
   The issue, friend, is stark farewell
With measured gratitude and hopes for the trek;
But—thank God maybe—you're far past gone.

44. A VISIT THAT FEELS LIKE THE LAST, L.B., 7 FEBRUARY 1996

You do no more than answer pointless questions,
My impotent tries at filling the air;
And of course I'm dehydrating through the eyes,
A fact you register calmly as a mantis
Praying before the lunge at its victim
Or like a heartless oracle—still,
Bronze-lipped and true.
                                        Desperate finally
I take up the palm-sized Whitman by your bed
And read through the next five minutes at random,
Each poem somehow bullseyed on today—
Sweet-handed death. . . . the jocund love of comrades.
   When your sisters, parents and brother join us
(Just as I feel I can't read more),
Your mother—handsome as in her fresh girlhood
In that tan picture you kept on your desk—
Says "Lightning, this room is full of love";
And your blind Cyclops gaze sweeps us all in
Before you speak to say "I know it."
   What I think I know is that, barring a summons,
I've watched a life crest and will leave you now.
I touch your brown bone wrist—"See you soon."
   Long past even the memory of a smile,
You nod my way—"Yes. Well, all right."

45. GONE, L.B., 12 FEBRUARY 1996

All the last day before you lapsed
Into comatose silence, then slipped away,
You told your sister "They're waving at me.
Everybody down there is waving at me."
   Nan plainly asked "Who are *they?*"
And you said typically "How should *I* know?—
They're just down there waving."
   Assuming "down there" is a good destination,
They waved you into that narrow door
You scratched on a thousand walls to find
These past eight months.
                                        Out for a nap
The instant you vanished, I actually felt
The line of a long slot open from neck
To groin, then the brush—like a short letter mailed,
No pain, no sound—of your slim shadow
Passing through me and eagerly on.
   Twenty minutes later when the phone rang to tell me,
I was already watching the infinite wake
Of your last shape, entirely free.

46. SCATTERING LIGHTNING IN THE SLAVE CEMETERY, CHAPEL HILL, 16 FEBRUARY 1996

What white man on the planet but you
Would think to be strewn on the wide-spaced graves
Of human chattel, men and women
Enslaved by the local faculty, clergy,
Some century and a half ago?
Yet seeing the place in this driving snowstorm—
Old pines thicker than elephant thighs,
A squat wall, jagged fieldstone markers
(Bare of names) to a few dozen lives
Voiceless to speak the still inexplicable
Fact of bondage in a whole town chartered
For freedom and mercy—you seem a fit occupant,
Parched to essence by a fire you kindled
Knowingly in the midst of a life
Already smoking, hell bent on justice
For the birthright-helpless and the Earth herself.
We strew your sandy ochre dust,
The two slim quarts we'll all come to,
On frozen wind that blows you back
Against our legs before you settle;
And I recall your last four words
As you fined your aim down toward the end—
"Am I there yet?"
There, lost pal.
There at the least.

47. EROS TYRANNOS

Far from sure if a crackling joy
Or ashy humiliation is in order;
But it's been thirteen years to the month
Since every cell of my hair and hide—
Every hinge and chamber, sinus and tendon—
Was jolted by the literal instant
And made to shine this sanguine light
In the steady hope of drawing you near.
    Plainly absurd, given years and light years
Of distance between us; yet on you've come,
Slyly braving the glare—hopeful of what?
Gladness, we know, and crusted salt;
My measured praise and maybe (Tyrant!)
A battered veteran's warm wise hands.

48. AN UNEXPECTED PARENT

Young as you are, it's still unnerving
To see you here in my room with your mother—
The palpable cause of you, the oven,
And her slim head and onyx eyes
The unmistakable gratified matrix
Of your high prime, this welling heat.
   Yet occasional Titans were born in caves.

49. SCOURED

This snug hairshirt scouring my hide
Is hardly fresh—self-woven, self-worn—
Though twelve years without it have tenderized
My back to the essence of baby veal,
Cringing raw as I stroke myself
With reeking scraps of the spring-lit fact
That your bare body oars its pleasure
On bodies fitted out for your goal,
While I wait beached by age and balkage
With this full cargo useless to serve.
  What else then but strap the shirt tighter,
Grow again that gator suit
I've grown before with its thin-lipped
Take-anything armed grin?

52. SMALL ASTONISHMENTS

Common courtesies—the brief phone call
To stitch a short gap, the funny gift,
Three lines (E-mail) to fix a thought
About our hopes or register thanks,
The unseen print of your face as it presses
Against whatever space hangs between us:
Space or flesh or the sheer abyss
That stands at hand just there by the door,
Readier even than you to oblige—
Common as condensations of the lost
Or palpable visits from the sudden dead.

53. ECLIPSE

How many years since I first agreed
To let this maniacal itch consume me?—
Forty-five, to the month, since I sat
In a rocker (Chinese red) in my Raleigh bedroom,
Hung both arms down, clamped both eyes
And gave the ceiling one long dumb howl
For lack of a single promised phone call,
A face withheld.
                    Here this far on,
Full moon outside being rapidly eaten
By the sun's black shadow, I offer this similar
Howl to the face you fail to show.

54. WANT

Want as pure as a week old baby's,
A scarred-up fox hound's baying the scent.
Want so perfect it lacks arms, legs;
Is only this mouth, this bore and vent
For processing want—
which now is you.
Two choices—flee or surrender quietly
And learn, in time, the warm perfection
Of life at the turbulent core of greed.
I have, to be sure, a further choice—
Heeling this hound or bawling child,
Yielding you freedom with the deathbed grace
Of Marse George Washington, Marse Tom Jefferson
Freeing the drained slave loose on a new life
Weird and chancy as the back moons of Pluto.

55. STUCK IN GEAR

That I've aimed this furnace blast at you
In the past few weeks is owing mainly
To who you are and how that being
Is visibly, audibly, palpably housed
In noble elegant good-smelling quarters;
But more than a meager real component
Of the shine and roar, the devastation,
Derives from that old ninth-grade law—
The conservation of energy.
                                        Fifteen months
Of tending Lightning in, finally, raw futility;
Then watching him rammed in overwhelmed silence
Through this frail membrane—Earth and air—
Has left me stoked to the pitch of fury
With no wheel to turn, no alp to budge.
  No apology then but clarification—
Call it the next gear onward past love.

56. QUIET EVENING

Yet here we sit and plan a life—
Or a year of life—with the equanimity
And cool-eyed care of soul for soul
That would have done credit in any century
To two gray Stoics, poor as the poor
But self-possessed as the leanest hermit
On Patmos and saner. The hopes we bare
With no embarrassment or fear
In words and grins, stops and chuckles,
Are handsomely matched, if high as condors.
   Older, I know how literally feasible
The whole hope is. Can you stand to believe it?

57. WHO?

Who honestly, ever—above ground—trusted absent love
A whole day?
A trustable love would doubtless cool to tepid in a day—
The love of an aunt
Or the speechlessly grateful rescued pound dog glued to my scent.
Could I manage, though,
To stretch this plausible confidence to thirty-six hours, say:
The entire life of a luna moth?

58. MAY DAY

In fact, I'm improving.
This staggering May Day—
Lacking your presence
A solid week—
I nonetheless hear
Your telephone voice
In a luxury of trust,
A swell of thanks
My memory bears
No precedent for.
Further, I seem
Near sane in the mirrors
I've passed since dawn.

59. AT FEARRINGTON

Never till now—on any night,
In any tangled noon or day—
Have I confronted eye to eye
This angel from the sounding heart
Of changeless light and told it every
Need I know and asked its help
And watched its grave descending Yes
And thanked it amply where it stood.

60. LEFT

You were five, on the island playing with kids
Near the sea, when you saw—just past shouting distance—
Your parents mount the horse-drawn buggy
In blue twilight and head home without you:
No backward glance.
                                        Full years later,
You recount the fact as an extant terror—
Your winded bitter watch from the hill,
Your certainty they'd never return
Though they'd gone no farther than half a mile
(Meaning to come at dark for you,
Whatever'd drawn them home).
                                                        The desolate minutes
Are scored so deep they chill old me,
Gray terrapin, and raise a hard question—
Which of our minds might yet be saved
From the wrack of hope, assured desertion;
Which is past rescue?

61. THE SWAP

Calm as breath from Vermeer's kitchen maid at dawn,
You tell how—over Christmas last year—
You dreamt the frequent dream of my friends:
That I'm inexplicably upright, wobbly
But walking. No chair, no cane.
                                        The fresh
Departure in your dream is that—since
I walk like the me you never knew—
You take to your bed, entirely frozen
To give me ample power again.
  No one else in a dozen years
Of selfless offers has offered that,
Day or night; so borne on thanks—
This broad ascending late spring thermal—
I return the gift.

62. WESTWARD

Lightly as Cortez crossed a tile floor
To cool his brow in a copper bowl
Not ten feet away, I board this plane
And skip a continent in one long nap—
Three thousand miles.
                                        The odds in general
Are stacked my way; but in the event
Of an alternate grind in the gears of things,
Recall this much—the pouring pleasure
You helped me tread, the hour-by-hour
Thanks I've clocked to your account:
My clear-eyed surety of your unmatched,
Unmatchable, grace in a brimming life.

63. FROM HERE

Yet here beyond those intervening
Tons of air—the Earth executing
Its knobbed arc beneath us (farms, deserts, the Rockies,
Countless robust Yanks at work)—
There stands between us a useful filter
That's lacking at any closer range;
And in clear silence, the boreal voltage
Of frequent auroras fades to memory;
And what I feel and think I see
In mental vision is trustworthy gist,
The durable root of what we've drawn
On the actual ground and need to build
In acts and thoughts as real as oak—
A low-slung, ribbed-roof Anglo hogan
Or Saxon hut to house a central
Cooking fire, a smoke hole cut
On clouds and stars, a circular vertical
Clay-and-stick wall to hold off torrents
And parching wind and at least two blanketed
Troughs for sleep, clean air between us
Through which we register as necessary
The promised likeness to God we show
Sufficient times in an average night
To brace this trust beyond a breach.

64. NOB HILL

Ninety minutes in church, the longest ecclesiastical
Stint I've worked in nearly seventeen years
(Since Christmas mass in the actual Bethlehem).
  Yes and *No* in hot succession
As the time slugs by—good music,
Flags to nothing, glamorizing robes,
Interesting glass in a single window,
Studied plummy self-listening voices
Embalming the hasty Greek of quasi-
Literate ancient Jewish pleaders
With fire on the brain, my nattering silent
Non-stop judgment.
                As we exit
The spotless underground parking deck,
A waving scarecrow thwarts our path—
A boy more nearly, not much past twenty,
Filthy raincoat, a torn cap
Against the slate sky chill for June,
His whey face studded (magenta lesions
The size of fingerprints, cancer gardens),
His dead eyes set on me through the windshield.
  I speeding on, ignoring his cupped hand;
Jesus plainly there beside him,
Watching me pass.

THREE

Jesus said to them "Fill the jars with water."

They filled them to the top.

He said to them "Now draw some and take it to the head servant."

They took it.

When the head servant tasted the water turned to wine, not knowing where it came from—though the servants knew, the ones who'd drawn the water—the head servant called the bridegroom and said to him "Everybody brings out the good wine first and once the guests are drunk brings out the poor stuff. You've kept the good wine till now." JOHN 2:7–10

THE DANCING AT CANA

FOR LIGHTNING BROWN
1947–1996

Of course we were there, the soberest guests—
You in your Mexican wedding shirt,
I in all-black with a blood-red belt—
And though (despite the lunatic killers
We housed in the secret deeps of our chests)
We'd more than drunk our liberal share
Of the sudden outburst of cold new wine,
It was we who led the first dance: moonlit,
Each of us to our secret amazement
Strong on our pins as a mailed Crusader
Yet light on the air as the courtliest boy—
That smoky oiled half-grinning slant-eyed
Asian boy we'd squired through the dinner:
The whole roast sheep, the squab and doves,
The honeyed almond ice and currants—
And we almost below the salt
Which caked in a red crock near the right hand
Of the magic guest, the boundless wine steward
Who (so I thought) had slightly smiled
In our vague direction as he stroked the great jars
And made this light new wine from the water
We'd seen four slaves bring straight from the well.
  All fed and slaked, you rose at last,
Put out your hand; and oh I stood,

Rigid at first, mildly shaky,
Scared you'd drop me if my knees failed—
I silently thought you frailer still—
And thrust my left hand out to the boy,
Who was gone by then: it was you and I;
All the others (plus Jesus and Mary)
Were wobbly and dozing.
                                        Fear struck up through me;
Still you fixed both gold eyes on mine
And—all but foaming at the ends of your mouth
From the boiling fury of the death dug in you—
You said "Mr. P, please lead."
    My legs firmed then, my mind half cleared,
My eyes looked out and I took the first
Strong step in a decade, turned a handsome
Dervish twirl on the sandy ground
And saw I'd drawn you in beside me—
Strong as any mountain mustang,
Prop and partner, mirror and lens:
We outdanced the moon.

THIS FIELD

This fallow field behind me here
Stretches for nearly fifty years;
And no other field I know of—Shiloh,
The Wilderness—saw a keener scything
Of riflemen, drummers, bystanders, cooks
Than my long field: this ground I've contested
By the millimeter and ticking instant,
Aching to howl at the butcher's bill,
The day's tub of skulls but endlessly glancing
At random mirrors and catching my stunned face
Seamed with laughter, two eyes hungry
As a shipwrecked dog.
                                        Here lately, as dusk
Becomes near-dark, and what I suspect
Is summer dew exhales from the innocent
Put-upon earth, I can all but make out
Actual faces—the coveted dead,
All comrades, all combatants
(Most of them breathing but past my reach),
The reckless scapegrace bare contenders:
Each a certified stunner and eager as I
To burn whatever flesh or bone
Might be required to fuse our joint
One further night, when all I can send
Is this pale signal—peace and a brand
Of cooling thanks, this hopeless
Undeterred slim hope, to their own wrecked remains.

ANOTHER MEAL

Gods often ache to join us in the dark;
The younger angels long to stroke our hair.
Notice—those cold evenings down drab streets—
How many windows open on last suppers,
How those normal hands enact the rite
Of bread to flesh and soon the warm wine thickens
Till (there among the clustered just-fed faces)
A single pair of eyes will rise and see
You frozen in the night beyond and nod
To the silent honor you extend:
Word of his coming tortured sacrifice
And how his racked abandoned public death
Buys you the world again, one further day.

after Rilke

THE LIST

Honest men admit to the list—
The scrap or actual reel of paper,
Names on the inside wall of a closet,
The mental roster scrupulously memorized
Through decades with faces, voices,
The pleasure islands of curl and heat;
Occasional names entirely faceless
Or mere inchoate sounds in dank sheets,
The taste of linen and briney skin.
  What percentage of guilt or pride
Do honest men feel, skimming the roll?
Many lists, after all, bear names that died
To notch their places in grisly lines
Of particular brands of eye, neck, hairdo
That triggered madmen.
                The number of my names
Dies with me; but the scales of guilt
And pride tip steeply toward pride: rank laughter
In polar summer nights, on evergreen
Shagged rocky shores, this vacant room
Containing now my beartrap memory
Barely marred.

FROM SO FAR

A SONG FOR MORTON GOULD

From so far down this road I think I see
A plain with one bare beech, a long low house;
And while the windows still are curtained dark,
I claim—from where I wait—they hide a home.

A HAVEN

FOR LEE GOERNER
1947–1995

The Wabash doesn't wash Oklahoma—does it?—
So I need to help you understand
What's waiting for you fairly soon.

First thing—the Wabash became the site, early,
In my main dream of a happy life:
Its shaggy banks would offer nothing less
Than total contentment to sit in a new world
And watch things pass at a comfortable distance,
Hear music safe behind my eyes
And be who I mean to be at my ease,
Fully employed by the air and the light.

The Wabash came to me, plainly, from the song—
The moonlight's fair tonight along the Wabash;
From the fields there comes the breath of new-mown hay;
Through the sycamores the candle lights are gleaming
On the banks of the Wabash far away.
I heard the song in a Forties movie,
"My Gal Sal," about Paul Dresser
From Tin Pan Alley by way of Indiana—
Theodore Dreiser's elder brother,
Of all things unimaginable.

For most of my childhood, I lived by a creek
And saw my share of murky rivers
From the windows of the family car on jaunts;
So the sound of the river in Dresser's song
Struck me indelibly in '42—
The river's pleasure as moonlight stroked
Across its gray skin and sped toward me.

Beyond the tune, I could see a wide stream
Dark as octopus ink, darker trees beyond it;
A sky darker still, waiting above

Two far-off candle flames—or was it three?
In theory, I could get there before the song ended
And moor my life—the years I'd get—
Just past those willows hugging the bank;
I could last there forever (or the years I'd get).
The ticket, I well understood, was courage;
The courage I badly needed as a boy
Prone to shy from trouble and run.

Fifty-three years onward, Lee,
I'm there in fact—*here*. And by the slow light
Of two candle flames (or is it still three?)—
I think I can almost make out near me
In the ringing dark your vanished shape
Awake again, the line of your large head,
Your sensible nose that you once told me
Was named "The Moose."

I understand, at first glimpse, why you're here.
I count the acts that earned you the right;
Oddly they add up to well more than needed.
You're plainly at ease, for the first full time
Since the day you also discovered pure music;
And any year I'll expect you to speak—
Meanwhile, this full and silent welcome:
Old sport, brave eye.

THE DREAM OF MOTHER AND MY CANE

Thirty years gone, last night you turned up
In a brief dream, looking sixty years younger
Than you'd be in life (your ninetieth birthday
Is three weeks off)—the strong black hair,
The endless eyes—with me upright
To welcome the visit.
                                        I'm all but swamped
By the shock of course—The Dream of Me Walking—
And all I can think to do in the seconds
We have together is show you my cane:
I've somehow walked through the room to greet you.
Then—no words at all—I extend the silver
And ebony eagle-head walking cane
I gave myself last month for Christmas
(Not for walking, it helps me fetch dropped objects
From under the desk or bed in style).
  You take it carefully, stroke the raging eagle's head
With unaccustomed gravity—matriarchal benediction
In lieu of your general fountaining laughter—
Then return it, silent.
                                        Not till then
Do I think *These steps are the first I've taken*
In ten years. Who else on Earth
Or wherever you wait could have brought me this far?

THE BUDDHA IN GLORY

Core of all cores, seed of seeds,
Almond that folds on itself and sweetens—
All matter to the farthest stars
Is your fruit's flesh: welcome here.

See, nothing any longer clings to you;
Your tender shell is in eternity.
There the rank juice gathers, yearns to stream
And from the deeps a gleaming lances it;

For, deeper still, your broad resplendent suns
Have wheeled in such full blaze that even now
There starts inside you what outlasts the suns.

after Rilke

SCORED BY LIGHT

The blindest man with numbing hands would have felt
The rushing line of these instants scored by light
On the lid of my skull, the stubbornest pictures left
From a nightmare twelve years old.

—The head and shoulders (surely a man's, surely
Real if untouchable) that waited by me
As I woke in the dark for those snail hours of dread
When the silent sleepless unassuaged eater
Bolted my spine in minuscule but ceaseless meals.
Like a listening mutely ticking priest,
The bearded head in unrelenting profile
Behind a screen of tan cloth faintly lit from behind
Would take my notice provided I never turned
My face and strained to pierce his fragile hideout.
He'd abide all questions, barely breathing—*Would I live*
Or die? In my sleep at home or in public torment?
Would I walk, crawl, sit or freeze entirely?
And where, what bed, what chilly floor attended by whom?
But he never answered—unless of course his presence
Was answer, his willingness to wait through dense nights beside
The terror of a single human, lending whatever
Ear he had, whatever mind to hear
My circling beg for time: endurance however
Docked or hacked. I figured he had no need
To answer, being the cause and end of all.
I guessed he was God.

—The late summer afternoon when Xander
Stood in shuttered sun at the foot of my brass bed
And, more than an hour, lightly brushed the soles
Of my bare feet with slow dry fingers and ringed my ankles
In long loose grips, not mouthing a word, not groaning
Or urging, in whatever sweep of prayer or command
His mind launched toward me down nothing stronger than a grown
Man's arm and cool fingers I could scarcely feel.

What I feel, this distance ahead—still beating—is the silence,
Flawless companioned silence, in which he worked
And his yielding no explanation whatever, only
The mystery of tacit care and a seamless trust
In his right and power to haul me back, to save
My actual battered skin when all but he
Had counted me gone and were gazing past me.

—The strangling fear near dawn when I woke (entirely
Stalled) to hear the shearing metal drone
Of an echoed voice from my quick clammy dream
Ringing in the August night with frogs and harmonic locusts,
A voice that proved in trim stacks of numbers that the healing
Vision I'd got in alternate vivid livable space
By the Sea of Galilee—pale sweet Kinnereth—
Was no trustable cure but a putrid leak from the fistula
Of Nazi deception somehow punched through the wall
Of my heart, hooked there and seeping its murderous lie:
Your vision was merely a skit contrived by Goebbels
To lull the last of your will—Goebbels or Himmler,
Some close-shaved monster common as table salt
And lethal as strychnine. Lunatic laughable credible
Dream.

—That poet stranger (flown from Chile into safe exile
With nothing but taut skin and corn-rowed hair,
Beyond the reach of night squads in sneakers)
Seeing me puffed to a toad balloon on steroids
And death and napping in my morphine haze
Came toward me with the curious hope he'd mustered—
Stripping in the unhurried languor of a prince,
Gently straddling my numb legs and, in the dire sunset
At my west window on sweltering woods, palming
Himself in what seemed an all but infinite torpor
Toward spouting life. Another vaguely baffling rite
I chose to bear if only on the chance of watching
Him burn at his furious peak to a fistful of ash
Or of feeling my legs jolt upright again and walk
Me back to my walled-off past (I await a miracle
Steadily as any cooped-up Romanov).
But he proved no more than a real-skin sacrificial

Saint far past control and spinning toward rapture
Three feet from where my blurred eyes focused and, laughing,
Saw his offer at last arc out and land
On my blue shirt in the midst of my chest
A foot due north of my killer's locus in the height
Of my spine—the same old lukewarm chlorinated balm
That would never pour from me again, me dry
As any mile of sand. Possible anyhow
To think, even now, that an inexplicable rite
At dusk from a man run out of a whole subcontinent
Saved my mind, my aim to last—no harm at least.

Pictures I shuffle less often now, peeled
From the hurtling nights and days by an eye in a mind
Outside my body, then hung before me in iron
Frames, potent to burn all chance of forgetting—
Stranger still and far more useful than what
My excellent eyes see here this noon at my window:
A rat-faced squirrel in furious dudgeon to eat
The balk off my birdfeeder fiendishly rigged
To starve him out.

THE PROSPECT

Granted one reliable wish
To serve as a boat from here on out
Toward death at the least, I'd ask for this same job—
A mind to work my hands till they freeze,
A body to cup the mind in safety
Till both go halt in the singular moment.

Given that, couldn't I manage
To keep this affable house and roost in it
With minimal help from any human
Not of my own free sensible choice
And no foul taste of the stingy hearted?

My oldest kin in three generations
Made it past eighty—twenty years and change
From tonight. Twenty years on, whatever mask
The world secretes in ceaseless cunning,
Couldn't I meet the all but surely
Reptile gaze, the reeking teeth,
And say what I see in words exact
And usable enough to earn my keep?

Fox-faced Titian somewhere near ninety
Painting on his ladder; Michelangelo
Building St. Peter's near eighty-nine
With wrenched splayed hands, eyes bright as adders'—
Swift partners to set my hopes beside;
But since some human model's likely,
Why reach for less?

To be sure, if you
Were a third alternative, precluding the masters,
I'd ask for you—to light and temper

This darkening room, to lend a final
Sight of the unaccountable worth
Of the world subsumed in tangible flesh;
Then some late hour with those dark fingers
Long as trees, to shut my eyes.

THE CLOSING, THE ECSTASY

A last considerable rift runs between us.
This might close it.
In a dim warm room
I'd sit in my chair, you'd stand precisely
Six feet away, our eyes would meet
(Granting we've shared the remainder that matters),
You'd shuck your clothes to the ultimate thread
And wait in the narrow bar of sun
That pierces the bullseye window above you,
Firing the white incalculable change—
Racking the slender wedge of your torso
Till truth leaks from it, then smokes, then streams.

First, glare and dark, an assorted turbulence—
Every notch of the visible spectrum,
The hot unfolding of new prime colors—
Boils out from the boundary line
Of where you end and, pouring toward me,
Frees my dubious eyes to see you
Shift through further unforeseen spectra
In headlong metamorphoses
(Every order of bristlecone pine
And Joshua tree, the endless forms
Of usable water and potent creature,
Chiefly the higher animals): becoming
In sequence an unbridled horse,
A famished leopard, the brute Cape buffalo,
Predators, raptors, lone storks and cranes,
Scores of other huge existences—
Each an aspect of both your self
And the single pulse of eager blood
Which beats at the crux of every life
That's drawn and held my eyes and care.
Then, in reach of my arm, the black-maned lion
Rears in a locked intent to spring.

*

Though each shape nods to mark my presence,
Each offers speedy death or blindness
Till I concede my fear, astonished
Thanks and trim expectant glee
At the promise I'm all but sure I read
In the fierce unfolding of your hid nature—
My luck accrued through patient watch
To witness this sequestered warning
In quiet domestic space as common
As kitchen doors or table lamps:
A luck from which I fail to run.
So while the triggering light withdraws,
You sink again to human form,
Far your most imposing phase.

The sight suffices; the rift grinds shut.
Yet one final feasible act—
None watching but we in this safe room
In brown still air—might seal the gap
Beyond a chance of widening
If you'll persist in the dare you've launched.

Start at the crown of your tall head
And—downward pointing with a dry forefinger
From brow to eyes to nipples, navel,
Your intricate tripartite groin—
Teach me the secret name of each part
In whatever language (Mandarin, Macedonian,
Tlingit) serves to chart the phenomena,
Concealed coordinates and heights,
Of nothing finer than a tended body
Near apogee: trusty guidance
Is what I've lacked. Adroit as a mellow
Turkish masseur, I know the uses
Of every cell.
And that topography suffices,
A grid for stringing memory,
Unless I choose the sizable risk

Of moving toward you or you toward me.
The mildest touch from these strong hands,
That held off death, could trace the path
You've named down your whole tender length:
Awarding more than negligible pleasure,
A canny homely durable ecstasy
If I can also bring your mind in this same hand.
That sober progress may convince
Your skin to flourish. In moments, minutes,
Hours, decades, shafts and vanes
May sprout and complicate and strengthen
Down your arms, every grade
Of color known in jungle birds,
Till—at the scary edge of burning—
You're more than rigged to take free flight
On wings sufficient to bear a ship
Or stay as the messenger I've persuaded
And you've agreed to be, here on.

We welcome each. This will not recur
Unless both our tenacious wills
Or the thrust of whatever eye may watch
From however high in the pitch of blue
Demand again this shared hazard
So gorgeous, profligate, selfless, new—
Not elsewhere known on Earth or under.

ACKNOWLEDGMENTS

Some of these poems appeared, in earlier forms, in the following places:

ALBONDOCANI PRESS *Angel; Anniversary, 9 January 1995; Archaic Torso of Apollo; Christ Child's Song at the End of the Night; Leaving the Island*

THE AMERICAN REVIEW *At the Gulf*

THE AMERICAN VOICE *At Sea; Paid; Sky, Dark*

AMPERSAND *Noon Rest, Best Day*

THE ARCHIVE *Again; Black Water; Half of Life; Initiation; I Am Transmuting; Midnight; Praise; Valentine. Heron.*

ATLANTA *Farewell with Photographs*

BLACK WARRIOR REVIEW *First Love*

CARÇANET *Winter*

THE CAROLINA QUARTERLY *Man and Faun; Naked Boy*

THE CHATTAHOOCHIE REVIEW *Easter Sunday 1989*

CROSS CURRENTS *Two Caves, A House, A Garden, A Tomb*

DOUBLETAKE *Besieged But Stronger; Brief Visit; The Dread; Forty-Eighth Birthday; Gone; The Issue; Lightning Brown Discovers He Shares a Birthday with Emily Dickinson; Near the Death of the Sun; Scattering Lightning in the Slave Cemetery, Chapel Hill; A Visit That Feels Like the Last*

ENCOUNTER *I Say of Any Man*

THE GEORGIA REVIEW *Divine Propositions*

THE KENTUCKY REVIEW *Samuel Barber; Stephen Spender*

LESSONS LEARNED *Monday, June the Sixth*

THE MASSACHUSETTS REVIEW *The Dream of Lee*

NEW LETTERS *Before the Flood*

THE NEW VIRGINIA REVIEW *An Iron Bed in Granville County*

THE NEW YORKER *The Claim; Rincón 2; Spring Takes the Homeplace*

THE NEWS AND OBSERVER *A Chipmunk Gone at Christmas, for K.W. on Her Birthday*

THE ONTARIO REVIEW *Ascension; Porta Nigra; Reparation; Resurrection; Seafarer; Three Dead Voices*

PALAEMON PRESS *The Dream of a House; Instruction; Lines of Life; Pure Boys and Girls; Sleeping Wife; Socrates and Alcibiades*

THE PARIS REVIEW *A Single Bed, A Back Street in Venice*
PERMANENT ERRORS *The Alchemist*
PHOSPHENES *Dead Man, Dying Girl*
POETRY *After an AIDS Benefit; Ambrosia; An Actual Temple; An Afterlife; The Annual Heron; Back; The Closing, The Ecstasy; Easter Sunday 1986; Good Friday; Hawk Hill; A Heaven for Elizabeth Rodwell, My Mother; A Heron, A Deer—A Single Day; Juncture; Lighthouse, Mosquito Inlet; Napalm; On the Road; Pictures of the Dead; Near a Milestone; Rescue; The Resident Heron; Rincón 1; Three Secrets; Unbeaten Play*
PRAIRIE SCHOONER *Antipodes; 1 January 1990; Spirit Flesh*
PRIVATE GREETINGS AND A BROADSIDE *Annunciation; Cumaean Song; For Leontyne Price after* Ariadne.
QUESTION AND ANSWER *Dead Girl*
THE SEWANEE REVIEW *First Green; Jim Dead of AIDS; Lights Out*
SHENANDOAH *Epitaphs; F.H. Again; Last Conversation; The Prospect; Recumbent, Sleeping; Remembering Golden Bells; Sleeper in the Valley*
THE SOUTHERN HUMANITIES REVIEW *13 February 1984–90*
THE SOUTHERN REVIEW *Bethlehem—Cave of the Nativity; The Dancing at Cana; 15 March 1987; For James Dean; For Leontyne Price; For Vivien Leigh; Giant; Jerusalem—Calvary; The Rack; 16 March 1987; To My Niece; Twenty-One Years*
THE SOUTHWEST REVIEW *Safekeeping*
TRIQUARTERLY *The Eel; House Snake*

INDEX OF TITLES

Actual Temple, An, 359
After an AIDS Benefit, 394
After the Annual MRI Scan, Clear, 392
Afterlife, An, 1953–1988, 348
Again, 255
Aim, The, 146
Alchemist, The, 18
All Will Be Whole, 372
Ambrosia, 101
Angel, 2
Anger: 1985, 240
Anniversary, 23
Anniversary, 9 January 1995, 398
Annual Heron, The, 89
Annunciation, 39
Another Meal, 450
Antipodes, 1969 and On, 310
Aphrodite, 187
Archaic Torso of Apollo, 66
Ascension, 58
At Fearrington, 438
At the Gulf, 19
At Heaven's Gate, May 1956, 305
At Sea, 271
Attis, 24
August 1939, 231
Aurora, 71

Back, 270
Back, D.V., 403
Back at Merton College, 391
Bed, 341
Before the Flood, 111
1. Her Choice, 111
2. His Discovery, 112
Ben Long's Drawing of Me, 260
Besieged but Stronger, 399
Bethlehem—Cave of the Nativity, 26
Birthday Party, 415
Black Water, 78
Boar's Hill, Spring 1958, 306
Brief Visit, 430
Buddha in Glory, The, 456

Caught, 154
Caw, 155
Cherokee, 108
Chipmunk Gone at Christmas, A, 388
Christ Child's Song at the End of the Night, 43
Claim, The, 160
Classical Friend, A, 421
Cleared Ring in the Blue Ridge Mountains. A boy aged twelve, now a middle-aged man., A, 336
Closing, The Ecstasy, The, 462
Cool, 136
Cumaean Song, 86

Dancing at Cana, The, 447
David's Lament for Saul and Jonathan, 116
Dawn (John 21), 244
Day Itself, The, 417
Days and Nights, 134
1. Salamander, 134
2. Flood, 135
3. Cool, 136
4. Hmmmm, 137
5. Luna, 138
6. Letter Man, 139
7. Relic, 140
8. Praise on Your Birthday, 141
9. Hecatomb, 142
10. Warned, 143
11. A Polar Simple, 144
12. Riddle, 145
13. The Aim, 146
14. Same Road, 147
15. Late, 148
16. Eels, 149
17. For Vivien Leigh, 150
18. Secret, 152
19. For Leontyne Price, 153
20. Caught, 154
21. Caw, 155
22. Transatlantic, 156
23. A Life in Dreams, 157
24. Rest, 158
25. For James Dean, 159
26. The Claim, 160
27. TV, 162
28. Neighbors, 163
29. Pears, 164
30. Vision, 165
31. The Dream of Refusal, 166
32. October Sun, 168
33. Mother, 169
34. Turn, 170
35. Late Visit, 171

Days and Nights 2, 254
1. Praise, 254
2. Again, 255
3. Rex, 256
4. The Dream of Salt, 257
5. Nocturne for a Wedding, 258
6. The Dream of Falling, 259
7. Ben Long's Drawing of Me, 260
8. 31 December 1985, 261
9. Thicket, 262
10. Samuel Barber, 263
11. Stephen Spender, 264
12. Valentine. Heron., 265
13. Near a Milestone, 266
14. Paid, 267
15. Good Friday, 268
16. Easter Sunday 1986, 269
17. Back, 270
18. At Sea, 271
19. Sky, Dark, 272
20. Two Caves, A House, A Garden, A Tomb, 273
21. A Heron, A Deer—A Single Day, 279
22. First Green, 280
23. 15 March 1987, 281
24. 16 March 1987, 282
25. Spring Takes the Homeplace, 283
26. The Resident Heron, 285
27. Lights Out, 286
28. The Rack, 287
29. Jim, with AIDS, 288
30. Tom, Dying of AIDS, 289
31. Fishers, 290
32. Yom Kippur 1983–88, 292
33. Jim Dead of AIDS an Hour Ago, 293
34. Two, 294
35. Easter Sunday 1989, 295
36. Tom Dead, 297
37. Down and Back, 298
38. Thanks, 299
39. Scanned, 300
40. The Net, 301
41. *New Music* in Cleveland, 302
42. J.H., 303
43. Mob Quad, October 1955, 304
44. At Heaven's Gate, May 1956, 305
45. Boar's Hill, Spring 1958, 306
46. A Heron, A Deer—Again, 308
47. Spirit Flesh, 1960, 309
48. Antipodes, 1969 and On, 310
49. Free Fuel, Byrd Street, 1948, 311
50. First Love, Hayes Barton, 1948, 312
51. Elegy, Byrd Street, 313
52. 1 January 1990, 314
53. Safekeeping, 1963 and On, 315
54. Giant, 316
55. Maya, 318
56. 13 February 1984–1990, 319

Days and Nights 3, 380
1. For K.W. on Her Birthday, 380
2. F.H. Again, 381
3. Durham, 4 June 1984–Fort Worth, 4 June 1993, 382
4. Home from the Cliburn Piano Competition, Fort Worth, 383
5. Twenty-one Years, 384
6. Recumbent, Sleeping, 385
7. Indoors, 386
8. Luck, 387
9. A Chipmunk Gone at Christmas, 388
10. Lion Dream, 389
11. For Hubert Dilworth Dead in His Sleep, 390
12. Back at Merton College, 391
13. After the Annual MRI Scan, Clear, 392
14. Lightning Brown Discovers He Shares a Birthday with Emily Dickinson, 393
15. After an AIDS Benefit, 394
16. Near the Death of the Sun, 395
17. On the Road North, 396
18. The Dying Belt, Douglas Paschall Gone, 397
19. Anniversary, 9 January 1995, 398
20. Besieged but Stronger, 399
21. Mere Fact, 400
22. The Wheeled Eros, 401
23. Two Friends, Parting, 402
24. Back, D.V., 403
25. Safe Home, 404
26. On the Road, 405
27. Stephen Spender Dead, 406
28. Napalm, 407
29. With A.T.M., Baltimore, 408
30. With T.M., Baltimore, 409
31. Tenth MRI, 410
32. In the Fall, 411
33. Near Thanksgiving, 412
34. Toward an Ending, 413
35. The Dread, 414
36. Birthday Party, 415
37. Forty-eighth Birthday, 416
38. The Day Itself, 417
39. Turtle Dance, San Juan Pueblo, 418
40. A Long Storm Passing, 419
41. Snow, 420
42. A Classical Friend, 421
43. The Issue, 422
44. A Visit that Feels Like the Last, 423
45. Gone, 424
46. Scattering Lightning in the Slave Cemetery, Chapel Hill, 425
47. Eros Tyrannos, 426
48. An Unexpected Parent, 427
49. Scoured, 428
50. A Reading, 429
51. Brief Visit, 430
52. Small Astonishments, 431
53. Eclipse, 432
54. Want, 433
55. Stuck in Gear, 434

56. Quiet Evening, 435
57. Who?, 436
58. May Day, 437
59. At Fearrington, 438
60. Left, 439
61. The Swap, 440
62. Westward, 441
63. From Here, 442
64. Nob Hill, 443
Days and Nights (A Journal), 133
Days and Nights 2 (A Journal), 253
Days and Nights 3 (A Journal), 379
Dead Girl, 44
Dead Man, Dying Girl, 121
Dionysos, 184
Director, 222
Divine Propositions, 76
Down and Back, 298
Dread, The, 414
Dream of the Court, The, 364
Dream Elephants, 246
Dream of Falling, The, 259
Dream of Food, The, 12
Dream of a House, The, 5
Dream of Lee, The, 8
Dream of Me Walking, The, 369
Dream of Mother and My Cane, The, 455
Dream of Refusal, The, 166
Dream of Salt, The, 257
Drowned, 113
Durham, 4 June 1984–Fort Worth, 4 June 1993, 382
Dying Belt, Douglas Paschall Gone, The, 397

Easter Sunday 1986, 269
Easter Sunday 1989, 295
Eclipse, 432
Eel, The, 227
1. 25 July 1984, 227
2. 26 July 1984, 229
3. 26–30 July 1984, 230
Eels, 149
Elegy, Byrd Street, 313
Entry, 373
Envy and Covetousness: 1952, 239
Epitaphs from the Greek Anthology, 128
Eros Tyrannos, 426

Farewell with Photographs, 345
F.H. Again, 381
Field, The, 85
15 March 1987, 281
First Christmas, 366
First Green, 280
First Love, Hayes Barton, 1948, 312
Fishers, 290
Flood, 135
For Hubert Dilworth Dead in His Sleep, 390
For James Dean, 159
For K.W. on Her Birthday, 380
For Leontyne Price, 153
For Leontyne Price after *Ariadne*, 88
For Vivien Leigh, 150
Forty-eighth Birthday, 416
Found, for my Brother, 67
Free Fuel, Byrd Street, 1948, 311
From Here, 442
From So Far, 452

Giant, 316
Gone, 424
Good Friday, 268
Good Places, 104
1. Warm Springs, 104
2. Rincón 1, 105
3. Rincón 2, 106
4. Cherokee, 108
5. Lighthouse, Mosquito Inlet, 109
6. Hawk Hill, 110

Half of Life, 226
Haven, A, 453
Hawk Hill, 110
Heaven for Elizabeth Rodwell, My Mother, A, 123
Hecatomb, 142
Helix, 194
Her Choice, 111
Hermes Psychopompos, 190
Heron, A Deer—A Single Day, A, 279
Heron, A Deer—Again, A, 308
His Discovery, 112
Hmmmm, 137
Home from the Cliburn Piano Competition, Fort Worth, 383
House Snake, 200
Hymn, 243

I Am Transmuting, 195
I Say of any Man, 70
Imprecation, 340
In the Fall, 411
Indoors, 386
Initiation, 237
Instruction, 55
Iron Bed in Granville County. A girl aged twelve., An, 328
Issue, The, 422

J.H., 303
Jerusalem—Calvary, 27
Jesus, 180
Jim, with AIDS, 288
Jim Dead of AIDS an Hour Ago, 293
Jonathan's Lament for David, 114
Joseph, 176
July 1956, 233
July 1946, 232
Juncture, 323

Last Conversation, 118
Late, 148

Last Visit, 347
Late Visit, 171
Laws of Ice, The, 129
Leaving the Island, 22
Left, 439
Legs, 367
Letter Man, 139
Life in Dreams, A, 157
Lighthouse, Mosquito Inlet, 109
Lightning Brown Discovers He Shares a Birthday with Emily Dickinson, 393
Lights Out, 286
Lines of Life, 175
Lion Dream, 389
List, The, 451
Long Storm Passing, A, 419
Lost Homes, 328
1. An Iron Bed in Granville County. A girl aged twelve., 328
2. A Single Bed. A Back Street in Venice. Two young men., 334
3. A Cleared Ring in the Blue Ridge Mountains. A boy aged twelve, now a middle-aged man., 336
Luck, 387
Luna, 138
Lust and Greed: 1962, 241

Man and Faun, 73
Mary, 179
May Day, 437
Maya, 318
Memoranda, 79
Toward Junction, 79
Memorandum 1, 80
Memorandum 2, 81
Memorandum 3, 82
Memorandum 4, 83
Memorandum 5, 84
The Field, 85
Mere Fact, 400
Mid Term, 370
Midnight, 199
Mob Quad, October 1955, 304
Monday, June the Sixth, 344
Mortal Seven, 238
1. Pride and Sloth: 1985, 238
2. Envy and Covetousness: 1952, 239
3. Anger: 1985, 240
4. Lust and Greed: 1962, 241
Mother, 169

Naked Boy, 46
Napalm, 407
Near the Death of the Sun, 395
Near a Milestone, 266
Near Thanksgiving, 412
Neighbors, 163
Net, The, 301
New Music in Cleveland, 302
New Room, 362
Night Speech, 29
Nob Hill, 443
Nocturne for a Wedding, 258
Noon Rest, Best Day, 249
November 1989, 236

October 1976, 235
October Sun, 168
On the Road, 405
On the Road North, 396
1 January 1990, 314

Paid, 267
Pears, 164
Photographer, 223
Pictures of the Dead, 63
1. Robert Frost, 1951, 63
2. W. H. Auden, 1957, 64
3. Robert Lowell, 1968, 65
Polar Simple, A, 144
Porta Nigra, 117
Praise, 98
Praise, 254
Praise on Your Birthday, 141
Pride and Sloth: 1985, 238
Prospect, The, 460
Pure Boys and Girls, 28

Questions for a Student, 17
Quiet Evening, 435

Rack, The, 287
Rainbow and a Day-Old Calf, A, 72
Reading, A, 429
Recumbent, Sleeping, 385
Relic, 140
Remembering Golden Bells, 120
Reparation, 41
Rescue, 31
Resident Heron, The, 285
Rest, 158
Resurrection, 53
Rex, 256
Riddle, 145
Rincón 1, 105
Rincón 2, 106
Road, 183
Robert Frost, 1951, 63
Robert Lowell, 1968, 65

Safe Home, 404
Safekeeping, 1963 and On, 315
Salamander, 134
Same Road, 147
Samuel Barber, 263
Scanned, 300
Scattering Lightning in the Slave Cemetery, Chapel Hill, 425
Scored by Light, 457

Scoured, 428
Seafarer, 14
Secret, 152
September 1961, 234
Single Bed. A Back Street in Venice. Two young men., A, 334
Six Consolations, 231
1. August 1939, 231
2. July 1946, 232
3. July 1956, 233
4. September 1961, 234
5. October 1976, 235
6. November 1989, 236
Six Memoranda, 340
1. Imprecation, 340
2. Bed, 341
3. Your Lies, 342
4. Your Debt, 343
5. Monday, June the Sixth, 344
6. Farewell with Photographs, 345
16 March 1987, 282
Sky, Dark, 272
Sleeper in the Valley, 122
Sleeping Wife, 51
Small Astonishments, 431
Snow, 420
Socrates and Alcibiades, 221
Spirit Flesh, 1960, 309
Spring Takes the Homeplace, 283
Stephen Spender, 264
Stephen Spender Dead, 406
Stuck in Gear, 434
Swap, The, 440

Teacher, 224
Ten Years, Four Days, 30
Tenth MRI, 410
Thanks, 299
Thicket, 262
13 February 1984–1990, 319
31 December 1985, 261
This Field, 449
Three Dead Voices, 222
1. Director, 222
2. Photographer, 223
3. Teacher, 224
Three Secrets, 176
1. Joseph, 176
2. Mary, 179
3. Jesus, 180
Three Visits, 184
1. Dionysos, 184
2. Aphrodite, 187
3. Hermes Psychopompos, 190
To Music, 375
To My Niece—Our Photograph in a Hammock, 68
Tom, Dying of AIDS, 289
Tom Dead, 297
Tomb for Will Price, A, 196
Toward an Ending, 413
Toward Junction, 79
Town Creek, 75
Transatlantic, 156
Turn, 170
Turtle Dance, San Juan Pueblo, 418
TV, 162
25 July 1984, 227
Twenty-one Years, 384
26 July 1984, 229
26–30 July 1984, 230
Two, 294
Two Caves, A House, A Garden, A Tomb, 273
Two Friends, Parting, 402
Two Songs for James Taylor, 243
1. Hymn, 243
2. Dawn (John 21), 244

Unbeaten Play, 217
Unexpected Parent, An, 427

Valentine. Heron., 265
Vision, 165
Visit that Feels Like the Last, A, 423

Want, 433
Warm Springs, 104
Warned, 143
Watchman. Tower. Midnight., 212
Westward, 441
W. H. Auden, 1957, 64
What Is Godly, 103
Wheeled Eros, The, 401
Who?, 436
Winter, 242
Winter 2, 346
With A.T.M., Baltimore, 408
With T.M., Baltimore, 409

Yom Kippur 1983–88, 292
Your Blood, 193
Your Debt, 343
Your Element, 77
Your Eyes, 327
Your Lies, 342

REYNOLDS PRICE

Reynolds Price was born in Macon, North Carolina in 1933. Educated in the public schools of his native state, he earned an A.B. summa cum laude *from Duke University. In 1955 he traveled as a Rhodes Scholar to Merton College, Oxford University to study English literature. After three years and a B.Litt. degree, with a thesis on the poetry of John Milton, he returned to Duke where he continues teaching as James B. Duke Professor of English.*

With his novel A Long and Happy Life *in 1962, he began a career which has produced numerous volumes of fiction, poetry, plays, essays, translations and memoir.* A Long and Happy Life *won the William Faulkner Award;* Kate Vaiden *won the National Book Critics Circle Award for fiction; and his poems have won the Levinson, Blumenthal and Tietjens awards from* Poetry.

He is a member of the American Academy of Arts and Letters, and his books have appeared in sixteen languages.